THE EVOLUTION OF THE TRADE RE W9-ASJ-221

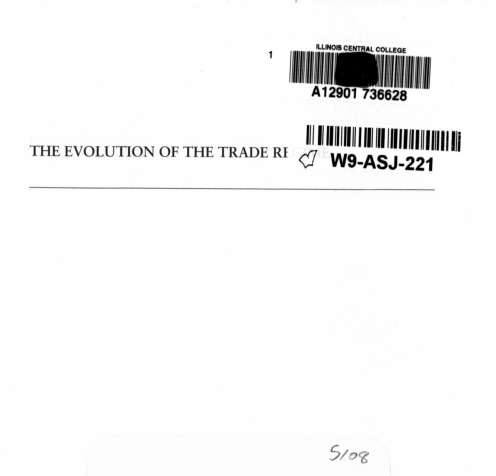

THE EVOLUTION OF THE TRADE REGIME

POLITICS, LAW, AND ECONOMICS OF THE GATT AND THE WTO

John H. Barton
Judith L. Goldstein
Timothy E. Josling, and
Richard H. Steinberg

PRINCETON UNIVERSITY PRESS   PRINCETON AND OXFORD

Copyright © 2006 by Princeton University Press
Requests for permission to reproduce material from this work
should be sent to Permissions, Princeton University Press
Published by Princeton University Press, 41 William Street,
Princeton, New Jersey 08540
In the United Kingdom: Princeton University Press, 3 Market Place,
Woodstock, Oxfordshire OX20 1SY
All Rights Reserved

Fourth printing, and first paperback printing, 2008
Paperback ISBN: 978-0-691-13616-5

The Library of Congress has cataloged the cloth edition of this book as follows

The evolution of the trade regime : politics, law, and economics of
the GATT and the WTO / John H. Barton ... [et al.].
p.   cm.
ISBN-13: 978-0-691-12450-6 (cloth : alk. paper)
ISBN-10: 0-691-12450-7 (cloth : alk. paper)
1. General Agreement on Tariffs and Trade (Organization)
2. World Trade Organization. 3. Free trade. 4. Foreign trade regulation.
5. Regionalism. 6. Trade blocs. 7. Free trade—Political aspects. I. Barton, John H.

HF1713.E96 2006
382'.92—dc22   2005045400

British Library Cataloging-in-Publication Data is available

This book has been composed in Sabon

Printed on acid-free paper. ∞

press.princeton.edu

Printed in the United States of America

10   9   8   7   6   5   4

Contents

Chapter 5
Extending Trade Rules to Domestic Regulations:
Developing "Behind the Border" Instruments   125

Chapter 6
Expansion of GATT/WTO Membership and the Proliferation
of Regional Groups   153

Chapter 7
Accommodating Nonstate Actors: Representation of
Interests, Ideas, and Information in a State-Centric System   182

Chapter 8
Conclusions   204

Illustrations, Box, and Tables

Figures

Box

Tables

Preface

THIS BOOK originates from a series of conversations among the authors initiated shortly after the debacle of the 1999 ministerial of the World Trade Organization (WTO) in Seattle, which met with violent protest in the streets and discord among negotiators. Our central question was, "After Seattle, what next?" As is typical of academics, our thinking evolved into the preparation of a book.

Our fundamental concern was, and is, to understand the working of the multilateral trade system. We graduated from thinking about responses to the institution's immediate problems to consideration of how the institution actually works, the reasons for its apparent success, and why it now faces new kinds of political tensions. We brought a mix of skills to the analysis. John Barton is an academic lawyer who emphasizes in his work the role of international organizations and brings experience as a panelist in the North Atlantic Free Trade Area dispute settlement process. Judith Goldstein is a political scientist who has worked on the history and politics of the trade regime, and was instrumental in bringing the WTO/General Agreement on Tariffs and Trade (GATT) document depository to Stanford. Timothy Josling is an economist who has written about the various rounds of GATT and WTO trade negotiations, with particular emphasis on the issue of agriculture. Richard Steinberg is both a lawyer and a political scientist, and brings experience from working as counsel within the office of the United States Trade Representative. For all of us, the learning process in our discussions was exhaustingly exhilarating. Collective ownership and responsibility is indicated by the alphabetic listing of our names: senior authorship is not assigned.

Our hope is to provide academics, students, and practitioners with an accurate analytic framework for an understanding of the workings of the WTO system, with particular attention to the role of power in the actual operations of the system and to the political implications of the immense expansion of the WTO's authority that took place as part of the Uruguay Round. But we have not given up our initial concern with the evolution of the system—for we believe that the future of the organization can be shaped only on the basis of a solid understanding of the past. We see two major issues arising in the next decade: the legitimacy of the WTO system and the possibility that globalism will shift to regionalism. Both are explored in this book.

Trade liberalization depends upon the WTO's being viewed as a legitimate agent. At the heart of the legitimacy problem is that many old as-

sumptions about the role of the trade regime no longer fit. The WTO/
GATT system was once oriented toward free trade—and thus served a
goal believed to be globally beneficial. But as it entered into other areas,
it became a rule-oriented institution—and therefore needed a new form
of legitimacy, since there are politically significant trade-offs involved in
writing rules, and one can no longer assume that the rules are beneficial
to all. This outcome is seen, for instance, in European fears of WTO decisions affecting consumer standards—and in U.S. critiques of WTO decisions affecting antidumping law. And now many members of the WTO
seek a more development-oriented goal, and many European and U.S.
nongovernmental organizations demand a more environment-friendly or
more labor-friendly institution. The precise new vision of the WTO that
emerges will be defined in political debate, but the new themes could certainly emphasize both global economic growth and fairness or equity. In
the context of trade, "fairness" is often used to couch arguments against
free trade. But in the context of moving beyond the organization's original
goal of the removal of trade barriers—the context that is now crucial for
the WTO—fairness is essential, for there is otherwise no guarantee that
either legitimacy or mutual benefit will result.

Within the system of world trade there is great pressure toward regionalism, that is, an emphasis on trade agreements between countries within
specific regions. In the short term it may serve the interests of the United
States and other countries to seek agreements bilaterally that they have
difficulty obtaining globally. Regionalism arises from a variety of factors,
including the ability to open markets faster than is feasible at the global
level. Such agreements can increase trade, and trade diversion—away
from countries not party to the agreement—may be small compared to the
amount of trade growth. In addition, the mechanisms of market opening
developed at the regional level may provide experience useful in similar
opening at the global level.

But there are risks. Regionalism may be a means for developing countries to serve as a center for low-wage manufacture for export to specific
developed-country markets—as happened with the maquiladora factories
near the U.S.-Mexican border. A network of these bilateral arrangements
could ultimately undermine interest in more global trade relations. Likewise, there are serious implications for developing nations that are left
out of such free trade regions, and strict rules of origin may exacerbate
the diversion of trade that arises from such preferential access.

It is unclear whether or not the mix of politics and economics that
underlies regionalism is contributing to a decline in interest in a global
trade regime. Every preferential or regional arrangement contradicts the
most-favored nation principle (the principle that all GATT parties will
receive the most preferential trade access), and one of the fundamental

economic benefits of this principle is that it makes access to markets harder to use as a tool to seek broader political concessions.

These issues are extremely significant for the developing nations. The notion of universal rules may be too utopian. It is nearly impossible to imagine that, even with time, nations will move toward identical trade structures, given the vast differences in legal and political traditions. The WTO may have to reinstitute a multispeed approach, as in the Tokyo Round, or negotiate special treatment within common rules. The alternative, using dispute settlement or other means to force compliance, may only push the South into more politically acceptable regional arrangements. Yet for the South to eschew universalism seems shortsighted. The acceptance of WTO agreements increases the visibility and importance of the South and provides a basis for future North-South negotiation. Further, in some areas of trade, regionalism makes little sense—it is hard to envision ways for nations to negotiate regional agreements regulating product or environmental standards without undercutting the benefits of global trade.

The WTO as an institution has become one of the centerpieces of the international economic order—but that order is changing rapidly. The WTO must respond to these changes to maintain its relevance and legitimacy in both the developed and the developing worlds. Indeed it may be the forum for new negotiations that attempt to deepen the integration of developed and developing countries in a way that encourages mutually supportive and beneficial growth.

In the longer term, the WTO faces a more serious potential problem, an outcome of the diffusion of power within the organization. Since the establishment of the GATT, a concentration of market power has been in the hands of the United States, later shared by the European Union countries and Japan. This has enabled a relatively small number of like-minded diplomats to advance the agenda of global trade liberalization. Over time, however, as more countries have joined the WTO, market power has been diffusing. If this diffusion continues, diplomats from several more countries—including China, Brazil, and India—will all need to cooperate in order to advance an agenda in the WTO. As the number of powerful players grows, cooperation becomes more difficult, particularly if their interests diverge. In the long term, the WTO's success in facilitating development, which has led to a diffusion of global economic power, may present the organization with its greatest challenges.

The authors of this book have many debts. We wish to thank the European Forum of the Stanford Institute for International Studies, and the European Union Center for California at Scripps College, which supported a workshop on the EU, the United States, and the WTO in winter

2003, where we discussed a draft of the book and received very helpful comments and criticisms. We have also received encouragement and advice from many colleagues, including Claude Barfield, A. Jane Bradley, Marc Busch, Seung Wha Chang, Mac Destler, Geza Feketekuty, Anthony Gooch, Andrew Guzman, Robert Howse, Robert Z. Lawrence, Richard Morningstar, John Nash, Kal Raustiala, Eric Reinhardt, Ronald Rogowski, Jeff Schott, Andrew Stoler, Stephen Woolcock, and anonymous reviewers for Princeton University Press. We have also been aided by excellent research assistants, including Kathryn Judge, Natalya Shnitser, Adi Greif, Rachel Rubenfeld, Ju-young Park, Myles Morrison, Peter Nilson, Lisa Hodges, and Adam LaVier. Finally, we wish to thank the editors and staff at Princeton University Press for their assistance and support in bringing this book into print.

One

Political Analysis of the Trade Regime

1.1. Introduction

In 1995, with high hopes and great fanfare, the World Trade Organization (WTO) was established. Its champions extolled its many virtues. It was to be a global organization, not just a club of Western trading nations. It would be a legitimate multilateral institution, with formal legal status as an international organization and formal diplomatic status for its secretariat. Its detailed rules and automatic and binding dispute settlement mechanism would make it one of the most legalized international institutions in the world. Its rules were touted as covering "commerce" construed more broadly than ever—not just trade in goods, but also services, intellectual property, investment, unfair trade practices, and other economic issues. And its rules were largely liberal, promising to raise standards of living, welfare, and gross domestic product globally and in each member country. The institutional embodiment of global liberal trade had come of age.

Since then, the assessments of many have changed. Antiglobalization groups protested at the third WTO ministerial meeting in Seattle in 1999. Environmentalists from Europe, the United States, Australia, and elsewhere marched in the streets in opposition to the WTO and its rules. Labor unions were complaining that the WTO ignored their interests and was creating a "race toward the bottom" for labor standards. Members of the U.S. Congress, joined by activists and academics, demanded a solution to the "democratic deficit" in Geneva. Diplomats from developing countries stormed a ministerial caucus that was dominated by developed-country diplomats, complaining that the WTO legislative process was nontransparent and unfair. The "Group of 77," representing over a hundred developing countries, complained of an "imbalance" in WTO rules that favor the interests of the developed world. And by 2002, both the EC[1] and the United States were failing to implement some significant WTO dispute settlement decisions. During U.S. congressional hearings in 2002 to consider renewed delegation of trade negotiating authority to the president, several witnesses and members of Congress complained about judicial "activism" in the dispute settlement system. While the Doha Round of trade negotiations was successfully launched, the negotiations almost immediately deadlocked along North-South lines. Measured by this political tension, WTO institutions have not been performing as hoped.

What explains these changing perceptions of the trade regime, and to what extent has increasing discontent undermined the purposes of the organization? We address this question in succeeding chapters, focusing on rising resistance to open trade and the extent to which the organization can be credited with both fostering and undermining the trade liberalization process. Although national leaders created the regime to facilitate the joint removal of national barriers to trade, their willingness to endorse rules that allowed the regime to make authoritative decisions has varied over time. In some periods, the regime moved to expand its authority and nations actively participated in the process of trade liberalization; at other times, the regime was impotent to effect behavioral changes in members.

This book argues that this "authoritative gap" reflects the regime's inability to recast its rules and norms of behavior in line with the changing interests and power of its members. Although the organization has not been stagnant and, in fact, went through a substantial reinstitutionalization in 1995, we argue that the regime's "contract" regularly falls out of step with the interests of members and the circumstances of international trade. It may be true that international regimes solve problems of cooperation through the creation of common rules and norms; however, it is also true that shifts in the nature of the interests of powerful domestic constituencies in member countries may make past "cooperative solutions" difficult to sustain. When the regime was created in 1947, its small size, cohesive membership, and shared vision meant that aspects of the trade agreement could be left underdefined. Members did not worry whether the decision-making system could accommodate fundamental differences in interests since the organization itself was a club of like-minded nations. In the early years of the General Agreement on Tariffs and Trade (GATT),[2] this structure was a virtue. Ambiguity and exceptions allowed governments flexibility to deal with political issues at home. Nations were willing to enforce agreements because of shared norms.

The irony of the trading system is that many of the features that explain the early success of the regime later turned out to be its Achilles heel, creating demand for institutional change. Shifting patterns in both the direction and the type of world trade had unanticipated effects on the regime. While the existence of shared rules was a prerequisite for this expansion in world trade, the rules chosen in 1947 to open trade generated political challenges for the organization in the ensuing decades.

First, and most important, trade liberalization created a dynamic for the expansion of the organization's membership that could not be easily accommodated. The GATT/WTO[3] has had network effects, whereby the addition of every new member makes the organization more valuable to members and more desirable to nonmembers. The diversion of trade and investment associated with exclusion from the regime generated global demand to join and led to an expansion of the GATT from a small club of nations into the WTO, with nearly 150 members. The growth of the number of members was accompanied by a second shift: U.S. dominance in world trade and production declined, and the EC shares increased. Both of these changes occurred with no resultant shift in the formal governance practice that had relied upon consensus decision-making since the late 1950s. As long as EC and U.S. interests were largely aligned, members were able to cooperate in using sources of power extrinsic to the consensus decision-making rule to drive outcomes they favored. But to the extent that the EC and United States have focused on internal politics, and EC-U.S. competition and tensions have intensified, transatlantic cooperation has proven more challenging and governance under consensus decision-making procedures has been more difficult.

Trade liberalization not only led to more and different trade relations among members but also brought new trade issues, such as intellectual property, and new actors, such as nonstate organizations, into the center of the regime. As international trade moved from manufactured items to services, and from commercial transactions to foreign direct investment, the interests of the membership began to separate along North-South lines. Attention to new trade issues, such as protection of intellectual property rights, exacerbated this divide since the developing world often was required to change its domestic rules and institutions. The expectation of compliance increased in the post–Cold War years since there was no Communist threat to counter the ideological fervor of those who supported free markets. At the same time, the reduction in trade barriers and the creation of global markets made salient the argument of "a race to the bottom," activating new groups who did not favor the regime's purpose. Labor and environment groups have been among the many nonstate actors whose self-declared purpose has been to constrain or undermine the integration project that was the ideological basis of the regime. Their activity has also required institutional change.

Second, while the GATT encouraged members to open up home markets to all members, the organization's rules made it acceptable for nations to join preferential regional trading groups. GATT Article XXIV permits the establishment of free trade areas and customs unions, despite their inconsistency with the GATT's most-favored nation (MFN) cornerstone. The result has been an explosion of such arrangements, even though the trade and investment diversion resulting from regionalization, and the political tension associated with it, often conflict with the goals of the multilateral regime. The GATT's founding members saw regionalism as akin to an "insurance policy" for the smaller nations; being a member of multiple trading organizations re-equilibrated some of the asymmetries between large and small trading partners. But that flexible rule encouraged countries to find solutions to their trade problems in venues other than the multilateral regime. Such "exit options" may now make it more, and not less, difficult to conclude trade agreements.

The ambiguity of the original rules became a problem in the WTO structure for a third reason. In the GATT, imprecision in the "law" created space for countries to placate powerful domestic groups, when necessary, without endangering their general commitment to the regime. Disputes were most often settled without formal procedures, reflecting the fact that members shared a common vision of the purposes of the regime. Flexibility, however, granted new members, such as Japan and other Asian developing countries, license to ignore the spirit of the rules. Moreover, the EC and United States invented new vehicles of protection, such as voluntary export restraints and the Multi-Fiber Arrangement, which seemed to fall within shadows of the trade regime's rules. This led to increasingly complicated negotiations as the norms of MFN and national treatment became insufficient guides for behavior.

The response to this problem was to better specify the rules and procedures of the regime. Increased legalization led members to specify with greater detail aspects of the trade contract. Still, gaps and ambiguities remained, often a result of an inability to agree on details. This ambiguity posed a challenge to the new judicial system established in the WTO. Consistent with a view taken by many national judicial bodies, the WTO Appellate Body has seen its mandate as clarifying and ensuring the completeness of WTO law. The result has been a new judicial culture in the WTO that favors making law—a role for the Appellate Body far different from what was expected by its creators. In any individual case, law made by the Appellate Body may not accord with the interests of the powerful members of the organization—or with the negotiators' political compromises. However, on balance, the Appellate body has not fundamentally shifted the balance of WTO rights and responsibilities against the interests of powerful members.

In sum, a great transformation is under way in the global trade regime. We argue in the ensuing chapters that the GATT/WTO has succeeded politically to the extent that its rules, principles, practices, and norms[4] have kept up with the politics of a deeper and geographically broader integration of world economies. Yet many aspects of the trade regime are not currently politically functional. Some institutional changes are bringing the regime into accord with its environment, but substantial political turbulence remains. As opposed to the early regime, in which membership made the opening of markets easier for decision makers, aspects of the regime may now make further liberalization more difficult.

This book focuses on the politics of institutional change in the GATT/WTO system. The central question we pose is whether GATT/WTO-related institutions have evolved in ways that match underlying material and ideational changes so as to maintain and rebuild constituencies for an increasingly open, global trading system. We argue that power politics, reflecting the interest of the United States (and later, the EC) as the largest market, fundamentally shaped the creation and evolution of the GATT/WTO system. Shifts in underlying material interests and ideas, and the challenges presented by expanding membership and preferential trade agreements, have applied pressure for the regime to change. We trace how the institution has evolved from flexible rules to greater legalization, and from liberalization of trade barriers to regulation of a much broader range of economic issues.

Chapter 2 offers the historical context in which the subsequent chapters evaluate the evolution of the regime. Chapter 3 looks at the WTO's legislative and judicial structures. Chapters 4 and 5 consider new problems and issue areas that have emerged over the course of GATT/WTO history: chapter 4 examines traditional border measures, while chapter 5 looks at newer domestic regulatory issues, suggesting why application of the older rules, principles, and processes to the newer missions may not work.

Chapter 6 evaluates the implications of increased diversity in the types of states and entities that participate in the GATT/WTO system, and suggests how WTO rules may bolster liberal reform efforts within member states. The chapter also considers the emergence and proliferation of regional trade agreements and their implications for the multilateral system. As new issue areas have emerged and the diversity of state membership has grown, new nonstate actors have begun to engage in trade politics. Chapter 7 considers institutional design and the entry of those new nonstate actors into trade politics. Chapter 8 concludes with implications for analysis and policy.

1.2. Understanding the Political Economy of the GATT/WTO Regime

The GATT is a multilateral trade agreement among autonomous entities (not necessarily states)[5] aimed at expanding international trade. As described in greater detail in chapter 2, the GATT was signed originally in 1947 as an interim agreement, and it became the key international agreement and institution concerned with global trade. In 1995, the GATT 1947 was replaced with the GATT 1994, which is substantively

TABLE 1.1.
Flow of Ideas: Cost of a Three-Minute Telephone Call from the United States to the United Kingdom

	1927	1956	2003
Technology	Radiowaves	Cable	Satellite
Nominal cost of call	$75	$12	$0.21
U.S. Urban CPI (1927 = 100)	100	156	1056
Cost of the call in 1927 dollars	$75	$7.69	$0.02

Source: AT and T and U.S. Bureau of Labor Statistics.

identical but a legally distinct instrument, and the WTO was created as an international organization to administer the GATT and related trade agreements.

Much about the international environment has changed since the GATT took effect in 1948. The United States remains the world's biggest market, but the EC, which now includes twenty-five members, has grown into a market almost as large as the United States; Japan and China have emerged as among the world's strongest economies, each with a national economic system structured in ways significantly different from those of the Western nations. Issues never given much consideration when the GATT was negotiated—such as multilateral environmental protection and intellectual property protection—are now central to trade negotiations. Yet the rules and principles of the regime—the central rules and principles that govern the world trading system—remain largely unchanged.

The world is far more integrated today than in the middle of the twentieth century, in part as a result of technological changes in the information, communications, and transportation sectors. One indicator, the declining cost of transatlantic phone calls, illustrates the magnitude of these changes. Table 1.1 shows how much the cost of a telephone call from the United States to the United Kingdom has fallen over the last seventy-five years, in contrast to a tenfold increase in the general price level in urban areas in the United States, suggesting how much more cheaply and rapidly ideas can flow across borders now.

Cross-border flows of capital are another measure of this growing economic interdependence. Figure 1.1 shows the sharp increase in foreign direct investment (FDI) over the past forty years—both in nominal terms and in terms of share of global output—indicating that capital flows more freely today than before. Trade in goods and services has also increased as a share of GDP. In the early postwar period, world GDP growth averaged 5 percent and international trade grew at 8 percent. Figure 1.2 shows

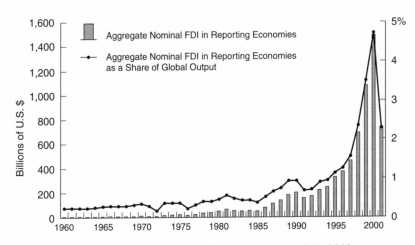

Figure 1.1. Aggregate nominal foreign direct investment, 1960–2002

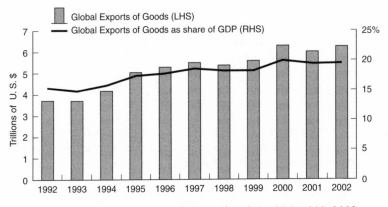

Figure 1.2. Global export value and share of trade in GDP, 1992–2002

that the rise in the value of global exports continued through the 1990s, rising from $4 trillion to $6 trillion (in current dollars) and now accounts for about 20 percent of economic activity in the WTO member countries.

Much of the international flow of capital and goods is within rather than between corporations, reflecting the development of cross-national networks as a central form of production in the global economy. Table 1.2 shows an absolute increase in intrafirm imports and exports during the last years of the twentieth century.

In general, one would expect institutional attributes of an international organization to correspond in some logical way to the international envi-

TABLE 1.2.
Intrafirm Trade and Its Share of Total Trade, Various Countries and Years
(billions of U.S. dollars and percentages)

Country and Year	Intrafirm Exports		Intrafirm Imports	
	Value (bill U.S.$)	Share in Country Exports (%)	Value (bill U.S.$)	Share in Country Imports (%)
Japan				
1983	33	22	17	15
1993	92	25	33	14
Sweden				
1986	11	38	1	3
1994	22	38	4	9
United States				
1983	71	35	99	37
1993	169	36	259	43

Source: UNCTAD, *World Investment Report 121*, note 3 in notes on chapter 4 (1996).

TABLE 1.3.
Institutional Attributes of the GATT/WTO

	Prescriptive	*Mandates and Constraints*
Written	Principles	Rules and procedures
Unwritten	Norms	Practices

ronment that it purports to govern. We conceptualize institutional attributes in terms of whether they are prescriptive (i.e., general concepts of appropriateness) or mandatory and whether they are written or informal. Table 1.3 presents a matrix of these institutional attributes: principles are written prescriptions for behavior, whereas norms are unwritten prescriptions; similarly, rules and procedures are written mandates for or constraints upon behavior, whereas practices are unwritten mandates for or constraints upon behavior.

The ensuing chapters assess the effects of environmental shifts, both exogenous and endogenous, on the written and unwritten institutional attributes of the GATT/WTO. The GATT/WTO is treated as a legal system, which has been defined in terms of the relationship and interaction between its legislative, judicial, and administrative functions (Hart 1961). These institutional components and structures should not be viewed in isolation from other parts of the larger system. Hence, change in particular GATT/WTO institutional rules or procedures, such as the creation of an Appellate Body, should be analyzed in the context of other parts of the WTO structure.

The absence of fundamental change in GATT rules and procedures, noted above, is not surprising. Analysts have shown that different institutional arrangements can be designed to perform the same function (Koremenos, Lipson, and Snidal 2001). This multiple-equilibrium view of institutional design has a number of implications. Two are most important. First, the rules of the regime may not be optimal; rather, a whole range of possible rule structures could be consistent with a cooperative outcome. Second, moving among rule sets may be dictated by political considerations, outside the liberal institutional model.[6] Scholars of institutions well understand the difficulty of changes in procedures and norms within an organization. Rules create beneficiaries whose interests lay in the status quo. The organization may have to be very inefficient—that is, even the actor most benefited by the system is disaffected—before change is possible.

The challenge for any institution is to devise, ex ante, a mechanism that allows the organization to respond to environmental change, ex post. Regimes that do not adapt will become irrelevant; in the extreme, the political disorder engendered by inadequate institutional adaptation may cause a collapse of the institution. Thomas Jefferson made a similar point about the need to amend or reinterpret a national constitution as society changes.[7] Samuel Huntington's work on maintaining political order in changing societies demonstrated the need for state institutions to evolve with societal change as countries develop economically (Huntington 1968). Organizational theorists have made similar arguments.

International organizations are confronted with changes in their environment as profound as, or more profound than, those that challenge domestic institutions. The League of Nations was doomed to irrelevance and eventual collapse because it failed to include constitutional rules championed by one of the great powers—the United States. The World Intellectual Property Organization (WIPO) became less relevant in the 1980s and 1990s, when it seemed unable to cope with demands from two powerful actors—the EC and the United States—to increase global intellectual property protection, and unable to offer an institutional solution to their demands for enforcing Berne Convention and Paris Convention obligations (Beier and Schricker 1989). Similarly, the International Telecommunications Union lost much of its relevance in the 1990s as rapid technological developments outstripped its institutional capacity to set international policy (Borrus and Cohen 1998).

Moreover, the converse holds: institutions survive and remain a focus of international activity if they adjust well to environmental change. So, for example, NATO has thus far survived the collapse of the Soviet Union and the Warsaw Pact—the elimination of its raison d'être—by redefining the functions it performs and reorganizing to do so. And the EC has widened and centralized its political authority since 1957 through a series of major institutional reforms—most notably, the Single European Act, the Maastricht Treaty on European Union, and the treaties of Amsterdam and Nice—each aimed at solving new economic and political challenges.

Three environmental shifts—of state power, interests of nonstate actors, and ideas about trade—bear on WTO politics and design, and serve as benchmarks for measuring the extent to which GATT/WTO institutions have evolved as these environmental factors have changed. Subsequent chapters offer a more complete analysis of these relationships in an effort to understand the extent to which WTO-related institutions maintain and regenerate political support for multilateral liberalization of trade.

1.3. State Power and International Trade Institutions

Despite recent obituaries for sovereignty and the central role of the state in international affairs, states are still the primary actors in the international system. States and customs territories, and no other entities, have standing in the WTO. International institutions are voluntary organizations; states adhere to their mandates out of self-interest. Given a world of sovereign nation-states, we would expect that decision-making processes will either formally reflect the interests of powerful states, or will be supplemented by informal action that allows their expression of power.

However, operationalizing state "power" poses a central challenge to this line of argument. While there is some consensus that power should be defined as the ability to get others to do what they otherwise would not do, measurement is another problem (Keohane and Nye 1977). Some analysts evaluate state power in the aggregate, considering total military and economic might in order to classify countries as "great powers" or not (Waltz 1979; Gilpin 1981). But in a specific negotiating context, like trade negotiations, in which only some dimensions of power are likely to be brought to bear, the measure of power must be more tailored.

In analyzing trade relationships, market size—the capacity to open or close a market—may offer the best first approximation of bargaining power (Steinberg 2002b). Most political scientists and trade economists agree that governments treat foreign market opening and associated increases in export opportunities as a domestic political benefit and domestic market opening as a cost (Schattschneider 1935; Bauer, de Sola Pool, and Dexter 1963; Putnam 1988). Hence, for example, the greater the export opportunities that can be attained, the greater the domestic political benefit to the government of the country attaining them. Market opening and closure have been treated as the currency of trade negotiations in the postwar era (Hirschman 1945; Waltz 1970; Krasner 1976).

Whether trade bargaining takes the form of mutual promises of market opening, threats of market closure, or a combination of both, larger, developed markets are better endowed than smaller markets in trade negotiations. The proportionate domestic economic and political impact of a given absolute change in trade access varies inversely with the size of a national economy. Larger national economies have better internal trade possibilities than smaller national economies. An additional value of exports offers proportionately more welfare and net employment gain to smaller countries than larger ones. The political implication is that a given volume of liberalization offers proportionately less domestic political benefit to the government delivering it in the larger country. Table 1.4 shows the twenty countries with the highest proportions of world trade and the twenty countries most dependent on world trade. None of the five countries with the highest proportion of trade appear on the list of countries most dependent on trade: smaller countries depend more on trade. Therefore, smaller countries may be more "impatient" to reach agreement on trade liberalization than larger countries. Similarly, in trade-liberalizing negotiations, the internal trade possibilities of larger, developed countries give them a better "best alternative to a negotiated agreement" than is available to the smaller ones.

Conversely, in negotiations entailing threats of trade closure, a threat of losing a given volume of exports is a relatively less potent tactic when used against a large country than when used against a small one. Hence, it is well established that developed economies with big markets have great power in an open trading system by virtue of variance in the relative opportunity costs of closure for trading partners (Krasner 1976).

By this measure, the United States must be considered the most dominant state in shaping GATT and WTO institutions over their history. However, its role has waned, and increasingly it has needed to cooperate with other great powers in order to govern the system. While the United States may be hegemonic on security matters, it now shares power with the EC on trade. Figure 1.3 shows the proportion of GDP of GATT/WTO members accounted for by the United States and the EC, respectively, from 1947 to 2001. While such figures are only an approximation of power in the trading system (e.g., they do not account for the effects of the fall of the Soviet Union or the increased size and diversity of GATT/WTO membership), the graph illustrates the relative loss of U.S. market power, and the rise of Europe, in the GATT/WTO since 1947. In 1948, the first year the GATT was in force, U.S. gross domestic product (GDP) accounted for about 65 percent of the total GDP of all GATT members, and combined U.S.-UK GDP accounted for about 75 percent of the total.[8] By 1970, U.S. GDP share of the GATT total had fallen to 46 percent, and EC share was 14 percent;[9] hence, by the early 1970s, political analysts

TABLE 1.4

Importance of Trade and Dependence on Trade, by Country

Twenty Countries with Highest Share of World Trade	Percentage of World Trade	Trade Dependence (Imports + Exports) as Percentage of GDP
United States	19.90	20.72
EU	17.81	30.17
Japan	8.38	17.74
Canada	5.09	75.80
China	4.63	43.87
Hong Kong	4.07	256.15
Mexico	3.41	60.16
Korea, Republic of	3.25	72.11
Taipei, Chinese	2.81	92.97
Singapore	2.66	295.28
Malaysia	1.76	201.21
Switzerland	1.61	68.86
Australia	1.32	34.71
Thailand	1.28	107.13
Saudi Arabia	1.12	66.11
Brazil	1.11	19.13
Indonesia	0.93	62.80
Norway	0.92	58.35
India	0.91	20.31
Poland	0.79	47.87
Overall	83.76	32.19
Twenty Countries Most Dependent on Trade		
Singapore	2.66	295.28
Hong Kong	4.07	256.15
Malaysia	1.76	201.21
Bahrain	0.10	152.53
Swaziland	0.02	144.04
Botswana[a]	0.05	136.82
Angola[a]	0.08	135.73
Papua New Guinea[a]	0.03	129.85
Mongolia[a]	0.01	121.50
Congo, Republic of[b]	0.02	109.66
Nigeria	0.44	109.29
Thailand	1.28	107.13
Nicaragua	0.02	103.77
Philippines	0.72	98.48
Costa Rica	0.12	94.99
Lesotho	0.01	93.74
Bulgaria	0.11	93.52
Ghana	0.05	93.21
Taipei, Chinese	2.81	92.97
Namibia[c]	0.03	91.79
Overall	14.38	154.75

Sources: WTO International Trade Statistics 2001, IMF, International Financial Statistics, Dec. 2001.

[a]Data from 1999.
[b]Data from 1998.
[c]Data from 1997.

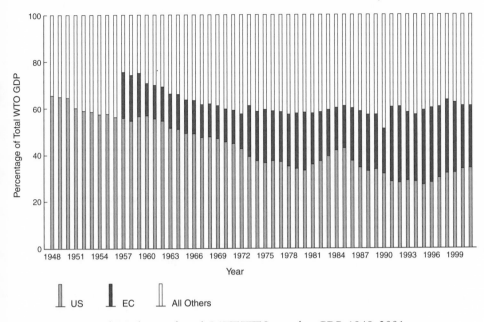

Figure 1.3. U.S. and EC shares of total GATT/WTO member GDP, 1948–2001

observed that the United States and the EC together ran the GATT (Curzon and Curzon 1973).

As the turn of the millennium approached, U.S. share continued to fall, while the EC market had become almost as large as that of the United States: in 2000, U.S. GDP accounted for about 33 percent of the total GDP of all WTO members and EC GDP about 31 percent. The combined share of the "Quad countries" (United States, EC, Japan, and Canada) was roughly 81 percent of the total.[10] Some of the decline in relative U.S. market size is attributable to an increase in the number of states that are members of the GATT/WTO: the organization grew from 19 members in 1948 to 145 by 2002. The EC share has increased in part as a result of enlargement. Thus, U.S. power at the GATT/WTO has been on the decline, and cooperation with other players there—especially the EC—has become crucial to determining the shape of WTO institutions.

This change in power structure has not been accompanied by change in the GATT/WTO's fundamental constitutional rules or practices. Moreover, changes in judicial rules and practices, discussed in chapter 3, do not seem directly related to power shifts. Some *formal legislative rules* have been tinkered with over the years: for example, three-fourths of the WTO membership is now required to affect a waiver, instead of the two-thirds required in the GATT system. But most *formal legislative rules* are essentially unchanged—one nation, one vote; majority rule for "joint action" by the parties; unanimity required to amend Part I of the GATT (most-favored nation treatment); three-fourths vote to amend any other part of the GATT. And the main legislative *practice* has not varied since the 1950s: despite the formal rules just listed, most action is taken by a "consensus" of GATT/WTO members—a motion carries if no member formally objects to it (Steinberg 2002a).

1.4. Nonstate Actors and Domestic Institutional Design

We have spoken as if states or governments have clear or well-understood "interests" in international trade policymaking. But understanding state interests is not straightforward. Interests are generally exogenous to "pure" models of international relations: few interests other than survival can be ascribed to all states. Some other theory, observation, or assumption about interests is necessary to supplement a pure international approach.

The most common analytical approach is to join a state-centric international story with a liberal domestic political model of national preference formation (Moravcsik 1991, 1997). Hence, classic political analyses of international trade policy in the twentieth century were often stories about how powerful domestic actors in the United States or Europe—business organizations and trade associations—shaped national trade policy (Schattschneider 1935; Bauer, de Sola Pool, and Dexter 1963). Economists have generally gone along with this argument, analyzing the consequences of protection of special interests on the greater good. The result is often a "two-level" explanation of the actors influencing international institutions and the interests at play: a domestic political story about how state interests are defined and an international story about how powerful states secure their state interests (Putnam 1988).

The domestic political analysis of trade should begin with an explanation for the constitution of domestic institutional arrangements that aggregate to trade preferences. How do national rules and procedures channel the voices of various trade interests? Are certain groups encouraged to have voice? Do government policies explain variation in the impetus to organize? For example, if national law offers no opportunity or incentive for the organization of such interests (e.g., no right to collective bargaining), then those interests are likely to be unorganized and weak. And even if national laws do provide opportunities and incentives for the organization of such interests, but they are excluded from national trade policymaking processes, then the resulting trade policy and associated institutions will be doomed to constant domestic political opposition from the excluded actors. To produce a broadly supported national trade policy, domestic political institutions must intermediate between the interests of all organized interests.

To maintain support for liberalization, domestic and international institutions also must together solve the problem of aggregating and intermediating interests in a way that is not protectionist. Various institutional mechanisms may be used to facilitate the aggregation of interests favoring liberalization over those that would permit domination by protectionist interests. For example, processes of treaty making and treaty implementation that encourage a national government to logroll a package of market-opening policies are more likely to catalyze powerful support for liberalization than processes that allow piecemeal consideration of each element of the package (Bailey, Goldstein, and Weingast 1997).

Domestic and international institutional arrangements should be analyzed simultaneously. They may operate in a consistent and mutually supportive manner, or they may operate at cross-purposes. For example, when a foreign government is failing to comply with its WTO obligations and that failure nullifies or impairs benefits that would otherwise accrue to the United States, WTO dispute settlement rules may operate in conjunction with a U.S. statute (Section 301 of the Trade Act of 1974, as amended) to target trade retaliation threats in a way that improves the likelihood of the foreign government's compliance with WTO obligations (Goldstein and Martin 2000; Martin 2000).

Not only must domestic and international trade-related institutions function effectively together, they must do so over time. For example, GATT/WTO enlargement has increased the diversity of types of nations that are GATT/WTO members and that increased diversity has strained the multilateral institution. A majority of the original GATT 1947 contracting parties were developed, capitalist economies. The countries that have acceded since the early 1950s have tended to be of a different type—developing countries and, now, countries transitioning from central planning to a form of capitalism. Over a hundred of the WTO's approximately 150 members are developing countries. Increased diversity in the composition of GATT/WTO membership raises a host of institutional problems. For example, consider a comparison between tariff reduction and the harmonizing of competition policy from the perspective of the demands on states engaging in the exercises. Politically, negotiations over tariff reduction demand that a state negotiator balance the demands of import competitors and export-oriented producers—not a trivial task, but one that has proved feasible. Administratively, lowering tariff rates requires simply changing the rate charged by an existing bureaucracy (the customs authority). No judicial action is required, except perhaps to review the processes by which the tariff was reduced. In contrast, harmonizing competition policy entails for most states the establishment of an entirely new governmental institution; its enforcement requires establishing the rule of law; and the policy itself potentially challenges the industrial structure of the national economy—daunting political, judicial, and administrative challenges. For rules and principles that perform many of the new trade functions, it may be that a "one size fits all" approach is not appropriate and that a two-speed or multispeed system may be required. Rules and procedures must account for different levels of state capacity.

Similarly, liberalization typically begets functional or political demands for further liberalization (Haas 1958; Burley and Mattli 1993). For example, the elimination of tariffs and quotas—a once classic definition of trade liberalization—exposes the trade-constraining effect of different technical regulations across countries, creating demand to reach international agreement on what constitutes a legitimate technical barrier to trade. These "spillovers" from previous liberalization demand institutional change not only because there are new functions to be performed, but also because they are accompanied by the participation of new actors in the politics of the system. New functions and issues do not often stand on principle alone: they have become new issues because interested parties have brought them onto the stage. For example, as border measures have fallen, environmentalists and labor unions have raised an additional set of trade issues—protection of the environment and of labor rights. A threshold institutional question concerns how to accommodate these new actors in the political system that governs global trade. They must be given procedural avenues for participation at either the national level or at the WTO, and their interests must be mediated with those of other actors—or they will likely remain in the streets, protesting against the system.

1.5. Ideas and Institutional Design

Changes in the environment may be cognitive as well as material. Institutions may confront changes in ideational structures, both within their own organization and in their operating environment. From a merely materialist base, it is often impossible to understand both the choice of particular rules and procedures and the impetus for change. For example, it may be true that the United States dictated the initial form of many postwar institutions, but only an analysis of American goals and strategies can provide an explanation for the particular choices made (Goldstein 1993).

The institutional arrangements embodied in the GATT 1947 reflected the vision of the postwar world found in the United States and the United Kingdom. Diplomats from both countries wanted to establish rules and an international organization that could avoid repeating the catastrophic closure of world trade that was symbolized by the Smoot-Hawley Tariff Act and that exacerbated the Great Depression. But they recognized that contemporary domestic political realities would make orthodox liberalism infeasible: some protection was a political necessity. For example, the U.S. Congress grandfathered a set of laws to protect domestic producers. The British, for their part, objected to U.S. demands and did not give up imperial and commonwealth preferences.

Substantively, the United States and United Kingdom converged not on a set of substantive rules and principles of pure free trade, but rather a system designed to move in a liberal direction, with ongoing efforts to reciprocally reduce tariffs and to lock in those tariff reductions while simultaneously maintaining various forms of protection (Ruggie 1983). Organizationally, U.S. and UK diplomats sought to create an International Trade Organization (ITO), which was to be established through the Havana Charter. By 1951, it became clear that the U.S. Congress would not ratify the Havana Charter, so it was never submitted to Congress and never came into existence (Jackson 1969). The GATT—an instrument negotiated largely by U.S. and UK diplomats, never formally approved by Congress, containing weak and ambiguous rules of governance, and claiming only twenty-two original contracting parties—was left to govern multilateral trade.

Just as generals who adopt plans based on how the last war was fought are often ill-prepared for the next conflict, international institutions designed to remedy the failures of previous policies and institutional arrangements may be ill-equipped to address new exigencies. The drafters of the GATT created rules, principles, and procedures intended to foreclose the border measures that had been a vehicle for the beggar-thy-neighbor policies of the 1930s. They largely succeeded in meeting that objective. But trade associations, trade policymakers, and states behave strategically, and any given institutional arrangement creates opportunities for strategic behavior intended to confer advantage on those engaging in it.

Thus, for example, the mercantilism of the 1980s and 1990s looks very different from the mercantilist battles of the 1930s. In the more recent period, the relative "competitiveness" of national economic systems became a metric for good trade policy in many countries. Several scholars have identified a new rationale for national policies intended to foster the development or maintenance of a particular sector (Tyson 1992; Cohen and Zysman 1987; Krugman 1991). "Strategic trade theory" was premised on the idea that analysts could identify "strategic sectors," which offer high rents and positive externalities not associated with other sectors. With traditional border measures—tariffs and quotas—disciplined by GATT rules, states could use industrial policies to block imports or maintain an undervalued currency to stimulate exports, building and maintaining strategic sectors (Prestowitz 1988). These policies seemed to many to be neomercantilist contradictions of the foundational "free trade" principle upon which the GATT was built. Yet they were not effectively disciplined by GATT rules.

Similarly, many issues raised in the context of the Doha Round of trade negotiations relate to effects *of* trade rather than effects *on* trade. Most trade policy debates in the first forty years of the GATT/WTO system centered on national policies that create barriers to trade. Since 1990, debates have expanded to consider principles, rules, and procedures pertaining to the relationship between trade and the environment, organized labor, and human rights. The scope of the debate has expanded.

1.6. Accommodating Changes in Power, Interests, and Ideas

Outcomes from international institutions may disproportionately benefit powerful states (Krasner 1991), but the outcomes may nonetheless make all states better off. Hence, many analysts have shown that international institutional arrangements may facilitate the conclusion of Pareto-improving contracts. Milgrom, North, and Weingast (1990), for example, show that the medieval institutions of the law merchant and trade fairs solved a fundamental credibility problem that had been a barrier to long-distance trade, providing crucial information about the reputation of sellers for delivering and buyers for paying. Others have shown more generally that international institutions may solve cooperation problems that otherwise would be an obstacle to reaching Pareto-improving agreements (Keohane 1982, 1984; Stein 1993). According to this logic, international institutions can solve cooperation problems by undermining ex post opportunistic behavior of members, through such mechanisms as monitoring, information gathering, and reducing transaction costs.

In this light, the GATT/WTO may be seen as performing important functions for its members, including facilitation of an important exchange of information. Reaching agreement about rules and principles that will be applied to nearly 150 countries is not a trivial task. It requires understanding the structure of each constituent national political economy and, in many cases, detailed information about its laws and regulatory structures. The continuous presence of negotiators from many WTO member countries in a single location—Geneva—greatly reduces the costs of obtaining that information. The GATT/WTO's Trade Policy Review Mechanism, which generates a detailed report on the trade-related laws, regulations, and practices of each member every four years, provides a wealth of information for these purposes. The secretariat's efforts to collect, organize, and distribute information specific to particular negotiations helps solve the information problem. And, although not all members of the WTO agree with the practice, creating informal negotiating groups from a representative sample of interested countries facilitates information exchange better than that which takes place in a group where all members are present (Steinberg 2002a).

GATT/WTO rules have facilitated the expansion of trade in other ways. For example, the assumption of international legal obligations has affected domestic politics by tying the hands of governments and leading policymakers who often cite such obligations as a basis for opposing protectionist measures (Goldstein 1996). Moreover, the assumption of market-opening obligations may tip a domestic political balance towards further openness by diminishing the power of a group that was enriched and empowered through protection.

Throughout much of the GATT years, international and domestic institutional mechanisms of interest aggregation and intermediation complemented and reinforced each other. In the United States, for example, Congress delegated authority to the executive branch, which packaged liberalizing deals at the international level in a way that built sound political coalitions at home. Perhaps the biggest single problem for trade today is that the domestic and international institutional mechanisms are no longer fully complementary: the range of domestic stakeholders has expanded, and the international issues have become more complex and demand more domestic institutional change. In this context, delegation to an executive branch committed to older notions of what should be contained in trade agreements now interferes with successful interest aggregation and intermediation.

The GATT 1947 was a child of its political time, but times change. Institutions may fail to adjust to political demands that they perform new or expanded functions. The main purpose of the GATT was to lower trade barriers at the border: tariffs, quotas, countervailing duties, antidumping duties, safeguards measures, together with their administration. But, as suggested above, early efforts at trade liberalization generated "spillovers"—a newer set of trade barriers and demands to liberalize them. One observer has likened these spillovers to peeling an onion: as one layer of trade barriers is stripped away, the next layer of barriers is exposed.

Since the GATT was written, deeper layers of trade barriers have indeed been exposed, creating dozens of newer functions for the GATT/WTO system to perform. In the 1960s and 1970s, demand grew for more elaborate rules to discipline antidumping and countervailing duty actions, voluntary restraint agreements, and government procurement. In the 1980s and 1990s, demand emerged to address many "new" issues, such as trade in services, intellectual property protection, and internal investment measures. Since the Uruguay Round, the WTO has also begun addressing issues relating to environmental protection and competition policy. In short, spillovers have increasingly generated "trade" topics that historically have been treated as internal regulatory measures. In noting this shift, Stanley Hoffman has taken issue with the onion analogy, declaring that trade spillovers are more like an artichoke than an onion: from 1947 to 1979, we peeled off the outer leaves, and we have now arrived at the heart of the matter—differences in national regulatory systems that have been reserved traditionally for sovereign control (Vogel 1986).

The GATT/WTO has faced great political challenges as its functional focus has shifted from border measures to internal regulatory issues. It is not at all obvious that the same principles, procedures, and practices for trade liberalization that worked in the case of border measures will be appropriate when applied to internal measures. For example, consider— once again—GATT tariff liberalization and WTO proposals to coordinate or harmonize competition policy, this time from the perspective of comparing the effectiveness of applying fundamental principles and procedures of tariff liberalization to a competition policy exercise. Traditional GATT/WTO principles, like most-favored nation (MFN) treatment and national treatment, and typical GATT/WTO practices, like the "horse trading" associated with request-offer negotiations, have been quite effective in and central to multilateral tariff reduction, but they are unlikely to be effective in or central to harmonizing competition policy.

As suggested previously, the GATT/WTO has needed to respond to changes in the types of trade problems the organization addresses, shifts in the power and interests of domestic and international actors, and new ideas about the benefits of free trade. Over time, these errant forces have been addressed, more or less successfully, by the organization. Geopolitical shifts, such as the emergence of the Cold War, initially limited GATT participation largely to countries in the Western bloc; conversely, the end of the Cold War has given the EC and the United States a freer hand in setting the rules of the WTO (Steinberg 2002a). Changing macroeconomic conditions, such as the Asian financial crisis of 1997, have provided leverage to the United States and Europe to open new markets through International Monetary Fund (IMF) agreements. Technological developments have led to the creation of truly global markets as well as the ability to sell services as well as manufactured products. This too has created an incentive to change WTO rules.

Institutional change has also been driven by endogenous factors. Spillovers from earlier rounds of liberalization created new participants as well as problems for the trade regime. Similarly, the pattern of opportunities and incentives offered by the WTO's rules and procedures for settling disputes may generate its own dynamic of increasingly expansive trade law (Keohane, Moravcsik, and Slaughter 2000). Rules adopted to serve one purpose may provide opportunities or incentives that create their own dynamics. Change in one aspect of an institution may generate outputs that feed back onto other parts of the institution, placing new functional demands on those parts—which they may or may not be able to accommodate.

Institutional redesign has been led most proximately by the community of trade negotiators, secretariat officials, and academics who involve themselves in GATT/WTO affairs. It is commonly asserted that the GATT/WTO is a "member-driven organization," suggesting that representatives of the members propose and negotiate the terms of institutional rules, principles, procedures, and practices. Several histories of GATT/WTO negotiations seem to support that view (Paemen and Bensch 1995; Winham 1986; Wilcox 1972). But the GATT/WTO secretariat has also offered proposals for institutional change,[11] perhaps most commonly with respect to GATT/WTO practice. And occasionally, nonstate actors and academics may propose institutional changes that are successfully adopted.[12] It is ultimately the ideas of such agents that specify the form that institutional change will take.

Many commentators have observed that the GATT/WTO has become increasingly legalized over time, most markedly via the Uruguay Round Dispute Settlement Understanding. Whether WTO dispute settlement is now "overlegalized" has been debated from many perspectives (Steinberg 2004; Barfield 2001; Goldstein and Martin 2000). Some commentators, such as Claude Barfield, have argued that the Uruguay Round created an overlegalized process, when viewed in the context of the WTO legal system as a whole. Barfield argues that legalization of the dispute settlement process has generated judicial activism and specificity in interpretation of WTO agreements. He claims this to be a "constitutional flaw": given the weak legislative capacity of the WTO under the consensus decision-making rule, the "political branch" of the WTO is unable to react efficiently to politically problematic dispute settlement decisions. Understanding whether or not Barfield is correct entails a much more complete analysis of formal and informal aspects of the organization than he offers. Judicial lawmaking could be a functional response to a particular problem in the regime; that is, it could be that such lawmaking fills gaps and clarifies ambiguities that are intrinsic to all legal texts and that the Appellate Body has performed those functions in ways that do not fundamentally and adversely change the balance of rights and responsibilities of powerful states. Analysts need to understand not only the impetus for a particular change in structure but also the implications of the shift for the larger political environment in which trade regulation occurs.

1.7. Alternative Perspectives on the Trade Regime

Political analysis of GATT/WTO institutions has not dominated U.S. commentators' views of the organization. Indeed, much of that analysis, and many of the prescriptions for institutional change have been driven by economic and traditional legal approaches. Increasingly, advocates of "democratizing" the WTO have joined the debate. The political approach employed here complements these alternative perspectives.

Economic analysis of international institutions has largely grown out of two related North American intellectual movements: trade economics in university economics departments and in think tanks, and the law-and-economics movement in law schools. Economic analyses of the efficiency of the GATT/WTO build on the classical and neoclassical formulations of comparative advantage and related theories. Trade economists have for a generation critiqued the rules of the world trading system and national trade laws in terms of the inefficiencies resulting from barriers to free trade. The second movement may be traced to the late 1950s and 1960s, when law scholars began applying economic methods and metrics to the analysis of law (Coase 1960; Calabresi and Melamed 1972). The approach blossomed in 1970s to become one of the most influential movements of the last half-century in the analysis of legal institutions. Alan Sykes, perhaps the best-known trade law and economics scholar, has repeatedly used economic analysis to advance free trade, critique the inefficiency and internal contradictions inherent in U.S. countervailing duty law, and identify types of product standards that may be internationally inefficient (Sykes 1998, 1989, 1995). Others use economic analysis to champion the liberalization of investment law, critique U.S. trade remedy laws, and distill the logic of arguments about trade and the environment (Boddez and Trebilcock 1993).

Efficiency is an important, appropriate, and central objective for the world trading system, and no movement in the North American academy has been more coherent, vocal, and influential in trade policy than trade economics. However, as with many normative metrics, a positive evaluation of the feasibility of its prescriptions is extrinsic to the metric. Maximization of efficiency does not maximize political support for liberal, multilateral trade, partly because efficiency maximization cannot explain interest groups' relative political power on trade policy issues. For example, consumers who benefit from trade liberalization often face a collective action problem in attempting to organize in support of pure free trade, whereas producers, some of whom are protectionist import-competitors, can more easily organize to bias the political calculations of elected officials (Olsen 1971). Moreover, to the extent that nonefficiency interests are unaccounted for, an efficiency-oriented approach cannot accurately estimate the political sustainability of the liberal trade orthodoxy it typically favors. While a safety net for economic and social dislocations resulting from liberalization may be paid for from efficiency gains, efficiency does not inherently imply the extent to which those equity problems should be resolved (Okun 1975). And many environmentalists have concerns that transcend traditional notions of economic value (Leopold 1990). Hence, the efficiency approach does not intrinsically explain or value the political sustainability function of maintaining "safety valves" (such as some trade remedy laws) or ways in which a generally liberalizing institution may have some illiberal rules because they are "embedded" in a particular sociopolitical context (Ruggie 1983). These are usually treated as second best institutional elements and explained by an appended political argument.

International law commentators and practitioners offer institutional prescriptions for the GATT/WTO system that differ from those of economists. While there are notable exceptions,[13] much of the work of European and U.S. trade law commentators has prescribed increased legalization for the GATT/WTO system: more precise rules; increased delegation of dispute resolution to judicial authority; and more obligatory compliance by members.[14] Various GATT/WTO legal commentators have been championing interpretive approaches that aspire toward completeness and predictability in the WTO legal system, largely through filling gaps and clarifying ambiguities, as well as compliance, coherence, and dynamism in the legal system (Pauwelyn 2001; Jackson 2000; Trachtman 1999).

Without doubt, the GATT/WTO system has become increasingly legalized since 1970, when a "legal culture" began to emerge among members. The Uruguay Round agreements clearly moved the system towards greater formalization of rules and enforcement. And since its creation, the WTO Appellate Body has rendered many decisions that rely on the broad expanse of public international law and have increased the precision of WTO rules (Steinberg 2004; Palmeter and Mavroidis 1998).

Many of these prescriptions and the nature of the legalization trend (discussed subsequently) may not be well aligned with the politics of the trade regime. For example, while there is a legal obligation to comply strictly with WTO Dispute Settlement Body decisions (Jackson 1997b), compliance may not be appropriate politically in all contexts. Under some circumstances, when domestic political forces are strongly or popularly aligned against compliance, a state may need to pay "compensation," by means of lowering its tariffs on products from countries suffering nullification or impairment of a WTO benefit as a result of the contravention (Bello 1996). Where compensation liberalizes a volume of trade equal to the trade closure resulting from the contravention, the result may have welfare effects virtually equivalent to those brought about by compliance. The difference is that the compensated breach is more efficient politically: the breaching state will have decided that it is better off breaching and paying compensation than complying, and the state victimized by non-compliance will be no worse off than under the status quo ant because it will have been compensated. Hence, the contractual, efficient breach approach permits resolution of trade disputes through a set of institutional alternatives that may be more politically sustainable than a legalistic, strict compliance approach.

Completeness, predictability, coherence, and dynamism are appropriate objectives for the WTO legal system. But achieving those objectives through Appellate Body action requires judicial lawmaking, which could either weaken or strengthen political support for the organization. Political analysis is necessary for understanding the parameters within which judicial lawmaking must operate if it is to avoid weakening political support for the organization.

Finally, some new nonstate actors and commentators complain broadly of a "democratic deficit" at the WTO. They complain about the WTO's lack of external transparency (i.e., its "secrecy") and limited opportunities for NGO (nongovernmental organization) participation in WTO trade policymaking and dispute settlement (Charnovitz 2002; Atik 2001; Raustiala 2000; Wallach 2000). One critic has argued that WTO decision-making processes should more closely resemble the "accepted and the legitimate practices that are broadly shared by liberal democratic states" (Raustiala 2000). At the same time, many developing-country negotiators complain of a lack of "internal transparency" at the WTO, claiming that the negotiating process is "undemocratic" and biased against them. Sophisticated analysts of democratic shortcomings at the WTO are quick to disaggregate "democracy" in an effort to measure WTO performance and prescribe solutions (Keohane and Nye 2003; Howse 2002b; Dahl 1999).

"Democracy" has undeniable rhetorical power in much of the world, and so democratic attributes of the WTO bear upon its legitimacy and political support for the organization. But from the perspective of those interested in maintaining or increasing political support for the WTO and trade liberalization, even the most sophisticated democratic critiques of the WTO are simultaneously underinclusive, since they approach legitimacy only as a matter of democracy and do not consider other factors affecting political sustainability, and overinclusive, since they may consider moral philosophy that is not central to political support for the organization. At the international level, a fully democratic process would be politically unsustainable: for example, powerful trading countries would withdraw from a trade regime with population-weighted voting; and developing countries are bitterly opposed to increasing external transparency, which they see as a vehicle for increased WTO penetration by northern-dominated NGOs.

In short, we do not deny the importance of efficiency, legal order, or democracy in the world trade regime. But none of those values can be advanced, and the regime itself cannot persist, if WTO institutions are not functional politically. Hence, in the ensuing chapters, we explore the evolution of the trade regime in terms of how its institutions have kept pace—or failed to keep pace—with changes in the underlying political environment.

Notes

1. *EC* is here used to refer to the European Community, the European Communities, or the European Economic Community, as appropriate. The European Economic Community was seated at GATT meetings from 1960 (Jackson 1969). The phrase *European Communities* refers to the three entities (the EEC, Euratom, and the European Coal and Steel Community) that were later merged as the European Community. The European Communities became a member of the WTO at its inception, though the individual member states are also members. We will refer to the European Union (EU) in context as the political manifestation of European integration that includes the European Community as well as other common structures.

2. There are two GATT instruments: GATT 1947 and GATT 1994. While the two instruments are legally distinct, they are substantively identical. The distinction between the two will be drawn here only when necessary.

3. We use the term *GATT/WTO* to refer to the GATT and its successor organization, the WTO, to emphasize the continuity of the trade regime.

4. Institutional developments refer to changes in WTO rules, principles, practices, or norms. The concept is similar to that of "changes in a regime," used by some political scientists (Krasner 1983).

5. By autonomous entities, we mean territories that are not necessarily states, such as the EC, and colonies and overseas territories that were nonmember participants in the GATT's early years.

6. In the liberal institutional model, institutions are cooperative solutions to collective action problems (Keohane 1984; Martin 1992).

7. Thomas Jefferson, "Letter to Samuel Kercheval," July 12, 1816, inscribed in the Jefferson Memorial. "I am certainly not an advocate for frequent changes in laws and constitutions. But laws and institutions must go hand in hand with the progress of the human mind. As that becomes more developed, more enlightened, as new discoveries are made, new truths discovered and manners and opinions change, with the change of circumstances, institutions must advance also to keep pace with the times. We might as well require a man to wear still the coat which fitted him when a boy as civilized society to remain ever under the regimen of their barbarous ancestors."

8. Calculated from International Monetary Fund 1977.

9. Calculated from World Bank 1972.

10. Calculated from World Bank 2001.

11. For example, see the "Dunkel text" of the Uruguay Round agreements.

12. For example, John Jackson's proposal to create an International Trade Organization is given much credit for inspiring creation of the WTO (Jackson 1990).

13. Robert Hudec was more cautious than most other trade law commentators about legalization of the WTO. See, e.g., Hudec 1999, 1992.

14. This treatment of legalization borrows from the definition in Abbott et al. 2000.

Two

Creating Constituencies and Rules for Open Markets

WHEN THE UNITED STATES INVITED fifteen nations to join in an initial round of trade talks in 1946, participants did not expect the meeting to yield the rules for commercial policy that would regulate trade for the subsequent century. Assuming that the regime's regulations were to be renegotiable, participants paid scant attention to the structure of the new organization. The GATT structure did survive, however, and with minimal changes over the following decades, influencing the trajectory of the trade regime in two fundamental ways.

First, the relationship between the principals (states) and the agent (the secretariat) remained underdefined. The resulting governance structure led to a small central organization with limited autonomy. Delegates granted little power to the secretariat to make policy and assigned to the membership governance issues normally relegated to a professional bureaucracy. The problem of authority was magnified over time as the numbers, type, and relative power of these principals changed. The inability of the principals to concur on oversight rules or to define the specific scope of the agent's powers created a tension among members that limited the effectiveness of the organization.

Second, the specific trade rules that were created were underspecified, making it difficult to determine whether or not a specific behavior was consistent with a country's obligation. Behavior was guided instead by a set of commonly held beliefs about the efficacy of open markets and reciprocity as the means to gain access to new markets. As trade regulation became increasingly technical over time, however, norm-based policymaking became impractical. The result was a reinstitutionalization of the organization in 1995.

The GATT's origin as a "stopgap" institution did not make it unsuccessful. The organization should be credited with the unprecedented reduction in national trade barriers that occurred in the period after World War II. In fact, the irony of the trade regime may be that its remarkable success is attributable to a lack of a strong and defined structure. As argued below, the regime's greatest strength may have been its flexibility, allowing the reconciliation of domestic interests in its member states with the general purpose of trade liberalization.

The previous chapter suggested that a trade regime will be unsuccessful if its purposes deviate markedly from the underlying interests of powerful member states. Defining domestic trade interests, however, and aggregating those interests into a single national policy is not easy. GATT/WTO member states have always held a number of often-conflicting preferences on trade policymaking. It may be true but unhelpful to say that nations define their trade preferences based on economic factors. According to such logic, the purpose of the trade regime would be to allow export interests to have entry into foreign markets and, reciprocally, to allow a wide range of goods to be sold at home. But economic interests alone rarely explain the position taken by countries on trade openness. More often, some combination of factors deriving from the economic, political, and social costs of openness explain a country's willingness to participate in the world economy. Powerful groups, often with little interest in competition from abroad, can lead countries to choose a trading position quite distant from one that maximizes objective "economic" efficiency.

However, recognizing that powerful groups influence the trading interests of GATT members does not mean that their interests translate in some simple way into international rules and norms. Interests are aggregated in multiple ways; the political process can undermine the power of certain groups and bring policy closer to the preference of the median voter. Domestic institutions will affect which groups or interests have voice, explaining some of the variation in national trade policies. As well, participation in an international institution may change the power of specific domestic groups by enlarging the size of a leader's constituency, making it more difficult for any one group to attain inefficient particularistic policy goals. Just as domestic institutions influence political outcomes, the international trade regime can be a vehicle through which officials manage domestic political pressures. Still, regime participation alone is not a sufficient counterweight to powerful domestic actors. If agreements on the international level are politically impossible to institute, they will not be observed. The trade regime succeeds only to the extent that powerful nations self-enforce agreements: nations must find it in their long-term interest to follow rules, even when inconvenient. To be self-enforcing, the regime needs to find a balance between the domestic political needs of members and the organization's rules and norms.

Lacking an empowered secretariat and a means to aggregate diverse member preferences, the regime has not responded adequately to the vast changes in the number and range of concerns over trade policy confronting the membership. As trade policy became embroiled in a wider set of production issues, the weakness in the rules that defined the regime became apparent in the lack of support for new trade initiatives. Further, the responsibilities of small market members shifted substantially over time. In the early years, smaller nations were allowed to free ride—they were never expected to give reciprocal access as the price of membership. This tacit agreement between the weak and the strong was undermined by the expansion of the regime into new areas, such as intellectual property regulation. By the 1990s, the desire for expanded access to markets created new pressures on the developing world and the decision to expand the obligations under the new WTO.

To examine this changing relationship between rules and politics, we organize this chapter as follows. We begin with an analysis of America's incentives for creating the GATT regime and the U.S. influence on the choice of regime rules and norms. The chapter then examines the tenets and functioning of the regime, and how the regime resolved the problem of assessing compliance, given the lack of clarity in GATT rules for behavior. A further section looks at alternative cooperative trade agreements during this period, and the chapter concludes with a look at the compatibility between the existing regime structure and the domestic politics of member states.

2.1. Why Create a Trade Regime?

A trade regime is both a political and an economic construct. At the economic level, a trade regime is a collective good provided by governments acting in cooperation to reduce the transactions costs of buying and selling beyond the borders of a national economy. At the political level the trade regime circumscribes the actions of individual countries and thus the domestic political institutions that determine those actions. The construct of a trade regime exposes differences between the approach to gains and losses from expanded trade as seen from an economic and from a political perspective. In economic terms, the benefits from trade accrue to consumers through greater choice and lower prices and to producers of exportable goods that find expanded markets. The importance of a transparent trade regime is that it increases the reach of the market and broadens consumer choice. The international market becomes more like the domestic market as rules and institutions alleviate uncertainty and risk. But from a political point of view, there may be little reward from the promotion of rules to lower the cost of trade, and potential costs from the restricted space in which domestic policy must operate. Global regimes and the benefits that they can confer on individual countries are recognized by political scientists, of course, but their calculus of gains and losses from such regime creation is likely to differ from that of economists.

Tension between the economic and the political nature of trade policy is highlighted by the difference in political and economic approaches to understanding free trade. While only a rare economist would find the move to freer trade anomalous, such a policy elicits both interest and often surprise for political analysts. Why? Economic theory suggests that openness is, in general, welfare enhancing. Open trade brings new products, better jobs, and higher levels of aggregate wealth. While not disputing the aggregate economic benefits of trade liberalization, politicians often find it difficult to defend such a policy in a democracy because the costs associated with collective action lead those who fear competition to dominate the political process, even though numbers favor consumers who benefit from lower prices. The problem derives from the nature of trade liberalization. When a market is opened to foreign goods, consumers benefit from cheaper products. However, not everyone benefits equally. Producers of goods that are now more cheaply available in the home market may find themselves out of business. Those employed in these sectors may lose their jobs. In economic models, such adjustments are an integral part of reaping the benefits: the free trade omelet requires some eggs to be broken. The politics of trade, by contrast, is largely determined by such frictional costs of adjustment as well as the benefits of expanded markets. For politicians, the distributional effects of liberalization are often far more salient than is the overall increase in wealth.

Distributional effects vary by nation and sector. Countries and products vary in their endowments, for example, as whether they are rich in capital, labor, or land. Depending upon the relative use of these factors in the production of a good, freer trade will either benefit or hurt those who hold the land or capital or provide the labor. In this way, the underlying technology will have a direct impact on trade because, as argued by Alt and Gilligan, the economic conditions determine the "stakes" of trade (1994, 171).[1] Who will benefit or lose from competition is often well known to political participants. Having a stake, however, does not necessarily mean political action, and there remains considerable uncertainty about which groups will choose to exert their influence over trade policy.

In general, the willingness of a democratic nation to sign a trade accord is associated with the number and interests of groups mobilized for or against the particular agreement. The willingness of stakeholders to mobilize will be a function of the cost of mobilization and the potential gains from collective action. Although import-competing groups may have a potential loss from a trade treaty, collective action costs may preclude their involvement. Similarly, reciprocity in trade agreements should lead to a greater political voice for exporters, thereby balancing out the "rent seeking" behavior of importer-competing producers. However, exporters may not always be interested in or willing to organize. Although interested in access to foreign markets, exporters' incentives are complex; they too have to overcome collective action costs, and they may decide these costs overwhelm the benefits of openness, either because there are limited gains from new markets or because they perceive their ability to affect government policy to be limited. Exporters could well decide that due to the uncertainty of economic gain, they are not willing to expend organizing costs in order to counter the rent-seeking behavior of import-competing groups. In short, considerations of economic interests alone do not lead to a straightforward prediction as to whether or not countries will favor trade liberalization. In all cases, trade is highly politicized, and politicians who want to keep markets open must assure that those who will benefit from openness have an avenue for political participation.

Understanding this logic of political participation is key to the explanation of the form and success of the postwar trade regime. In the nineteenth century, British trade liberalization was done unilaterally; with the repeal of the Corn Laws in Parliament, the British market opened up, in the absence of a simultaneous policy shift by trading partners.[2] In the twentieth century, U.S.-led liberalization was reciprocal. The United States agreed to lower tariffs only when it received reciprocal access to foreign markets. Support for open trade was more incremental in the United States than in Britain, occurring through a process whereby leaders traded off the interests of one set of market participants with another. If groups were well organized, they could veto such deals, and trade deals could not occur if the United States did not have a partner also willing to participate in liberalization.

America's decision to pursue reciprocal trade agreements had both political and economic consequences. As a result of the passage of the Trade Agreements Act of 1934, the United States entered into a series of bilateral agreements. Between 1934, when Congress first mandated such agreements, and 1947, when the GATT was negotiated, the United States concluded thirty-two agreements with twenty-eight countries.[3] Of the bilateral treaties that were signed, however, only those with Canada and Cuba were examples of deeper liberalization—the United States never completed second treaties with any of its other twenty-four treaty partners. In part, the inability to negotiate subsequent tariff reductions was due to involvement of producers. The 1934 act granted negotiating rights but stipulated that the president, before lowering a tariff, seek advice from the Tariff Commission, from the departments of State, Agriculture, and Commerce, and from all other appropriate sources. To accommodate this mandate a series of committees, including the Trade Agreements Committee, country-specific committees, and the Committee for Reciprocity Information, were assembled to give interested parties the opportunity to present views. They took briefs and held public hearings. Until 1937, a formal announcement of an intent to negotiate was accompanied by a list of the principal producers who could potentially get a tariff cut; afterward, the list was replaced by a general or "public" list that signaled all items that were under consideration in any negotiation. The result of committees, notices, and hearings, both before the negotiations and after a list of products was tentatively accepted, was a glut of information for producer groups. Interest groups now not only operated solely in Congress but pressured the bureaucracy throughout the negotiating process.

Through multilateral bargaining the United States was able to finesse some of the problems created by bilateral agreements; enlarging the number of participants at the table, the United States changed the information environment in which import-competing groups operated and increased the number of exporters with a stake in the process. The structure of multilateral trade negotiations made it more difficult to predict the depth of cuts for any particular product. Over time, the notification process became increasingly less predictive for producers, undercutting their ability to make an accurate forecast of their interests in political action. As result, officials heard less often from those hurt by open trade and more often from exporters, now willing to voice support for liberalization. The result was increased flexibility to conclude trade "deals" (see Gilligan 1997).

American leaders supported the creation of a multilateral organization for a second reason not associated with domestic mobilization. In the days after World War II, the international environment made less powerful nations wary of signing agreements to lower trade barriers with the United States. Although states realized that they were collectively better off with fewer trade barriers, America's past behavior provided evidence that the United States might not abide by its agreements. From the perspective of the smaller states, the absence of courts or a system of enforcement of international agreements was an invitation for the powerful to act in an opportunistic manner. Once the smaller state negotiated a trade treaty and made irreversible investments in export industries, even a small deviation from the agreement could have severe economic consequences. For the smaller nations, a trade treaty was rational only when the larger state could provide a clear and compelling signal that it was a trustworthy treaty partner. Sending such a signal, however, is difficult in the realm of commercial policy, where national policies, such as domestic subsidy programs, are difficult to monitor and are influenced by particularistic group pressures (Goldstein and Gowa 2002).

The GATT/WTO regime not only solved the pressure group problem within the United States but also obviated America's commitment problems. First, the trade regime created a mechanism by which the smaller nations could undermine the purposes of the institution if the more powerful acted in a predatory manner; the regime balanced the power asymmetries created by the difference in economic size through coordinated punishment. Second, the regime "bundled" together agreements so that the unraveling of one had implications for others. The effect was that groups, even within the larger economy, would suffer if a country reneged on an agreement. The interrelationship of these agreements was not just within sectors but joined together import and export interests across a range of producer and consumer groups. Third, the regime bound home producers even in powerful countries by encouraging them to make irreversible investments. In essence, the trade regime created a mechanism by which home producers as well as consumers were threatened if national policy deviated from that expected by even the less powerful members of the trade regime. The regime gave home producers a stake in open trade and thus produced an equilibrium whereby open trade became self-enforcing. Joining a trade regime was a credible commitment mechanism because of the implications of defection for a leader's own domestic coalition.

These twin concerns, finessing domestic political resistance and creating a "good" American reputation, explain the timing of U.S. interest in the trade regime. Although the United States had been a world economic power for a generation, it was only in the midst of the Great Depression that a coalition emerged in favor of trade liberalization. For the first 150 years of its history, U.S. trade policy was partisan and erratic; trade agreements were repeatedly enmeshed in larger disputes of party, region, and power haggling among the branches of government. A scarce year before Democratic Party control of government led to a shift toward an open trade policy in 1934, America had abandoned the London Conference; four years before, the government had enacted the Smoot-Hawley Tariff, one of the highest and the most inclusive tariff schedules in U.S. history.

The policy shift in 1934 led to two internal changes in tariff policymaking that presaged the trade regime that would be erected almost fifteen years later. First, Congress delegated authority to the president to lower rates if he received reciprocal reductions in the tariffs of America's trading partners. Congress mandated a lower limit for the reduction of the tariff schedule but did not specify what industries would be in the tariff bargain. The result was that export groups had an increased incentive to urge Washington to consider trade reform and import groups faced greater collective action costs, given the probabilistic nature of being included in the tariff "bundle." Second, Congress changed its procedures for oversight. Instead of requiring that tariff treaties gain a supermajority of support, tariff agreements that did not surpass the reduction mandated in the legislation did not need further congressional approval. Congressional oversight occurred through sunset provisions in the president's tariff-setting authority at relatively short intervals of time.

Changing the tariff schedule, line by line, in Congress was a time-consuming and difficult process; in addition, finding treaty partners and concluding trade agreements, even without the need for congressional approval, proved a difficult task for State Department officials. Although initially successful, the enlarged mandate in 1945 granting a 50 percent decrease in tariffs from those in effect in that year, not just from the Smoot-Hawley levels, put the president under considerable pressure to show progress on trade talks before the legislation came up for renewal in 1948 (Brown 1950, 18–20). This timing explains why the State Department embarked upon a double-track trade strategy after 1945. While negotiators were supporting the creation of a large and formal international organization to regulate trade, the International Trade Organization (ITO), the United States was issuing invitations to fifteen countries to participate in negotiations to reduce trade barriers in Geneva. The Geneva talks occurred under a set of rules agreed to during the first "round" of tariff negotiations, labeled the General Agreement on Tariffs and Trade (GATT). Less than a grand design for international trade, the GATT merely codified aspects of the treaties that the United States had negotiated since 1934. Many of the general clauses found in the GATT agreement can be traced to some principle the United States had agreed to in earlier treaties.[4] And although pieces of these agreements, for example, the use of MFN, were modeled on European treaties of the nineteenth century, the GATT agreement codified a far more diverse set of rules and norms, reflecting U.S. interests.

For example, the bilateral agreements negotiated under the original authorization consisted of two parts—a series of general provisions and the particular negotiated schedules. The general provision section was oriented toward making the tariff reduction meaningful: rules were set that defined what were and were not allowable exceptions and safeguards, that prohibited other forms of discrimination, and that described the conditions under which the agreements could be breached or terminated. The GATT included, in a somewhat more expanded form, this structure of rules. Part I of the GATT included the MFN provision and gave legal effect to the lower tariff schedules (Articles I and II). Similar to the earlier agreements, the GATT spelled out a prohibition against monetary manipulation as a means of protecting producers (Article II), specific rules in case of nullification of a tariff concession (Article XXIII), escape clause procedures (Article XIX), and exceptions for economic development (Article XVIII). The language and intent were familiar to all countries that had treaties with the United States. Unlike the bilateral agreements, there was a strict prohibition against an increase in preferences on all articles; earlier treaties only covered specified products. The GATT also prohibited export taxes, not covered in any earlier agreement.

Part II of the GATT also repeated language from the bilateral treaties. This section deals with barriers to trade and forbids the use of those that would undermine a tariff reduction. New were the extension of national treatment to imported articles (Article III), more narrow rules on dumping and countervailing duties (inserting the need for the product to not only be dumped or subsidized but also to hurt a domestic industry as a result of the action), and the details on custom rules (Article VII). The GATT also stipulated a balance-of-payments exception, reflecting the policy of the new IMF.

The most substantial differences in the GATT from earlier agreements are found in Part III (Articles XXIV–XXXIV). These are rules developed out of the consultative process over the creation of the ITO. For example, Part III includes an exception for free trade areas and customs unions, the voting rules in the trade regime, the period of time when modifications were possible, and the relationship between the GATT and ITO. All these provisions were new. Of these, the customs union exception (Article XXIV) and the period of time when modifications were possible (Article XXVIII) were the most important. The United States would use the customs union exception to push for European integration ten years later.[5] Article XXVIII allowed the partial renegotiations of the schedule. This section, a substitute for the sunset clause of the earlier agreements, was part of what stabilized the GATT reductions. As opposed to a general ability to rescind an agreement, the GATT allowed a country to move a concession from one product to the next, as long as the value of the overall agreement did not change. Making these small changes, however, was difficult since it either targeted a particular import-competing group or threatened an exporter. In essence, by taking out the reciprocal benefits from the negotiations, countries could not easily relieve one industry at the cost to another. The outcome was that few countries used Article XXVIII, even when under pressure from domestic groups (Goldstein and Martin 2000).[6]

While supporting the new GATT agreement, the State Department continued to act on its plans for the larger and deeper trade organization, parallel to those being created for finance (IMF) and development (International Bank for Reconstruction and Development). Even before World War II ended, the United States had begun planning for such an organization. In 1945, the State Department had formally endorsed the creation of the ITO in its *proposal* for an international trade organization. The ITO was to stipulate the rules and norms by which trade would occur and would provide oversight, through a large administrative structure, of the adherence to these rules. Commercial policy rules were envisioned broadly to include both the method of creating products for sale on world markets and the sale of those products. As opposed to the GATT, the charter was comprehensive and included provisions for things as diverse as competition policy, employment issues, investment guidelines, and rules on economic development. Until 1951, when the United States formally abandoned efforts to get the ITO charter through Congress, the GATT existed in the shadow of the charter. Although many aspects of the GATT parallel those in the charter, the ITO was far more detailed, in both what it expected of nations and in the specification of legitimate exceptions to its rules.

One of the differences in the two organizations was that the ITO would have delegated far more authority to an international institution than did the GATT. The United States agreed in the charter to abide by the majority will and accepted compulsory third-party adjudication of disputes. In many ways, the GATT decision-making system was inchoate; comparatively, the ITO rules specified a detailed and surprisingly egalitarian notion of representation. From the earliest meetings, countries had disagreed on how decisions would be rendered in the new ITO. Debate on three alternative voting schemes in the Preparatory Committee had preceded the Havana Conference and had ended inconclusively. The United States wanted shares of world trade to determine voting power. Britain and the Commonwealth states preferred a more "lightly" weighted voting that gave them more voice (Brown 1950, 145). Of the fifty-six delegates, thirty-five argued for one nation, one vote; only the United States supported the system it preferred (Brown 1950, 146). Similar battle lines had been drawn in Havana about the ITO's executive committee. The United States favored the creation of such a committee and permanent membership on it for a limited number of nations. Although small states did not dispute a permanent seat for Washington, they did demand wide representation of geographic regions.

The ITO procedures that the United States ultimately agreed to evidence a substantial softening of its position. Most fundamentally, it agreed to the one-nation, one-vote rule, although it insisted that certain decisions require the assent of a large majority. In the end, prospective members agreed that a simple majority of those in attendance at an ITO conference, the general assembly of member states, could approve a single member's request to waive the rules. To amend the charter, however, required a two-thirds majority, as did the selection of members to the executive board, the grant of exceptional waivers, and the creation of preferential trading blocs, among other issues (Brown 1950, 231–32). A similar willingness to compromise was evident with respect to executive board membership. Among its eighteen members, the board was to include eight serving three-year terms who were to be elected by the Conference with due, but not exclusive, consideration to national shares in world trade. In electing the remaining ten members of the board, the charter obligated the Conference to ensure that they reflected the membership at large. All decisions by the members were subject to oversight by the International Court of Justice. Although the United States had previously questioned the authority of international courts, it agreed in the ITO to allow any member to appeal a Conference decision to the ICJ. More unusual, the United States agreed to be bound by the court's judgment. Compared to its authority in the IMF, the United States had far less direct control over the ITO. Not only could it get outvoted on almost any issue, but the United States also agreed to adhere to the decision of an international court.

Within the United States, most observers had reservations about the potential loss of sovereignty. Others, however, dissented from the majority, arguing that experience in the UN General Assembly showed that smaller countries would not "gang up" on the United States. Writing in 1949, Bidwell and Diebold, for example, maintained that the principal risk "may be, not that we shall occasionally be outvoted, but rather that we shall always win." This would symbolize "domination" and would arouse "jealousy and hatred" among U.S. trading partners (Bidwell and Diebold 1949, 232). As Bidwell and Diebold suggest, at that point in time, the best interests of the United States were served by accepting constraints on the unilateral exercise of its economic power.

Even though the GATT agreement adopted the one-nation, one-vote structure, effective control moved back toward the larger nations. The agreement specified that a simple majority could support a nation's request for a waiver, but a two-thirds vote of the contracting parties was required to change anything fundamental in the Articles of Agreement. In fact, unanimity was required for changes in the most important three: Article I, MFN treatment; Article II, changes in concessions; and Article XXX, amendments of the GATT, all areas of particular concern to the United States. Admission of a new member state required a two-thirds majority, but any dissenting state could deny membership privileges to a newly admitted state. Although this differential voting system was mandated by the formal rules, under U.S. tutelage the GATT developed a consensus norm. Decisions were taken by consensus defined as having no member present object; American interests were thereby protected by its ability to wield a veto. As well as assuring U.S. interests, the norm granted less powerful nations the ability to undercut any GATT action. No nation needed to worry that a vote of the membership would abrogate costly investments it had made to open its markets. But while the voting rule protected all countries from the "downside" of membership, it made it impossible for small nations to craft any positive changes in the organization without U.S. assent. In addition, it became apparent by the 1960s that without permanent representation in Geneva, the perspective of the developing world and midsized nations was rarely heard. The voice of these countries would have been more effective had the ITO been created. Not only might the United States have been constrained by a majority vote, but also the executive committee could have given a voice to the small and midsized nations.

Why did the United States abandon support for the ITO and instead support the GATT over the next four decades? Both served U.S. interests of getting nations to the bargaining table, and of the two, the ITO was a better mechanism for making a credible commitment to trade liberalization. By 1951, when the United States formally abandoned the ITO, the structure of world politics had changed. The composition of a "free world" under U.S. tutelage changed the perceptions of U.S. allies about American intent. In the wake of the U.S. buildup of forces against communism, much of the commitment dilemma was solved. With the start of the Cold War, nations understood that their welfare would not be undermined by U.S. economic policy. The result was that the United States could rely on the less binding and friendlier GATT regime. Given domestic resistance to parts of the ITO charter and the ability to participate in the GATT under an executive order, Truman withdrew the charter from Senate consideration. The GATT, an agreement more reflective of the vision of trade policy legislated in 1934 than the rules and norms in the ITO's charter, became the backbone of the trade regime.

Throughout its existence, the GATT remained a victim of this odd history of birth. From the U.S. perspective, the GATT was part of a project of recasting U.S. institutions so as to allow the executive branch, and not Congress, to set the trade agenda. Executive delegation was precarious and required not only constant renewal by the legislature but evidence that U.S. interests were served in the tariff-setting process. The GATT's mission was not to fundamentally transform U.S. trade policy but rather to facilitate its mission of getting access to foreign markets and building domestic support for open trade. Since delegation was limited, the GATT was stymied by an inability to extricate itself from the interests of not only the United States but also of its other members. Indicatively, the president chose to bind the United States to the regime using his executive authority, not through a congressional oversight process. This lower-profile form of delegation finessed potential resistance, but it meant that there was no coalition in Congress to support either funding the GATT's secretariat or its general mission. Not until the end of the Kennedy Round, in 1968, did GATT funding appear on a budget line.

2.2. The GATT 1947 Trade Regime

In inception, the GATT was a bargaining vehicle.[7] The initial tariff talks in 1947 were initiated by the United States and conducted in a style adopted from earlier American negotiations. Countries negotiated on selected items or products, and the gains from a reduction were reciprocated not in a product but by value. As would become the norm, the Geneva talks began with countries sending product requests to each other for potential concessions. This was followed by the presentation of a list, to each country, of the concessions the other was willing to grant. Countries were expected to balance the value of concession with a commensurate value of access to their home market. For the most part, countries made demands on products for which they were a principal supplier, although it was not unusual for the secondary supplier to have a product on a "demand" list. Countries that benefited from the bilateral swap between two countries were expected to contribute a concession equal to their gain. In the end, all concessions were listed as changes on each participant's home tariff schedule, and all signatories to the GATT had access at this MFN rate.

Underlying these procedures were three commonly accepted principles or norms: MFN, reciprocity, and economic liberalism. More than formal rules, these implicit and explicit rules of behavior dictated policy for the ensuing forty years. The multilateral aspect of the regime was captured in the principle of most-favored nation status, extending all bilateral deals to members of the organization. By agreeing to MFN, trading partners grant the same tariff treatment given to their preferred trading partner to all others. The norm is one of equality of treatment or, in the reverse, a pledge against discriminatory trade relationships. The rule has long historical roots, dating at least to the eighteenth century in trade relations appearing as part of the agreement between Great Britain and Spain in the Treaty of Utrecht. There was an MFN clause in the Cobden-Chevalier Treaty between England and France in 1860, and, thereafter, most European trade agreements included such a promise. The United States was slower to accept the premise, arguing in the nineteenth century in favor of a "conditional" MFN status for its treaty partners. In 1923, by executive agreement, the MFN norm became accepted as part of U.S. policy and was incorporated into all trade agreements concluded under the auspices of the 1934 act.[8] Indicatively, the Atlantic Charter of 1941 stated that the principle was to be part of any postwar trade regime.

The MFN principle of multilateral and nondiscriminatory trading relationships has been a principle subject to exceptions. Even in the original ITO agreement, rules on preferential trade agreements (PTA) allowed parties to the agreement to discriminate by not extending the same privileges to all regime members. Likewise, the developing world has regularly been exempt from MFN obligations under the notion of a two-track system for trade obligations. Thus developing countries get asymmetric trade benefits under the Generalized System of Preferences (GSP), and they have been granted waivers for specific obligations that other members undertake. One of the most systematic deviations from MFN in the GATT was repeated in the WTO in the ability of existing members to choose not to extend benefits to a new member. Article XXXV of the GATT and Article XIII of the WTO prescribe that new members can be excluded from MFN treatment by another member through a process of nonapplication. This provision ensures that new members must negotiate the terms of accession with every member to whose markets it wants access.

While MFN treatment, the multilateral aspect of the regime, was subject to numerous exceptions, developed nations rarely deviated from the norm of reciprocity. Reciprocity, or the idea that governments would extend similar concessions to each other in order to "balance" out the exchange of benefits, was foundational, dating to Article 17 of the ITO, where no country was required to grant a concession unless other members were adequately compensated through a concession of equivalent value. Although the concept of reciprocity is not defined in the GATT, negotiations from the earliest period were conducted on the basis of reciprocal swaps of benefits. Not only were bilateral tariff deals based on the value of trade, but any supplier who constituted at least 15 percent of the market was expected to offer a concession equal to the value of the trade deal received because of MFN. The notion of reciprocity extended to the removal of tariff benefits as well. If a country reneged on a deal because of domestic resistance, the GATT specified the means to make the other country "whole." The GATT specified an "open" period when members could renegotiate their concessions, constrained only by the reciprocity norm. If they wanted to move a concession around, that is, they wanted to renege on a concession worth a specific amount, they could compensate a partner by giving it a tariff reduction in another sector. If no other concession were offered, the other party would raise a tariff in order to balance the level of concessions.[9]

As with MFN, the idea of reciprocity was challenged by unequal economic development. In the enabling clause, that is, the agreement on Differential and More Favorable Treatment, Reciprocity and Fuller Participation of Developing Countries, GATT members were encouraged to give more favorable treatment to developing members. Part IV of the GATT was negotiated during the Kennedy Round and explicitly stipulated that developed countries did not expect reciprocity for tariff reductions and the removal of trade barriers where the trade involved developing countries. The three articles (Articles XXXVI, XXXVII, and XXVIII) do not impose any legal obligations on the more developed countries, although they purport to create a two-tier trading system by making the reciprocity norm applicable to some but not all members.

The third tenet of the regime, economic liberalism, was implicitly accepted by members upon accession. Although no one expected the regime to yield free trade among participants, entering the regime signified agreement with the principle of economic openness or the value of encouraging the free flow of goods across national borders. The ideal of economic openness and the reality of economic regulation, both across and within states, created a tension in the original ITO charter and remain an issue in current WTO policy. Still and from the start, the organization and its members were formally committed to the freeing of world trade and the abandonment of isolationist and nationalistic economic policies, such as those that characterized the interwar years. Accepting the goal of openness proved easy; far more problematic was the implementation of the ideal. Not only were certain goods, such as agricultural products, never on the negotiating agenda, but early on, the United States adjusted its support for trade liberalization by adopting advocacy for "free and fair trade." According to the American interpretation, free trade policy did not extend to countries with different styles of economic management. Countries that did not allow a "level playing field" for all producers were not entitled to the same concessions granted to other nations. The United States was not alone in its challenge to a universalistic vision of trade liberalization. During the Uruguay Round, the regime considered and adopted policies less oriented toward opening markets and more to their regulation. While members agreed that the free trade vision covered policies relating to goods after they left a national border, the regulatory issues of production, ranging from intellectual property to competition policy, mandated policies often inconsistent with the organization's original purposes.

2.3. The Early GATT

The initial GATT round of trade talks in 1947 occurred over a nine-month period. The round was a success, largely due to American willingness to open up its own market, given that its trading partners' tariff concessions would not be meaningful until their currencies became convertible. When the United States went to the table in 1947, about 60 percent of the value of its imports entered the United States free. Of the 40 percent that were dutiable, the United States offered to reduce 53 percent of its duties and bind or freeze at their current level another 20 percent.[10] Only 27 percent of the products on the tariff schedule were considered politically too sensitive to offer increased market access (U.S. Government 1947). Further, the proposals were substantial. Fifty-nine percent were for reductions of 36–50 percent (U.S. Government 1947, chart 2). Although the negotiations required numerous bilateral meetings, the Geneva talks were far less divisive than were the preliminary talks on the ITO.[11] The final GATT agreement was signed by twenty-three contracting parties, of which eight countries' new tariff schedules went into effect on January 1, 1948. As opposed to the ITO charter, the protocol applying the GATT specified that signatories were bound only "to the fullest extent not inconsistent with existing legislation" (Kock 1969, 65). Not only was the agreement limited by past legislation but also countries were allowed to withdraw with six months notice.[12]

The GATT structure developed in the ensuing five years. At the second round, in Annecy, eleven new members began the process of acceding to the GATT. In the third, in Torquay in 1950–51, the United States announced its decision to rely only on the GATT mechanism and not to resend the ITO charter to Congress. By 1952, thirty-four countries were GATT contracting parties, representing 80 percent of world trade. Thereafter, the organization was the cornerstone of the liberal trade regime.

The growing number of members did little to ameliorate the GATT's organizational problems. The GATT's legal status remained underspecified. Although some countries approved participation as if the agreement were a treaty, the American Senate never ratified, nor even considered, the GATT. The GATT's formal legal status derived from a resolution at the UN Conference on Trade and Employment in 1948 where the International Committee for the International Trade Organization, or ICITO, was mandated to carry out specific functions until the ITO came into existence. ICITO was the entity that was entitled to privileges and immunities and had a legal personality, not the GATT. In March 1948, the committee had met and elected an executive secretary and an executive committee of eighteen members to ICITO. The committee then delegated all its powers to the new secretary. In its first and only subsequent policy meeting in September 1948, ICITO approved a financial arrangement that conferred authority on the executive secretary of the ICITO to provide secretariat and conference services for the contracting parties to the GATT. The formal head of the GATT was its director-general, a person nominated by the contracting parties. However, the choice of the director-general needed to be formally sanctioned by the ICITO, which simultaneously named that individual to be its executive secretary.

Since no one in 1948 thought the arrangement between the two entities would be long lasting, little preparation was made for financial or organizational support of the GATT. The lack of secretariat support, however, was consistent with the wishes of the contracting parties who under U.S. tutelage agreed that the organization should remain "member driven." Members adopted informal and often ad hoc administrative procedures that were often defended as a pragmatic response to the problem at hand. For example, there was no procedure for the succession of the director general (executive secretary), a problem encountered for the first time when Wyndham White, the first director-general, announced his intent to step down in 1967. The contracting parties settled on Olivier Long as the replacement, but although he was appointed by the membership in November 1967, it was not until the following March that the ICITO executive committee voted his concurrent appointment.[13] The same parallel procedure occurred in 1980 with the appointment of Arthur Dunkel. The ICITO committee, until the creation of the WTO, remained the legal entity with fiduciary responsibility for the organization.

The relationship between the GATT, ICITO, and UN influenced other aspects of the organization.[14] The lack of a clear organizational structure meant that both the executive and legislative functions of the institution, poorly articulated in the GATT agreement, were slow to change, even when inefficiencies developed as a result of a vastly increased membership. When created, the secretariat of the Preparatory Committee had acted as the secretariat for the GATT. No secretariat was created in 1948. The lack of supporting materials, normally provided by an international agency secretariat, was not lost on delegates; as early as during the GATT's second trade round in Annecy, members demanded information be available in preparation for negotiations and suggested tasks to be carried on between sessions. But neither at Annecy nor in Torquay were members willing to create, or pay for, any kind of standing committees to do the work of the GATT. Arguing against all forms of delegation, the contracting parties claimed a need to "retain and exercise final authority in all policy matters" (Kock 1969, 77). Only in 1958 did a consensus develop on the need to create a permanent committee of members to act in the name of the organization between rounds. In 1960 the Council was established and any interested member could participate. All members ultimately joined and the Council became the legislative arm of the membership. The Council developed a dual responsibility, both being the meeting place for the contracting parties and providing oversight of the secretariat. The secretariat, whose number in the 1960s was still under fifty, did preparatory work for trade rounds and provided oversight of the membership's trade practices. On a day-to-day basis, however, it was the countries with permanent representation in Geneva that had the greatest voice in the organization. The result was a Janus-faced personality. During trade rounds, a large number of countries attended and did "due diligence" of the organization. Between rounds, a small secretariat, under the watchful eyes of the largest members, focused the organization on an ever-expanding agenda of trade issues.

Although remaining more "member driven" than the IMF or World Bank, the secretariat's executive functions and authority expanded slowly, in line with the growth of the regime. Until the 1980s, the secretariat remained organized into relatively few divisions, changing little from its original structure. The director-general appointed one deputy, and until the Kennedy Round, the GATT was divided into only two divisions: Trade Intelligence and Trade Policy.[15] With the Kennedy Round, the Trade Policy Division divided into functional areas. The general division dealt with tariff and nontariff barriers, an agricultural division dealt with farm product issues, a development division supported projects for the developing world, and an administrative division dealt with internal management. As dispute settlement became regularized, a legal office was created (1980) and became the collective legal memory of the group.[16] Tariff negotiations required increasing amounts of data and other technical information resulting in the creation and expansion of a statistics division to provide members with tariff information both during and between trade rounds. The secretariat grew to over five hundred persons and an internal structure with over twenty divisions and four deputy directors-general. The increase in staffing not only reflects an increase in the level of complexity of trade regulation but also the incorporation of membership divisions into staffing allocation. For example, by implicit agreement, an American has always held one of the deputy director-general positions but never the director-general role. Instead of challenging the U.S. position in the secretariat, directors-general satisfied different constituencies by adding more deputies.

The American presence in the GATT took a number of forms, in addition to providing a permanent deputy director-general. Until Doha, no new round was initiated without authorization from the U.S. Congress of a grant to the president of negotiating authority. The political battles over such authorization often spilled over onto GATT politics. In Torquay, negotiations stalled waiting for an extension of the 1951 Trade Agreements Act. That extension came in 1955 and was renewed, but the limited mandate explains the minimal result of the tariff round in Geneva in 1956. In part, congressional intransigence reflected problems with the mode of tariff reduction adopted in 1947. U.S. duties had declined almost 19 percent from their 1945 levels as a result of the 1947 negotiation. This reduction was not matched by concessions from trading partners. Since 1934, the United States had received concessions on 62 percent of its exported products, but of these, half were mere bindings at current rates (Evans 1971, 11). Annecy had led to few reductions (on 8.3 percent of dutiable imports) representing concessions from ten of the eleven countries acceding to the GATT (Evans 1971, 13). From the U.S. perspective, Torquay had been more successful, in large part because of the addition of West Germany, and the United States had reduced tariffs on about 35 percent of its products. But thereafter, the process slowed. A Republican administration in Washington, the lessened need for import concessions to supply dollars around the globe, and an increasing number of nations participating in the organization resulted in small rounds in 1956 (Geneva) and in 1960–61 (the Dillon Round).

U.S. interest appeared to be rekindled with the election of John Kennedy. With significant negotiating authority, the United States pushed its trading partners for expanded trade discussions (see Evans 1971; Preeg 1970). The Kennedy Round was a turning point in the history of the regime. The reduction in tariffs was about 35 percent, no more than in the 1947 Geneva Round or at Torquay in 1950–51, but the size and scope of the effort made this a far more international undertaking than earlier rounds. Three aspects are noteworthy. First, the round moved away from the bilateral bargaining approach of earlier years, and members applied an agreed upon reduction formula to their tariff schedules. Much of the politics of the round involved negotiations over specific formulas, although the ability to select products on an exceptions list meant that bilateral bargaining continued over specific products.[17] Second, the negotiating agenda expanded to include nontariff barriers. Although the U.S. Congress subsequently failed to ratify an agreement on dumping, its existence paved the way for the inclusion of a range of new trade issues in future rounds. Third, the number of actors and the breadth of products on the table increased the role and visibility of the secretariat. Wyndham White, the director-general, played an instrumental role in assuring the success of the round, and his successors undertook the same responsibilities, relying on the secretariat to supply trade data, technical support, and policy advice.[18]

While the Kennedy Round still focused on reciprocal tariff concessions on manufactured goods, the Tokyo Round, concluded in 1979, focused on nontariff barriers to trade.[19] As is explained in subsequent chapters, delegates dealt with a range of new issues such as government procurement, customs valuation, and technical standards. On U.S. insistence, problems in aircraft and counterfeit goods made their way onto the negotiating agenda.[20] But as suggested previously, the reconciliation of these diverse issues was accomplished through a derogation of GATT norms; that is, only a subset of countries assumed the obligations of the codes, and they did not always lead to more open markets. By the late 1970s, basic GATT principles had been compromised on a number of fronts, in part a reaction to changes in the world economy. Not only were countries subject to two oil shocks causing unprecedented budget deficits, but also American economic supremacy was challenged by the emergence of both Japan and Germany as economic rivals. Domestic support within the United States and elsewhere eroded as governments were pressured by an expanding number of constituents for protection from world market pressures. Within the GATT, a group of developing countries, including the fast-growing Asian economies, joined with other regime members,

TABLE 2.1.
GATT/WTO Senior Secretariat Officeholders, 1947–2005

Executive secretary (1948–65)	Eric Wyndham White (UK)
Deputy (1947–48)	Julio Lacarte-Muro (Uruguay)
Deputy (1948–61)	Jean Royer (France)
Director-general (1965–68)	Eric Wyndham White (UK)
Deputy (1962–67)	Finn Gundelach (Denmark)
Director-general (1968–80)	Olivier Long (Switzerland)
Deputy (1973–80)	MG Mathur (India)
Deputy (1973–80)	Gardner Patterson (US)
Director-general (1980–86)	Arthur Dunkel (Switzerland)
Deputy (1980–86)	MG Mathur (India)
Deputy (1980–86)	William B. Kelly (US)
Director-general (1986–89)	Arthur Dunkel (Switzerland)
Deputy (1986–89)	MG Mathur (India)
Deputy (1986–89)	Charles R. Carlisle (US)
Director-general (1989–93)	Arthur Dunkel (Switzerland)
Deputy (1989–91)	MG Mathur (India)
Deputy (1989–93)	Charles R. Carlisle (US)
Director-general (1993–95)	Peter Sutherland (Ireland)
Deputy (1993–95)	Anwar Hoda (India)
Deputy (1993–95)	Jesus Seade (Mexico)
Deputy (1993–95)	Warren Lavorel (US)
Director-general (1995–99)	Renato Ruggiero (Italy)
Deputy (1995–99)	Anwar Hoda (India)
Deputy (1995–99)	Jesus Seade (Mexico)
Deputy (1995–99)	Warren Lavorel (US)
Deputy (1995–99)	Chulsu Kim (Korea)
Director-general (1999–2002)	Mike Moore (New Zealand)
Deputy (1999–2002)	Andrew Stoler (US)
Deputy (1999–2002)	Paul Henri Ravier (France)
Deputy (1999–2002)	Miguel Rodriquez Mendoza (Venezuela)
Deputy (1999–2002)	Ablasse Ouedraogo (Burkina Faso)
Director-general (2002–5)	Supachai Panitchpakdi (Thailand)
Deputy (2002–5)	Roderick Abbott (UK)
Deputy (2002–5)	Kiphorir Aly Azad Rana (Kenya)
Deputy (2002–5)	Francisco Thompson-Flores (Brazil)
Deputy (2002–5)	Rufus H. Yerxa (US)

Note: The title of the executive secretary was changed in 1965 to director-general.

notably, India, Brazil, and Egypt, to demand special treatment. American diplomats were little interested in forcing coherence in the organization and instead sanctioned a large range of exceptions in both GATT articles and in GATT norms, with the signing of the Short-Term Agreement in Cotton Textiles in 1961 and then in 1973, the more generalized Multi-Fiber Arrangement (MFA). The developing world had little voice in these agreements. In 1964, developing countries moved outside the GATT and formed UNCTAD, the United Nations Conference on Trade and Development, as the forum for their discussions of economic development. It was in good part a result of UNCTAD recommendations that Part IV was added to the GATT agreement, providing special and differential status for developing countries and exempting them from having to make reciprocal trade concessions. The Generalized System of Preferences was adopted in the early 1970s and added discrimination to the regime by institutionalizing a two-track system of obligations.

2.4. Creating the WTO

As detailed in the next chapters, the last round under the GATT led to a reevaluation of the regime's institutions and the recreation of the organization itself. As well as orchestrating the construction of the WTO, the round led to two critical changes. First, the agenda expanded to include trade-related intellectual property issues (TRIPS). Other new items on the agenda, such as negotiations on services (GATS), and investment issues (TRIMS) were more traditional additions to the GATT panoply of issues. In particular, the agreement on intellectual property signaled a new era for the regime, opening the door to a range of domestic regulatory issues. Where previous agreements regulated products only when they left the shore of the producer nations, TRIPS related to production issues within member states.

The second noteworthy change in the structure of rounds was the "single undertaking." Since the Kennedy Round, the principle of differential obligation had infused the liberalization process. The notion of a single undertaking was a throwback, an ideal more consistent with earlier reciprocal-MFN trade agreements. Joining the WTO now meant that all countries were subject to all the agreements covered by the organization. Where previous codes obligated only some of the membership, all WTO countries were now under the same regulatory system. Bundling the agreement in this way assured a tight and comprehensive trade accord. Perhaps because many of the leaders in the developing world did not fully foresee the difficulties they would encounter in adhering to the accords, they went along with the premise. Since many nations had still not met their obligations at the turn of the century, the organization was faced with two unpopular alternatives—either give extensions of time to the developing world and undermine the notion of a more tightly ruled regime or force already over-extended countries into multiple dispute settlement panels. As the WTO entered the twenty-first century, the difficulties experienced by members in adhering to Uruguay Round promises had led to an increase in criticism of the regime and an inability to find support for liberalization goals, both a reflection of the growing divergence of interests of the membership. These issues are taken up in subsequent chapters.

2.5. Making Authoritative Decisions

The GATT/WTO developed both legislative and judicial forms of decision making that were unpredictable from the original agreement. The GATT had been created to facilitate bargaining among participants on the regulation and liberalization of trade policy. American interests in the regime centered on its ability to reduce tariffs and not much more. Still, U.S. negotiators understood that to make tariff reductions meaningful, nations needed to abrogate the use of other measures, notably nontariff measures, or they would undermine the agreements just signed. The GATT at its inception therefore adopted the provisions on such measures that were agreed to in the ITO charter (Hudec 1991, 5). These rules were comprehensive, both prohibiting many nontariff barrier and domestic restrictions to trade as well as specifying exceptions for a variety of reasons, ranging from balance-of-payments problems to predatory dumping. These rules applied to all members who acceded to the GATT, whereas tariff agreements were binding only on those participating in a tariff reduction round.[21]

Although concerned that nations live up to their promises, the mechanism for assuring compliance depended upon a nation, in the name of a producer, complaining about a violation. The secretariat had neither direct oversight nor judicial powers. Although the secretariat compiled data on trade practices starting in 1989, through the Trade Policy Review Mechanism (TPRM), the data in these reports were not considered grounds for a dispute, nor did they constitute legal evidence of a country's trade practices. Monitoring occurred through domestic oversight; when a complaint was filed, the secretariat assisted in the formation of a panel. If the panel found in favor of one of the parties and both parties to the dispute accepted the report, countries were obligated to change their behavior. In the absence of a change in practice, little could be done other than sanctioning retaliation.

As explained in the next chapter, the organization moved over time to expand and specify procedures of oversight and dispute settlement. While the membership agreed to these arguably "judicial" reforms, they were far more reticent to change the character of the "legislative" or rule-making procedures established in 1947. In principle, when the WTO came into existence, small nations gained authority through formal constraints on the other members both in the Council and in dispute settlement procedures. Specific voting changes were agreed to during the Uruguay Round. Waivers required a three-quarters majority, purportedly constraining the ability of the larger nations to grant themselves exceptions from the rules of the game. To revise the general principles of the WTO requires unanimity, but a two-thirds vote can effect other changes. Unlike the GATT, if voting occurs in the WTO, the majority creates an international obligation on all members, regardless of the provisions of their domestic legislation. This is far more intrusive than was the GATT 1947 decision to allow the original contracting parties to "grandfather" domestic laws inconsistent with GATT rules. As opposed to the GATT, where trade concessions only obligated participants, WTO members all agreed to abide by all the rules covered in the Results of the Uruguay Round of Multilateral Trade Negotiations.

Since WTO membership is three-fourths developing nations, the result might have been a power shift toward these countries (see figure 2.1). Decision making in the GATT/WTO, however, is not dictated by formal voting rules. In principle, legislative matters are taken up during ministerial conferences, scheduled every two years. Each member has a vote, and decisions are rendered by the General Council. Details of the trade regime are decided formally in committees, open to all members. There is little delegation in this committee system—all interested and involved parties attend both the General Council and relevant committees. Crucially, as in the GATT, the WTO has continued the practice of making formal decisions through consensus. Voting is stipulated in the agreement, but, except for waivers and accessions, which are done by mail ballot, only consensus decision making is used. Issues are not decided by particular majorities but, rather, consensus is assumed unless someone speaks against a policy. Instead of granting all members a veto, the consensus rule assures that contentious issues are not brought forward to a vote.

This formal organizational structure has not been the locus of rule making in the trade regime. In practice, most of the decisions of the organization are effectively taken in informal caucuses. The inability to govern could have led members to delegate increasing powers to the secretariat, but members have consistently refused to allocate resources necessary to augment the professional staff in Geneva. The staff level at the turn of the century was still under six hundred, small compared to some international institutions, such as the World Bank, with a staff of eight thousand persons. Although the secretariat has grown over time, staffing numbers have

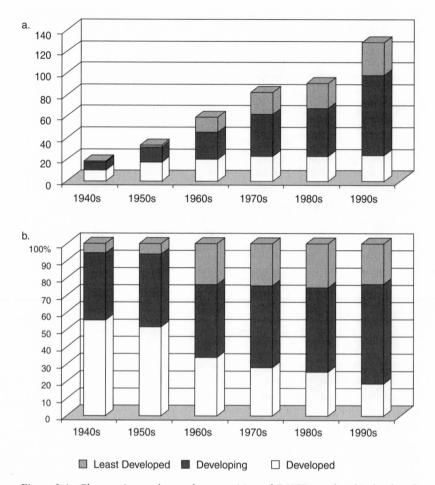

Figure 2.1. Changes in number and composition of GATT membership by decade

not kept pace with increases in trade. During the Dillon and Kennedy rounds, the staff tripled, from 71 in 1960 to 234 in 1968 (Blackhurst 1993, 38). The number of employees increased to almost 500 during the Uruguay Round negotiations. In the period between 1960 and 2000, world trade increased 1,097 percent; comparatively, the secretariat grew about 600 percent.[22] Similarly, the WTO's budget is small when compared to other agencies. For example, the World Bank's administrative budget alone was $1,052 million in 2002, compared to a $75 million total budget for the WTO. Indicative of the underlying authority relationships in the organization, its budget is funded by the largest trading countries.

The amount of formal delegation to the secretariat has always been limited. The director-general has the power of persuasion and can appoint the top echelon of the organization, including the deputy directors-general, but has limited direct authority. For example, director-general cannot initiate a dispute settlement case and has no votes in any committee; only rarely are members of the secretariat called on to be the chair of a standing committee. There is a legal office, but the office has no ability to either write or interpret laws. As noted in the preamble to the internal note provided to panel members on how to draft a report, the "responsibility of the GATT Secretariat is limited to providing the panel with a secretary and technical services and advice on legal, historical and procedural issues" (GATT Legal Affairs 1989). The legal office advises the panel that they should consider guidelines by the secretariat but that "the particular circumstances of a concrete case may provide good reasons for following a path different from the one suggested" (p. 1).

As Richard Blackhurst (1998) observes after a career in the research arm of the secretariat, even without formal powers the secretariat still has considerable influence on the regime. Although it is true that panel members can deviate from the structures for panel reports and investigations suggested by the legal division, they rarely do in practice. In between rounds and ministerial meetings, the members of the secretariat are in constant communication with delegates in Geneva. They provide the basic information used by members to interpret both their own and their trading partners' trade practices. The choice of division heads in the secretariat influences not only the efficiency of the organization but also has less visible effects on the organization's morale and willingness to fulfill its basic tasks of monitoring and information dissemination. For developing nations who have no permanent delegation in Geneva to attend to trade matters, the secretariat provides both administrative support and information. The secretariat runs seminars to educate trade ministers and provides technical assistance to enable countries to not only accede to the WTO but abide by their agreements. As the politically contentious election between Mike Moore and Supachai Panitchpakdi in 1999 for director-general suggests, members are willing to expend considerable resources in order to gain control of the secretariat.

On a daily basis, power in the organization moves between the larger members and the secretariat. The large nations have assured their voice in different ways over time. In the early years, through 1959, the contracting parties attempted to pursue policies that a large majority, if not all members, could agree to. Consensus was possible because of the clublike nature of the early GATT. By the mid-1960s, however, as the organization grew, a second type of informal decision-making was developed. Informally, the GATT agenda was set by a dialogue between the United States and EU, with some attention paid to the interests of Canada and Japan; if disagreement arose, particular members were invited to participate in the conversation, being chosen because their opinions were thought critical to an agreement. In 1975 the GATT created a formal version of this system in the Group of 18, mandated to make recommendations to the Council. The group was made permanent in 1979 and met twenty-nine times before it was disbanded in 1987 (Preeg 1995, 75).[23] The small-group decision-making that occurred during the tenure of the G18 continued even after it was disbanded. That process, associated with an invitation into the "Green Room," has been referred to by Blackhurst (1998) as the "concentric circle" model of decision making. This system allowed countries that cared strongly about an issue to gain membership in the inner circle that devised the policy. The specific decisions of this smaller group were then vetted by a larger group, allowing consensus to develop. Still, the disjuncture between the power of numbers, represented by the growth in the number of small developing-country members, and the asymmetric power of the few big countries was most evident during the Seattle ministerial meeting in 1999, when small nations reportedly stormed one of the informal "Green Room" meetings, demanding representation at the table.

In situations where the principals of an organization cannot agree, logic suggests that the agent, here the secretariat, would be able to enlarge its autonomy. In certain respects, the weakness of the decision-making system has granted the secretariat more authority than would be expected given its small budget and size. In 1977 the secretariat was authorized to publish what was called the *Review of Developments in the Trading System*. These reports were replaced by the TPRM in 1989, over the protest of countries such as India, which argued against granting the secretariat such oversight. The agreement meant that the four largest trading countries, EU, United States, Japan, and Canada (the Quad) were reviewed every two years, the next sixteen largest members reviewed every four years, and the rest every six years. The provision of information is one of a number of ways in which the secretariat's authority has grown. Not only does the secretariat provide data for trade negotiations, support committees, panels, and the Appellate Body and services for the smaller, poorer countries that might usually be done by trade ministers, but it also provides the institutional memory for delegates and panel participants.

2.6. Alternatives to Multilateralism: Preferential Trade Agreements

The trade regime was constructed on the premise that members could join narrower trading systems and not be in violation of either institutional rules or norms. Indicatively, Article I of the GATT allowed for the considerable array of preferential arrangements in force in 1947,[24] and Article XXIV created rules for customs unions and free trade areas. The vast increase in the number of preferential trade agreements (PTAs) that have evolved in parallel with the GATT/WTO system can be understood both in contradistinction to the multilateral regime and as a part of the overall trade liberalization process.[25] Such agreements do violate the basic MFN principle of the GATT/WTO system and may divert trade from the most efficient exporters. But they can also provide political support for more rapid liberalization of trade than would otherwise be possible. The interaction between the discriminatory and nondiscriminatory trade systems is complex and constantly changing. Moreover, no two discriminatory trade agreements are alike, and each differs in its relationship with the multilateral trade system.

PTAs have existed alongside the trade regime since its inception. Although the United States attempted to have the United Kingdom dismantle the system of imperial (later Commonwealth) preferences established on the eve of the Great Depression, they were ultimately recognized as a legitimate derogation from the principle of nondiscrimination. The system of Commonwealth preferences was weakened in the 1960s by British devaluation of the pound and dealt a severe blow by the decision of the United Kingdom in the 1960s to press for membership in the European Economic Community (EEC, later the EC). The creation of a collective institutional structure to preserve preferential access for all the former European colonies softened the blow, but the former dominions (Australia, Canada, and New Zealand) as well as the South Asian countries were essentially left out of these new arrangements.[26]

The development of the EU as a regional bloc is also tied in intimately with the development of the GATT/WTO system. Though few in 1947 would have imagined the impact that the EU would come to have on the multilateral trade system, there was interest already in the development of integrated markets in continental Europe. As early as 1922, Belgium and Luxembourg had formed an economic union (BLEU), and the Netherlands joined in 1948 to establish the Benelux Union. Thus the habit of integration, at least among small countries, was already established.[27] At first the integration movement focused on similar objectives to those set by the GATT: the removal of quota restrictions among countries and the reduction of tariff barriers. But encouraged by the Marshall Plan and the Organization for European Economic Cooperation (OEEC, forerunner to the Organization for Economic Cooperation and Development, or OECD), the foundations were laid for deeper cooperation that went well beyond the obligations of the GATT. This trend was given a major boost by the failure of the main continental countries to agree on a European political community and a European defense community and the subsequent decision to establish a Coal and Steel Community (ECSC) and an economic community (EEC) to accomplish the desired political entanglement of Germany and France and enhance the security of the Low Countries.

This integration was consistent with GATT membership as stipulated in Article XXIV,[28] but the impact on the multilateral system was sometimes corrosive, as more and more countries began to give regionalism priority over the development of the GATT. As with the Commonwealth preference system, it was in the area of agricultural trade that the conflict became most apparent. For domestic European reasons the inclusion of agriculture in the EEC was essential.[29] Trade in agricultural products was to be free within the EEC, but internal markets were to be regulated to stabilize price levels, under a Common Agricultural Policy (CAP). To get agreement on the price levels, border protection was needed. Attempts to reduce such protection in the GATT were therefore stillborn. The flexible GATT yielded to the realities of domestic politics and the need, supported by the United States, for the development of an integrated European Common Market.

The development of the European Union has in many ways mirrored that of the GATT.[30] By the 1970s the focus was on nontariff barriers and contingent protection, as markets became less transparent in the wake of economic instability. By the 1980s the emphasis was on expanding the range of trade-related areas of policy: in the EC the development of the Single Market broadened the competence of the Community to include intellectual property and services, as well as to harmonize and reconcile standards; in the GATT the Uruguay Round tackled many of the same issues at essentially the same time. Just as the GATT was expanding in membership, so too the EC accumulated new countries: first the United Kingdom, Denmark, and Ireland in 1973, then Greece (1981), Spain and Portugal (1986), and Sweden, Austria, and Finland (1994) joined. In May 2004, ten new members (Czech Republic, Cyprus, Estonia, Hungary, Latvia, Lithuania, Malta, Poland, Slovakia, and Slovenia) joined the EU, and accession negotiations were expected to be concluded for two more countries (Bulgaria and Romania) within a few years. Turkey is awaiting the EU agreement to start the application process, and the remaining Balkan countries are actively pursuing eventual membership. Thus both "widening" and "deepening" have characterized the EC as well as the GATT/WTO in the past three decades.

What explains the coexistence of PTAs and multilateralism? While many analysts suggest that preferential arrangements result from a dysfunctional global trade system, and regionalism often derives from political factors as much as economic factors, these smaller, more discrete agreements may often be best understood as a functional part of the trading regime. First, PTAs are often a precursor of more generalized liberalization. There may be different trade-offs available locally, as reflected in the agriculture/industry trade-off between France and Germany that helped shape the EU, and there may be stronger noneconomic motivations at the local level, as exemplified in the EU and in U.S.-Mexican desires to create the North American Free Trade Agreement (NAFTA). Here, PTAs set the stage for multilateral arrangements by changing the political support for open trade, through shifts in the power of particular domestic groups. Second, when PTAs involve groups of developing countries, they could be thought of as the institutional equivalent of buying an insurance policy. Smaller nations have greater bargaining power in the multilateral arrangement to the extent that they have exit options. Such options are not a disincentive to sign other agreements, but the reverse is true given the power asymmetries present in the world economy. The existence of alternative trading systems for the smaller countries makes multilateral agreements less risky. Although PTAs create an intellectual tension between the discriminatory and the nondiscriminatory trading areas, this tension is not evident in the rules or in the practice of the regime.[31]

Generalizations on regionalism should be made with care.[32] There is little evidence that the EU has allowed GATT and WTO talks to influence the process of either widening or deepening. On the other hand, widening of the EU has generally stimulated a general round of trade talks, in part to offset the trade-diversionary effects—over and above those talks required to compensate trade partners for tariff increases. Similarly, the efforts at regional trade liberalization in Latin America over the past forty years have little connection with the health of the trade system. By contrast, progress in the Free Trade Area of the Americas (FTAA) and in quasi-regional agreements such as the Asia-Pacific Economic Cooperation process (APEC) is much more dependent on the state of the multilateral trade system.

Further, PTAs have contributed to the expansion of the regime into "new" areas of trade cooperation, such as technical standards, intellectual property, service trade, investment, and competition policy. The EU has taken many of these issues to a high level of cooperation and harmonization, but other groupings such as the Closer Economic Relations (CER) agreement between Australia and New Zealand have taken coordinated action on standards, recognition of professional qualifications, and the rights of establishment. Even environmental and labor policies have been the subject of limited agreements in some regional pacts, as for instance in the side agreements in NAFTA. PTAs as test beds for multilateral action can be useful and may have contributed significantly to the "agenda creep" of the GATT/WTO system discussed in the next chapter.

2.7. Conclusion: The Trade Regime, Domestic Constituencies, and Free Trade

The next chapters review particular aspects of change in the trade regime. Three sets of issues are highlighted: the evolution of the formal and informal institution, changes in the constitution of the membership, and the changing nature of the problems on the regime agenda. This chapter has stressed the continuity in regime rules and norms over time. Although reconstituted as the WTO in 1995, the regime shares the strengths and problems of its predecessor. As in 1948, the relationship among members and between members and the secretariat is defined informally. In part, this reflects the political nature of trade—delegation to an international authority is difficult for national leaders. In addition, the preceding review suggests that the weak regime may exist because it serves the U.S. and EU interests. The United States and EU may each have only one vote in the WTO, but the size of their collective market gives each a predominant voice.

Still, there has been change. While the early years were dominated by the need to reduce tariff schedules, since the 1970s the key issues undermining trade liberalization have been regulatory. Trade in items such at telecommunication services demanded different procedures; reconciling the interests of these producers was far different from the process of reconciling variations in the level of tariffs. Neither reciprocity, MFN, nor free trade norms are easily appropriable to the problems posed by service companies attempting to enter new national markets.

Underlying political transformations have also influenced the trade regime. First, the international system has witnessed a radical shift in power relations since the regime's creation. Although formal decision-making procedures did not shift with changes in the relative power of members, informal procedures evolved to accommodate the interests of powerful members. The WTO remains in effect an informal bloc of powerful nations. Smaller nations, which dominate in numbers, remain formal "veto players." The WTO's ability to undermine, but not necessarily create, policy was clearly evident in the fight over who would be director-general in 1999 (Kahler 2001). Even here, coalitions were not divided between the developed and developing world, since the United States and Europe found themselves supporting different candidates.

In addition, diverging interests of the major nations have led the regime to take on a new character. Less a club, the WTO is a forum for countries experiencing increasing levels of competition and a declining arsenal of policy tools to assuage the fears and resolve the economic problems of their constituents. While contributing to cooperation among Quad members, the WTO is also a forum for dissention among the major nations. At various times, dissention has been significant, especially when the end of the Cold War and the two Iraq wars led to a return of the mistrust of American intentions akin to that which occurred at the close of World War II.

Most important in an explanation of changes in the regime are shifts occurring in coalition patterns within member countries. Two changes are noteworthy. First, in many Western nations, a coalition of the far Left and far Right has made it difficult to find continued support for free trade. Whereas the Right fears that delegation to the WTO has led to a loss of sovereignty, the Left fears that the organization is undermining the rights of labor and the protection of the environment. Thus the United States, long the motor of trade liberalization, is itself constrained by a public with limited interest in dealing with the market disturbances that could accompany deeper liberalization. The second change involves the growing activity of transnational actors. Related to shifts in domestic coalitions, new transnational actors challenge the fundamental underpinnings of the state-led organization. Answerable to no constituency, these groups pressure the secretariat, member governments, and individual negotiators, undermining the process of "horse trading" that characterized the reciprocity norm in the organization. The result has been a rise of interest in alternatives to the multilateral trade regime.

The evolution of domestic preferences and the rise of new transnational actors are central variables in the analysis of the regime that follows. While much of trade policymaking still occurs under the WTO's formal umbrella, it is impossible to understand the working of the organization and its ability to mobilize support for trade liberalization and regularization without consideration of the interests and power of those forces that influence the behavior of the member nations.

Notes

1. Economic theory predicts that freer trade will bring relative product prices together, benefiting directly the producers of exportable goods. The distribution of the resulting benefits among factors depends on the technology employed. The real incomes of the owners of factors that are most abundant and that are used most intensively in the production of an exportable product will rise. Trade will over time tend to equalize factor returns across countries, though in practice productivity differences will mask such factor price equalization. International competition tends to reduce the gap between product prices more noticeably than between factor returns.

2. By unilateral we mean that Britain changed policy by fiat, not through a process of negotiated agreements. Certainly, policymakers knew that they could control the trade policy of the colonies, and thus the change in London was mirrored in the colonies and territories; still, it was not until late in the century that Britain signed "liberal" trade treaties with European countries. British trade policy after 1933, the period discussed in the preceding, was far from its free trade

roots, being instead based on a system of imperial preferences with both current and past colonies.

3. Data on the effective tariff rate after these treaties is suspect. By one measure, that is, the ratio of total duties collected to total value of dutiable imports, the U.S. tariff declined from 53.6 percent in 1933 to 25.5 percent in 1946. This reduction of 53 percent in collected customs duties represented both the success of trade treaties and the significant increase in price levels (U.S. Tariff Commission 1948, 4).

4. One of the most important of the treaties signed was an agreement with Mexico in 1942. That treaty had seventeen general articles, and every one of these had a counterpart in the GATT.

5. At the time, the exception was probably a way to assuage fears on the part of smaller trading partners that the United States would renege on an agreement after its partner had become dependent upon world trade.

6. For a more complete analysis of the differences between treaties and the GATT see U.S. Tariff Commission 1948.

7. There are a number of good analyses of the history of GATT and the process of tariff negotiation. Among others, see Bagwell and Staiger 2002a; Irwin 2002; Hoekman and Kostecki 2001, and Dam 1970.

8. See Goldstein 1993 for an explication of the reasoning behind the U.S. acceptance of the MFN principle.

9. In fact, few nations reneged on agreements. Most found it difficult to find another industry on which to lower the rate (in the absence of an export deal at the same time), and in the absence of finding such a product, export interests were implicated by a potential tariff hike by a trading partner. See Goldstein and Martin 2000.

10. GATT negotiations began on a selected number of products. Participants agreed to either bind the tariff rate on certain products at their current or applied rate or at a lower rate. The bound rate was not necessarily as low as the applied rate, i.e., a state would agree on an upper bound for its tariffs during negotiations but could choose for economic reasons to use a lower rate. Over time, applied and bound rates merged for most of the larger developed economies as a result of repeated negotiations. For the smaller and developing member nations, however, a significant difference remains for most products.

11. One metric of the difficulty with gaining consensus on the ITO talks is the number of meetings attended. In the first session, in London, there were 115 meetings between delegates; in Lake Success there were another 58. In Geneva, the second session of the Preparatory Committee, there were 453 individual meetings (Preparatory Committee 1947).

12. The Chinese government on Taiwan withdrew in 1950. Lebanon and Syria withdrew in 1951.

13. Three non-GATT countries were members of eighteen-member ICITO committee: China, El Salvador, and Mexico. All were invited to participate in the election of new executive secretaries. In 1968, only El Salvador failed to show up (GATT Legal Affairs 1968).

14. One indicator of this unusual relationship was that the pension system remained under UN control until after the WTO's creation—the GATT never existed as a legal entity and so could not set its own personnel system.

15. Table 2.1 shows the officeholders at a senior level in the GATT and WTO.

16. The legal office was created only after considerable conversation and dispute; to reconcile the interests of those who did not want a significant presence for lawyers with the need for some legal advice, the first head of the division was not an attorney by training.

17. With the move to formulas, the regime retained the underlying understanding that specific countries would get credit for a reduction and that they would be compensated if a trading partner reneged on its obligations. Countries that were the principal supplier of a product to another country received an initial negotiating right (INR) on the concession, just as they did in bilateral negotiations. The INR gave the partner a right to compensation if the value of the tariff reduction changed.

18. No history of the GATT could be told without reference to the importance of Wyndham White. He not only was able to talk representatives into making concessions but also became a missionary, preaching the value of open trade in speeches and at meetings.

19. Countries at the Kennedy Round negotiated on four nontariff measures: American Selling Price, rejected by Congress; an antidumping code, rejected on grounds that earlier legislation had legal standing; some European user taxes on autos; and Swiss regulations on canned fruit imports (Krasner 1979, 499).

20. The round led to the following agreements: a series of tariff cuts; changed rules relating to dispute settlement; an agreement on trade restrictions for balance-of-payment reasons; codes dealing with dumping and countervailing duties, customs valuation, government procurement, technical barriers and standards, and import-licensing procedures; a sectoral agreement for civil aircraft; and agreements on trade in dairy and bovine meat products (Krasner 1979, 508).

21. Prohibited were all internal restrictions that discriminated against imports and all nontariff barriers, including quantitative restrictions. Three exceptions were made-for quotas linked to production subsidies, preferential government procurement, and quotas on movies. In addition to these exceptions to the use of internal means to thwart imports, the prohibition against quantitative restrictions could be ignored for balance-of-payments purposes, for economic development purposes, for protecting local industry from serious injury due to increased import competition, and for serious public policy purposes such as health, safety, morals, and national security (Hudec 1991, 6).

22. Trade data derived from IMF Direction of Trade series and WTO employment from the WTO website.

23. In 1985, the group was enlarged to twenty-two members.

24. The 1947 agreement had six annexes with exceptions to the MFN principle. Annex A gave benefits to the United Kingdom–related trade bloc, B to the French bloc, C to the Belgium-Luxembourg-Holland bloc, D to the U.S. bloc, E to a Chile bloc, and F to a Lebanon-Syria bloc.

25. For background see WTO Secretariat 2002.

26. The problems that the Commonwealth preferences posed for the multilateral system were highlighted by agricultural trade. The United Kingdom had previously imported agricultural goods from Commonwealth countries as if from a kind of "overseas farm." This posed a challenge both to excluded countries such

as the United States and to the United Kingdom's attempts to form closer trade ties with continental Europe, whose exporters also wished to have access to the large UK import market.

27. The nineteenth century had seen extensive trade and monetary agreements, some resulting in nation building and some in almost global alliances. These had atrophied by the end of the century and were finally rendered moot by the collapse of the political and diplomatic (as well as the social) infrastructure by World War I.

28. Article XXIV insisted that only those free trade areas and customs unions that included "substantially all trade" would be allowed to discriminate against nonmembers, and that the regional agreements should not raise protection against nonmembers. The GATT rules also provided for information to be given to the GATT for consideration by a panel. However, no adverse ruling on the compatibility of any notified free trade area or customs union has been submitted. This is another clear example of a situation of constructive political ambiguity on the part of the countries concerned. One would have difficulty imagining an adverse ruling from the GATT being allowed to change materially a deal struck by countries in the formation of a free trade area.

29. The Netherlands had insisted on the inclusion of agriculture: the Benelux Union had partially excluded Dutch farm exports from Belgian markets. And the French wanted access to the growing German market for agricultural goods (the most efficient German farms were in the east) as a condition for access for German manufactures.

30. Similar developments occurred in Latin America and Asia but with less impact on the GATT/WTO system. The broader issue of regionalism is discussed in chapter 6.

31. This politically desirable flexibility poses a challenge to the increasingly legal nature of the system. It is noteworthy that very few dispute settlement cases have been brought that charge a violation of Article XXIV. Countries have stayed well clear of testing the legal basis for regional trade agreements.

32. Many excellent studies exist on the extent and purpose of preferential trading agreements. See, for example, Frankel 1997; Mansfield 1993; and Mansfield and Milner 1999.

Three

The Politics of the GATT/WTO Legal System: Legislative and Judicial Processes

THE PRECEDING CHAPTER reviewed the development of the GATT/WTO system. This chapter describes and analyzes legislative and judicial rules and processes at the WTO, and considers critiques of those processes.[1] Part 3.1 examines the WTO's *legislative* rules and processes, showing how developed countries (principally the EC and the United States) have dominated WTO legislative decision-making. Part 3.2 describes and analyzes the WTO's *judicial* rules, norms, and processes in light of the legislative process. Trade negotiators from powerful countries see the primary function of the WTO dispute settlement system as helping enforce the terms of agreements reached through the WTO legislative process—even if those agreements appear to have asymmetric consequences. Judicial action consistent with that function reinforces the balance of rights and responsibilities agreed upon by WTO members and embedded in the WTO agreements; the judicial function thereby helps maintain powerful states' political support for the WTO. Judicial lawmaking that upsets that balance would likely be met by political action to check the Appellate Body.

Part 3.3 concludes that despite limited judicial lawmaking that has generated some political turbulence at the WTO, the WTO legal system continues to reflect a balance of rights and responsibilities generally favored by powerful states and so facilitates political support for the organization. However, the chapter ends with observations about the prospects for continued EC-U.S. influence over lawmaking processes at the WTO: increased dispersion of power and divergence of interests among the WTO membership will make it increasingly difficult to sustain the transatlantic cooperation that has been essential to effective operation of consensus decision-making and that has served as a political constraint on judicial lawmaking. In that context, the consensus decision-making rule is likely to come under increasing pressure, and judicial lawmaking will likely pose an increased threat to political support for the institution.

3.1. Legislative Rules and Processes—and Transatlantic Power

In practice, almost all legislative decisions at the WTO are made by consensus.[2] A consensus decision requires no manifested opposition to a motion by any member present. That decision-making rule endows weaker countries with formal power to block the legislation of important hard law that would reflect the will of powerful countries. Why would powerful entities like the EC and the United States support such a rule in an organization like the GATT/WTO that generates mandatory legal obligations?

3.1.1. The Working of Trade Rounds

In all WTO meetings, the formal rules provide that diplomats must fully respect the right of any member representative to attend; intervene; make a motion; take initiatives (raise an issue); introduce, withdraw, or reintroduce a proposal (a legal text for decision) or amendment; and block consensus support required for action. If an empowered state representative fails to object to (or reserve a position on, or accept with qualification— for example, *ad referendum*) a draft at a formal meeting where it is considered, that state may be subjected to an argument that it is estopped by acquiescence from any subsequent objection to the draft.

Although GATT 1947 formally provided for voting, and the General Agreement required different majorities of the contracting parties for approval of different types of actions, decision-making practice differed from these formal requirements. From 1948 to 1959, the GATT often used an informal version of consensus decision-making instead of formal voting. At least as early as 1953 the chairman took a sense of the meeting instead of resorting to a vote (Patterson and Patterson 1994). Since 1959, virtually all GATT/WTO legislative decisions (except on accessions and waivers) have been made by consensus (Porges 1995). The development of the consensus practice at the GATT is explained in part by the en masse accession of developing countries in the late 1950s. If a bloc of developing countries had formed, constituting a supermajority of the contracting parties, then that bloc might have been able to assume many of the legislative functions of the organization, even if all the industrialized countries stood together in opposition (Jackson 1969).

When the WTO was established, consensus decision-making was not only retained, but was adopted as the formally preferred method of decision making: Article IX of the Agreement Establishing the World Trade Organization requires that only "where a decision cannot be arrived at by consensus, the matter shall be decided by voting." It defines consensus the same way it had been defined in GATT practice since 1959: a decision by consensus shall be deemed to have been made on a matter submitted for consideration if no signatory, present at the meeting where the decision is made, formally objects to the proposed decision. There has to date been no voting at the WTO.

Empirically, bargaining at the GATT/WTO has taken one, or a combination, of two forms. When bargaining is law-based, a consensus would seem to require legislation that will be Pareto-improving, obliging the "organ to seek a formula acceptable to all" (Riches 1940), since legislation that would make any state worse off would be blocked by that state. Moreover, the consensus rule permits weak countries to block positive-sum outcomes that they deem to have an inequitable distribution of benefits. Equity has been, of course, a persistent international theme, particularly in postwar economic organizations, and developing countries have often blocked consensus in the GATT/WTO on grounds that a proposal did not sufficiently address their special needs.

In contrast to the law-based approach, many see legislative bargaining and outcomes in the GATT/WTO as a function of interests and power. In this view, it is possible for powerful states to simultaneously respect procedural rules and use various practices to escape the constraints on power apparently intrinsic to those rules. Power-based bargaining takes place when states use sources of power extrinsic to procedural rules as a source of leverage, "invisibly weighting" the formal process. As suggested in chapter 1, in trade bargaining, power may be approximated by GDP, and by that measure the EC and the United States are—by far—the most powerful members of the WTO.

Trade negotiating rounds are the means by which the vast majority of GATT/WTO law, including the various codes, has been legislated. Trade rounds may be analyzed in three stages. Rounds are launched (i.e., initiated) by a law-based consensus on the topics that will be negotiated. Trade rounds are closed when GATT/WTO members reach a consensus on the formal, binding legal texts that become the legal results of the negotiations; rounds are typically closed through power-based bargaining. The core negotiating process, in which legal texts are formulated, takes place between launch and closure.

Since at least as far back as the Kennedy Round, trade rounds have been launched through law-based bargaining. The easiest way to launch a round has been to attain consensus on a vague mandate for negotiation that includes virtually all initiatives offered by any member. This approach has enabled all parties to believe that the round could result in a Pareto-improving and equitable package of outcomes, with domestic political liabilities from increased import competition offset by foreign market-opening. Negotiators typically haggle over alternative ways to frame issues and objectives in the mandate, but to reach consensus, the less prejudice in the mandate, the better. In some rounds, there have been one or two issues that simply could not appear in the mandate because of domestic political constraints. But typically, a consensus on the draft negotiating mandate has been blocked until virtually all topics of interest to members have been included, and until the language has been made sufficiently vague so as not to prejudice the outcome of negotiations in a manner that any country might oppose (Steinberg 2002b). From the perspective of powerful countries, invisible weighting can be used at later stages, and the agenda-setting process has historically operated in the shadow of the coercive power that will be used by the EC and the United States to close the round. Moreover, only at later stages, after years of negotiations, do powerful countries have enough information on state preferences to fashion a package of asymmetric outcomes that they can be confident will be accepted by weaker countries. Hence, bargaining to launch trade rounds has been law-based.

After launching a round, the core negotiating process has three overlapping stages: (1) carefully advancing and developing *initiatives* that broadly conceptualize a new area or form of regulation; (2) drafting and fine-tuning *proposals* (namely, legal texts) that specify rules, principles, and procedures; and (3) developing a *package* of proposals into a "final act" for approval upon closing the round, which requires the major powers to match attainment of their objectives with the power they are willing and able to use to establish consensus. The process frequently involves iteratively modifying proposals in minor ways (for example, providing a derogation, floor, or phase-in), fulfilling unrelated or loosely related objectives of weaker countries, and adjusting the package that will constitute the final act.

The process has taken place on a formal basis in proposal-specific working groups, negotiating committees, the Trade Negotiations Committee, special sessions, and occasional ministerials. But important work takes place on an informal basis in caucuses, the most important of which are convened and orchestrated by the major powers. Most initiatives, proposals, and alternative packages that evolve into documents presented for formal approval have usually been developed first in negotiations between Brussels and Washington, then in increasingly larger caucuses (for example, Quad countries, G-7, OECD), and ultimately in the "Green Room."

These Green Room caucuses, named after a room in the WTO building in which they have sometimes taken place, consist of twenty to thirty-five countries that are interested in the text being discussed and include the most senior members of the secretariat, diplomats from the most powerful members of the organization, and diplomats from a roughly representative subset of the GATT/WTO's membership. The agenda for most important formal meetings, round-launching ministerials, midterm reviews, and round-closing ministerials has been set in Green Room caucuses that usually take place in the weeks preceding and during those meetings. The draft that emerges from the Green Room is presented to a formal plenary meeting of the GATT/WTO members and is usually accepted by consensus without amendment or with only minor amendments. This "concentric circles" model (Blackhurst 1998, 2001) of GATT/WTO decision making has been the primary object of concern by developing countries that want greater internal transparency.

In closing trade rounds, the EC and the United States have employed varying degrees of market power to attain consensus on a final act that may have asymmetric distributive consequences. The United States did not fully employ its trade bargaining power in closing the Tokyo Round because of geostrategic concerns relating to the Cold War. At the end of the Tokyo Round, the developing countries demanded that they be afforded MFN treatment in various codes (e.g., the antidumping and countervailing duty codes) that they refused to sign. When negotiators from Brazil, India, and Egypt declared that they would block a consensus to conclude the round and formalize its outcomes unless the codes were applied on an MFN basis, some senior U.S. trade officials sought an alternative: they threatened to exit the GATT and conclude the codes on a non-MFN basis under a new "GATT-Plus" regime, which had been proposed a few years earlier by the Atlantic Council of the United States. But when proponents of this approach conferred with their State Department counterparts, the proposal was withdrawn: State Department officials did not want to risk further alienation or "UNCTADization" of the developing countries in a bipolar world. The result was that the codes were concluded on an MFN basis, so that developing countries could gain the benefit of the codes without undertaking their obligation (Steinberg 2002b).

In contrast, by 1994 the Cold War had ended, so maximum bargaining power was used by the EC and the United States to close the Uruguay Round. Since the beginning of the Uruguay Round negotiations, most developing countries had stated their intention not to sign onto the agreements on intellectual property, investment measures, or services. U.S. negotiators considered developing-country acceptance of these agreements crucial to U.S. interests and to congressional support of a final package. Moreover, they were determined to avoid the free ride for developing countries that had characterized conclusion of the Tokyo Round.

To effect their desired result, the EC and the United States agreed in October 1990 to use their market power to close the Uruguay Round on terms they favored. Specifically, they agreed to adapt to their purposes a "single undertaking" approach to closing the Uruguay Round. GATT director-general Arthur Dunkel agreed to embed this mechanism in the secretariat's draft Final Act, which was issued in December 1991. As ultimately embodied in the Uruguay Round Final Act, the agreement establishing the WTO constitutes a "single undertaking" and contains "as integral parts" and "binding on all members": the GATT 1994; the GATS; the TRIPS agreement; the TRIMS agreement; the subsidies agreement; the antidumping agreement; and every other Uruguay Round multilateral agreement. The agreement also states that the GATT 1994 "is legally distinct from the General Agreement on Tariffs and Trade, dated 30 October 1947." After joining the WTO (including the GATT 1994), the EC and the United States withdrew from the GATT 1947 and thereby terminated their GATT 1947 obligations (including its MFN guarantee) to countries that did not accept the Final Act and join the WTO. The combined legal and political effect of the Final Act and transatlantic withdrawal from the GATT 1947 was to ensure that most of the Uruguay Round agreements had mass membership rather than a limited membership. Hence, the round was closed through power-based bargaining.[3]

The result of the Uruguay Round was a set of agreements with highly asymmetrical consequences for the developed and developing countries. Studies have shown high variance in the net trade-weighted tariff concessions given and received: some territories, such as the United States, received deeper concessions than they gave; other territories, such as India, South Korea, and Thailand (some of which had given relatively few concessions in the past), gave much deeper concessions than they received (Finger, Reincke, and Castro 1999). Moreover, several computable general equilibrium models have shown that the Uruguay Round results disproportionately benefit developed-country GDPs, and that some developing countries (particularly in sub-Saharan Africa) actually suffered a net GDP loss from the Uruguay Round—at least from 1995 to 2005 (Goldin, Knudsen, and van der Mensbrugghe 1993; Overseas Development Institute 1995; Harrison, Rutherford, and Tarr 1996). More broadly, it is hard to argue that developing-country governments uniformly enjoyed a net domestic political boost from the various agreements contained in the round. They assumed new obligations in the TRIPS and TRIMS agreements, the GATS, and the Understanding on Balance of Payments— which most long opposed; they gained nothing of significance from the revised subsidies and antidumping agreements; and they were required to assume the obligations of those two agreements—in contrast to the Tokyo Round codes, which had voluntary membership. And while the textiles agreement provides for elimination of quotas on textiles and apparel, it is heavily back-loaded, and U.S. tariff peaks of around 15 percent on those products were not eliminated. Most developing countries got little and gave up a lot in the Uruguay Round—yet they signed on (Ramakrishna 1998; Srinivasan 1998a, 99–101; Srinivasan 1998b; Oloka-Onyango and Udagama 2000). As measured by their own objectives going into the last two rounds, by their complaints about the shortcomings of the outcomes, and by the preceding analysis the negotiated outcome could not please developing-country negotiators nearly as much as their EC and U.S. counterparts. Developing countries accepted this outcome because rejection of the WTO agreements would have made them still worse off, eliminating their legal guarantee of access to EC and U.S. markets.

The foregoing discussion shows how power can be used to invisibly weight legislative outcomes at the GATT/WTO, despite the consensus rule. In that light, the most important function of the consensus decision-making rule may be to help generate information about country preferences. The task of a negotiator from a powerful country in GATT/WTO agenda setting is to develop a final act that will maximize fulfillment of the country's objectives, given the power that the country can use to attain consent from all states—a process that one former WTO official has described as "filling the boat to the brim, but not overloading it" (Lavorel 1995). The agenda setters from powerful states must have good information about each country's preferences, the domestic politics behind those preferences, and risk tolerances—across all of the topics that might be covered—to understand potential zones of agreement on a package acceptable to all.

Under the consensus rule, diplomats need to understand those preferences if they are to fashion a substantive package and design legal-political maneuvers that will lead to outcomes acceptable to all. Conversely, under the consensus rule, diplomats from weaker states have opportunities and incentives to provide information on preferences to powerful states. If weaker states perceive that the information they provide will be taken into account by the major powers in their agenda-setting work, then weaker states have an incentive to offer detailed information about their preferences. Even if many weaker states perceive that some of their preferences will be ignored, they have difficulty cooperating to obstruct the information-gathering process because of wide variance in their interests on different issues, and because of defensive and offensive incentives to provide the information.

The consensus rule, of course, serves other functions. It ensures that all have the opportunity to be heard and that different interests can be raised, even if in reality the United States and the European Union dominate because of their market size and power. Perhaps most important, the consensus rule lends legitimacy to the actions of the organization, because those actions may be said to reflect the interests of *all* the members of the organization.

3.2. Implementation and Dispute Settlement: The Expansion of Judicial Lawmaking—and Transatlantic Power

Upon creation of the WTO, the U.S. government favored automatic and binding dispute settlement because most thought such a judicial process would help enforce the set of substantive rules legislated in the Uruguay Round—which the United States favored.[4] This was an important change from the GATT, in which dispute settlement was neither automatic nor binding. The operation of GATT/WTO dispute settlement, the expansion of judicial lawmaking by dispute settlement panels and the Appellate Body, and the Appellate Body's strategic space are analyzed and evaluated subsequently. Thus far, the Appellate Body has engaged in lawmaking that has created some political protest, but it has not fundamentally upset the balance of rights and responsibilities embodied in the Uruguay Round outcomes, so it has not exceeded the bounds of its strategic space.

3.2.1. GATT Dispute Settlement Rules and Processes

The WTO's dispute settlement rules and processes must be understood in the context of the GATT's dispute settlement rules and processes. As shown in chapter 2, the GATT was created to facilitate bargaining among participants over the regulation and liberalization of trade policy. Although concerned that nations live up to their promises, the mechanism for oversight depended upon a nation, in the name of a producer, complaining about a violation. The secretariat had neither oversight nor judicial power. Although the secretariat compiled data on trade practices starting in 1989 through the Trade Policy Review Mechanism (TPRM), the data in these reports constituted neither formal grounds for a dispute nor legal evidence of a country's trade practices. Monitoring occurred through oversight by individual contracting parties; when a complaint was filed, the secretariat assisted in the formation of a panel. If the panel found in favor of the complainant and the complainant did not block a consensus to adopt the panel report, then the contravening party was ordered to change its behavior. In the absence of a change in practice, little could be done other than sanctioning retaliation—though that too required a consensus.

While the choice of a dispute settlement procedure had been an important element of ITO talks, the issue gained scarce attention in the GATT 1947. The actual dispute procedures in the GATT were based on Article XXIII, which specified procedures in cases when parties could not agree after consultations. The article references a contracting party's right to go to the contracting parties for a ruling on a violation. The practice of establishing a panel to assist the contracting parties in understanding a case was initially specified not in the articles but in the Annex that describes the customary practice of the GATT. Over time that Annex became more detailed, covering issues such as notification, rules for the selection of panel members, and the role of member governments. By the 1980s, dispute settlement procedures had been formalized in a series of understandings among contracting parties, which specified in great detail the structure, timing, and rules for the resolution of disputes.

Even with these changes, the fundamental nature of dispute settlement remained constant in the GATT. The contracting parties had to agree by consensus to establish a panel, to adopt the report of a panel, and to authorize any retaliation if a contracting party maintained rules inconsistent with a panel report. Of course, respondents sometimes blocked the consensus required to move through each stage of the process.

The weakness of the GATT dispute settlement procedure became increasingly apparent in the 1980s. In the early years of GATT, 1948–59, contracting parties brought relatively few (53) legal complaints against each other. The panel procedure previously mentioned was developed in these years, and it was used in over half of these cases (Hudec 1992). As the number of contracting parties grew, the number of conflicts increased. Perhaps reflecting dissatisfaction with the settlement procedures, the number of formal complaints did not rise and, in fact, fell after 1963. While there were almost 60 cases that were dealt with by the secretariat through 1962, only one new case was brought forward through 1970. Hudec argues the issue was legitimacy—the process was viewed as unfair (Hudec 1991). Legitimate or not, the caseload increased in the 1970s to a total of 32; in the 1980s the panel process began to be regularly invoked (Hudec 1991). Of the 115 complaints filed in the 1980s, 47 led to panel reports. However, only about two-fifths of rulings for the complainant resulted in full compliance by the respondent (Busch and Reinhardt 2002, 473). Nonetheless, the increased caseload forced the secretariat to create a separate legal division, which had the effect of encouraging even more legal complaints. As the number, visibility, and importance of cases increased, so too did the number of cases in which consensus was blocked.

During the 1970s and 1980s, in response to a growing trade deficit, perceptions of unfair trade practices abroad, and frustration with the sclerotic GATT dispute settlement system, the United States increasingly turned to domestic law to deal with its trade disputes. Specifically, a "unilateral" approach to addressing trade disputes was enacted by the U.S. Congress in the form of Section 301 of the Trade Act of 1974. Section 301 permits (and in some cases, requires) the president to impose retaliatory trade sanctions on countries engaging in practices that are "unjustifiable, discriminatory, or unfair"—as determined by the United States Trade Representative (USTR). Thus, when a foreign government blocked the GATT dispute settlement process, the U.S. government often found itself in a position of threatening unilateral trade retaliation against that government unless it agreed to change its trade practices in accordance with Washington's demands. This American approach to the settlement of trade disputes was not viewed favorably by the rest of the world.

3.2.2. Uruguay Round Reforms and the Creation of the WTO Dispute Settlement System

The United States thus championed a change in dispute settlement procedures as early as the Tokyo Round. American interest in reform was based on a belief that the United States was far more often in conformity with GATT rules than were its trading partners. By the middle of the Uruguay Round, however, it was not only U.S. interests that fueled reform efforts but the perception by others that reform would constrain unilateral U.S. action.

Early in the Uruguay Round, the USTR supported specific changes, arguing that the dispute settlement system had "diminished its credibility and, with it, confidence in the larger institution." Four reforms were suggested. First, the United States argued for a need to increase the role of the director-general or a designate as a mediator in bilateral disputes. This reform was tied to a more comprehensive defense of consultation as a substitute for formal panels. Second, the United States suggested that in cases in which the parties so desired, they could ask for mandatory arbitration. This would not mean that a country found in contravention of its legal obligations would have to change its practice. The United States argued that nations should have the right to accept retaliation or pay compensation (USTR 6). Third, the United States argued that the time period for dispute settlement needed to be shortened. Last, the United States recommended that panel members be chosen from a roster of neutral nongovernmental experts.

The U.S. position at the close of the Uruguay Round was not inconsistent with its earlier position, although by 1990 the United States had endorsed an even more radical shift in policy. Given that a new dispute settlement understanding had been adopted in the 1989 Midterm Review of the Uruguay Round, no one would have been surprised if the issue stayed off the agenda for the rest of the round. However, by December 1990, the United States saw an advantage in appearing to champion a more radical shift in authority away from home governments to the trade regime. The underlying theme was that it was time for member nations to agree to give up their right to block a consensus in the establishment of panels, the adoption of panel reports, and retaliation. Initially aligned closely with Canada but not the other Quad members, the United States proposed not only the automatic adoption of panel reports, but also a right to appeal to a new Appellate Body whose purpose was to oversee the work of panels on questions of law. The time limits established in this process would be modeled on its own Section 301 statute. For the United States, this seemingly radical position was contingent on a crucial proviso—that the substantive rules adopted in the Uruguay Round had to adequately reflect U.S. policy objectives.[5]

At home, increased delegation under these terms was argued to be consistent with American interests: the United States would remain more often in compliance with WTO rules that reflected its interests and policy objectives than would its trading partners. If the WTO's substantive rules were to its liking, and the dispute settlement procedures were both consistent with the timeline for action under Section 301 and could ultimately authorize retaliation for noncompliance, then a more legalized WTO dispute settlement system would legitimize U.S. use of its market power to pressure other countries to comply with U.S. trade policy objectives. Tellingly, the United States shifted to this position on dispute settlement reform at the end of 1990, at the same time that it reached agreement with the EC to impose the results of the Uruguay Round on developing countries via the "single undertaking," described previously. Few nations agreed with the U.S. analysis of who would end up in front of panels. But curbing U.S. unilateralism was one of the most salient elements in both Japan's and the EC's publicly stated interest in the round, and both endorsed the reforms, which assured their adoption.

The WTO dispute settlement procedures are diagrammed in figure 3.1. These procedures occupy thirty-five pages of text and an elaborate accompanying description. The process is far more complex and precise than in the past and covers all areas of WTO agreements, including Section 301 actions by the United States. The Dispute Settlement Understanding (DSU) is far more obligatory, automatic, and apolitical than the GATT rules. The effect of the change—a vast increase in use of the dispute settlement process—was far broader than was anticipated by most. While 535 dispute settlement complaints were filed in the forty-six-year period of the GATT system, 269 complaints were filed in the first eight years alone of the WTO system.[6] The most substantive change in the judicial system in the WTO was the automaticity of the new process. A consensus is now required to *block* the formation of a panel, adoption of a report, or an authorization of retaliation for continued noncompliance—a reversal of the former rule that required a consensus to move through each of these stages. Of course, petitioners would not agree to block establishment of a panel they are demanding, and prevailing parties would not block the adoption of favorable panel reports.

The other significant change was the creation of a judicial body to which nations could appeal panel reports. The Appellate Body's mandate is formally limited to the review of legal findings made by panels, given the facts established by the panel. The Appellate Body has seven members, chosen by the members at large, and appeals are heard by a subset of three members.

The Panel Process

The various stages a dispute can go through in the WTO. At all stages, countries in dispute are encouraged to consult each other in order to settle 'out of court'. At all stages, the WTO director-general is available to offer his good offices to mediate or to help achieve a conciliation.

NOTE: some times are maximums, some minimums, some binding, some not

60 days	**Consultations** (Art 4)	
by 2nd DSB meeting	**Panel Established** by Dispute Settlement Body (DSB) (Art 6)	**During all stages** good offices, conciliation or mediation (Art 5)
0–20 days	**Terms of reference** (Art 7) **Composition** (Art 8)	
20 days (+ 10 if director-general asked to pick panel)		NOTE: a panel can be composed (i.e. panelists chosen) up to about 50 days after establishment (i.e. DSB's decision to have a panel)
	Panel examination (Normally 2 meetings with parties (Art 12) 1 meeting with third parties (Art 10) →	**Expert review** group (Art 13; Appx 4)
	Interim review stage Descriptive part of report sent to parties for comment (Art 15.1). Interim report sent to parties for comment (Art 15.2) →	**Review meeting with panel** upon request (Art 15.2)
6 mths from panel's composition, 3 mths if urgent	**Panel report** issued to parties (Art 12.8; Appendix 3 par 12(j))	
up to 9 months from panel's establishment	**Panel report** circulated to DSB (Art 12.9; Appendix 3 par 12(k))	**Appellate Review** (Art 16.4 and 17)	max 90 days
60 days for panel report, unless appealed	**DSB adopts panel/appellate report(s)** including any changes to panel report made by appellate report (Art 16.1, 16.4, and 17.4)	30 days for appellate report
'REASONABLE PERIOD OF TIME' determined by: member proposes, DSB agrees; or parties in dispute agree; or arbitrator (approx. 15 mths if by arbitrator)	**Implementation** report by losing party of proposed implementation within 'reasonable period of time' (Art 21.3) →	**Possibility of proceedings** including referral to initial panel on proposed implementation (Art 21.5)
	In cases of non-implementation parties negotiate compensation pending full implementation (Art 22.2 and 22.6)	
30 days after 'reasonable period' expires	**Retaliation** If no agreement on compensation, DSB authorizes retaliation pending full implementation (Art 22.2 and 22.6) **Cross-retaliation:** same sector, other sectors/agreements (Art 22.3) →	**Possibility of arbitration** on level of suspension, procedures, and principles of retaliation (Art 22.6 and 22.7)

TOTAL FOR REPORT ADOPTION: Usually up to 9 mths (no appeal) or 12 mths (with appeal) from establishment of panel to adoption of report (Art 20)

90 days

Figure 3.1. WTO dispute settlement procedures

When a member fails to comply with a WTO dispute settlement decision, despite opportunities to do so within a "reasonable period of time" (which may be determined by the DSB), the adversely affected complainant may retaliate. Retaliation takes the form of raising tariffs on goods originating in the territory of the contravening country to a level that is intended to have the effect of eliminating demand for the imports. Retaliation must be proportionate to the adverse effect of the contravening measures.

Even with the formalization and expansion of the dispute process, trade problems are solved in much the same manner as they have over the last fifty years. Complaints lead the parties to consult—about one-third of all complaints are settled here, either because a resolution becomes apparent or else because the intransigence or salience of the issue leads neither party to want an authoritative decision. The actual judicial findings most often lead states to change their behavior, if politically convenient. If not, states can ask to retaliate, but far more often they do not. It is more often the controversies among the major actors (such as over steel between the United States, EC, and Japan, and bananas, beef hormones, and foreign sales corporations between the EC and United States) that lead to sanctioned retaliation.

3.2.3. The Main Function of WTO Dispute Settlement as Originally Conceived

The negotiating history behind the move to legalization of GATT/WTO dispute resolution suggests that it was not intended to lead to expansive judicial lawmaking. The switch to automatic, binding dispute resolution and the establishment of the Appellate Body were seen by the United States as an opportunity to foster implementation of and compliance with the deals struck in the legislative process—even if those deals were not optimally efficient and even if they were not considered equitable. The dispute settlement process was to fulfill that purpose by offering a neutral judicial process to enforce the WTO agreements. Our previous analysis of the legislative process and outcomes shows that the EC and United States have been able to dominate bargaining and the outcomes that comprise the WTO agreements. The United States was willing, and remains willing, to delegate to WTO dispute settlement the authority to enforce those agreements. The U.S. government may win a few cases, and it may lose a few, but WTO dispute settlement losses are of little consequence if the overall effect of the system is to help enforce substantive agreements supported by the United States. Hence, to the extent that it is performed effectively, the judicial function helps reinforce political support for the WTO by powerful countries.

Other governments view the dispute settlement system similarly, although from a different angle. They, too, want the contract enforced. John Jackson has argued that legalization and adjudication helps weaker members by reducing the scope for arbitrary use of power (Jackson 1997a). Many weaker members view the increased legalization of GATT/WTO dispute settlement as constraining the United States' unilateral determination of the terms of the contract. From the U.S. perspective, that foreign perception is politically useful: the DSU provides a vehicle by which the U.S. government may legitimately challenge WTO-inconsistent practices by foreign governments, and it has simultaneously helped solve America's credibility problem arising from unilateralism.

The result is a DSU that works in almost perfect sync with Section 301 to create political incentives for foreign governments to comply with their WTO obligations—and to restrain U.S. unilateralism when foreign governments are complying. Under the terms of the statute, the USTR may not retaliate if the WTO Dispute Settlement Body (DSB) concludes that the foreign government is behaving in a WTO-consistent manner; but the USTR must retaliate if the DSB concludes that the foreign government is behaving in a WTO-inconsistent manner and does not comply with the terms of the DSB decision. As the DSU timetable was drafted to accord with the investigative and retaliatory schedule provided for in Section 301, in implementing the DSU, the United States needed to make almost no changes to Section 301.

The manner in which threatened retaliation is packaged usually induces compliance by the threatened party. For example, under regulations promulgated pursuant to Section 301, the U.S. government publishes a proposed retaliation list in the Federal Register thirty days prior to the effective date of retaliation. Typically, the U.S. government's proposed retaliation list targets scores of products made by politically powerful producers in the contravening country. This has the effect of pitting those politically powerful producers against the industry that champions the contravening measures. If targeted smartly, the proposed retaliation list mobilizes sufficient political muscle within the contravening country to result in WTO-consistent reform. In this way, the DSU works in conjunction with domestic laws, regulations, and politics to foster compliance with the legislative outcomes that are codified in the WTO agreements (Goldstein and Martin 2000).

Hence, from the U.S. government perspective, the radical judicial reforms of the Uruguay Round represented not a multilateralization of U.S. unilateralism, but an Americanization of the GATT/WTO dispute settlement process.

3.2.4. Evaluating WTO Jurisprudence: The Emergence of Liberalizing Judicial Lawmaking

Few, if any, architects of increased legalization at the WTO foresaw the institutional development that would follow: largely in the interests of completeness, coherence, and internal consistency of WTO law, WTO judicial decisions have created an expansive body of new law. WTO judicial lawmaking has two dimensions: filling gaps and clarifying ambiguities. Gapfilling refers to judicial lawmaking on a question for which there is no legal text directly on point, whereas ambiguity clarification refers to judicial lawmaking on a question for which there is legal text but that text needs clarification.[7] These dimensions of WTO judicial lawmaking are illustrated in more detail in what follows; the suggestion is not that these cases were decided incorrectly, nor that the Appellate Body has exceeded its authority, but that substantial judicial lawmaking is taking place at the WTO (Davey 2001).

JUDICIAL LAWMAKING: GAP FILLING

The DSU's silence on many procedural questions has been seen by some as an invitation to the Appellate Body to make procedural rules. In some cases, the Appellate Body has created law that fills procedural gaps in WTO agreements, even though the existence of the gap has resulted from sharp disagreement among members about how to fill it. For example, in *United States—Import Prohibition of Certain Shrimp and Shrimp Products* (2000), the Appellate Body decided—without clear guidance from WTO agreements—that dispute settlement panels could consider amicus curiae briefs submitted by nonstate actors. In so ruling, the Appellate Body relied on general language in DSU Article 13, which provides that panels have a right to seek information and technical advice from any individual or body that it deems appropriate. Regardless of the merits on the question, the Appellate Body's interpretation of Article 13 was made in the context of several years of North-South deadlock on the question of whether to permit amicus briefs: few developing countries would have consented to an agreement with that outcome, yet the Appellate Body chose to interpret the DSU as supporting it.

Similarly, in *European Communities—Regime for the Importation, Sale and Distribution of Bananas (1997)*, the Appellate Body established that private lawyers may represent members in its oral proceedings, despite EC and U.S. opposition on grounds that the practice from the earliest years of the GATT was to permit presentations in dispute settlement proceedings exclusively by government lawyers or government trade experts. The Appellate Body acted at odds with nearly fifty years of GATT practice, reasoning that nothing in WTO agreements, customary international law, or the "prevailing practice of international tribunals . . . prevents a WTO Member from determining the composition of its delegation in Appellate Body proceedings." At the panel stage, this practice of permitting participation by nongovernment lawyers was subsequently adopted in *Indonesia—Certain Measures Affecting the Automobile Industry (1998)*.

JUDICIAL LAWMAKING: CLARIFYING AMBIGUITY

The WTO Appellate Body has engaged repeatedly in a form of lawmaking by which it has given specific meaning to ambiguous treaty language. Such clarifications may cause a negative political reaction by members or nongovernmental stakeholders that engaged in behavior that was within a range of possible meanings, given the ambiguity. For example, in *U.S.— Shrimp-Turtle*, the Appellate Body decided whether the United States could rely on GATT Article XX(g) to ban the importation of certain shrimp and shrimp products from members that did not maintain laws that guaranteed particular methods of protecting endangered sea turtles in the process of shrimp fishing. Article XX(g) excepts certain measures from the GATT's affirmative obligations if they are necessary for the "conservation of exhaustible natural resources," but the provision is ambiguous through silence on the question of whether such exhaustible natural resources must be located within the jurisdiction of the country invoking the exception. Earlier decisions suggesting that they must catalyzed enormous debate by the members. The Appellate Body offered a dynamic interpretation of the conditions under which the Article XX(g) exception for conservation of exhaustible natural resources could be invoked, stating that it must be read "in light of contemporary concerns of the community of nations about the protection and conservation of the environment." After concluding that the measures in question fell within the meaning of Article XX(g), the Appellate Body interpreted the justifying clause or *chapeau* to Article XX and established at least five specific factors that would apply in considering whether a measure contravenes the terms of the *chapeau*. Some of the factors had no textual lineage (e.g., whether the respondent's actions have an "intended and coercive effect on the specific policy decisions of other members"). In short, the Appellate Body ruling provided an approach to balancing trade-environment issues, despite WTO members having been deadlocked for a decade about how to achieve balance on the question (Steinberg 2002c).

In other instances, the Appellate Body has given precise and narrow meaning to language that was intentionally left vague by negotiators, either because they could not agree on more specific language, or in order to permit a range of alternative behaviors or national practices. For example, in three decisions, *United States—Safeguard Measures on Imports of Fresh, Chilled or Frozen Lamb Meat from New Zealand and Australia (2001)*, *United States—Definitive Safeguard Measures on Imports of Wheat Gluten from the European Communities (2000)*, and *United States—Definitive Safeguard Measures on Imports of Circular Welded Carbon Quality Line Pipe from Korea (2002)*, the Appellate Body fleshed out the causation analysis to be used in safeguards cases, which Uruguay Round negotiators intentionally left ambiguous.[8] In the *U.S.—Lamb Meat* case, for example, based on the obligation not to attribute injury from other causes to imports that were the subject of a safeguards investigation, the Appellate Body established an affirmative requirement that national authorities analyze not only the nature but also the "extent" of other causes. A similar approach was taken in the antidumping context in *United States—Antidumping Measures on Certain Hot-Rolled Steel Products from Japan (2001)*. The U.S. government and commentators have identified several other cases in which the Appellate Body or dispute settlement panels have given a specific and narrow interpretation of language in WTO agreements that was intended by at least some of its negotiators to be ambiguous and to permit a range of national practices (U.S. Secretary of Commerce 2002; Tarullo 2003; Barfield 2001). Decisions like these might enhance efficiency (Sykes 1991), but they are certain to engender negative political reactions in countries that intended to consent to broader interpretations.

Finally, a conflict between GATT/WTO texts (or between text and GATT practice) may create an ambiguity. In a handful of cases, the Appellate Body has read language across GATT/WTO agreements cumulatively in a way that has generated an expansive set of legal obligations. Perhaps most controversially, in *U.S.—Lamb Meat* and *Argentina—Safeguard Measures on Imports of Footwear (1999)*, the Appellate Body ruled that national authorities imposing a safeguards measure must demonstrate the existence of "unforeseen developments." In the 1952 *U.S.—Hatters' Fur* case, a GATT Working Party had agreed that the application of Article XIX safeguards measures could be based on an argument that an unexpected degree of change in consumer tastes that increased imports constituted demonstration of "unforeseen developments." Given that implicitly broad interpretation of the phrase, which would seem to allow almost any increase in imports to constitute "unforeseen developments," subsequent GATT panels did not require national authorities to demonstrate "unforeseen developments" prior to imposing safeguards measures. Moreover, the WTO safeguards agreement makes no reference to a requirement to demonstrate "unforeseen developments," and the negotiators expressly considered and rejected inclusion of any such requirement. The cumulation of GATT practice, relevant texts, and negotiating history created an ambiguity over whether "unforeseen developments" must be demonstrated in safeguards cases. Focusing on GATT Article XIX:1(a), the Appellate Body read all of the relevant GATT/WTO law and practice cumulatively in a way that led to the conclusion that a demonstration of "unforeseen developments" must be shown if a safeguards measure is to be applied.

3.2.5. Explaining Judicial Lawmaking at the WTO: Defining the Appellate Body's Strategic Space

While these are not a random or representative sample of cases of judicial lawmaking at the WTO, it is noteworthy that virtually all of these instances of lawmaking facilitated market-opening interpretations of WTO law—only one decision (*U.S.—Shrimp-Turtle*) created law that may support market closure. Others have argued that the Appellate Body's decisions on trade remedy cases have frequently leaned in a market-opening direction (Tarullo 2003). Liberalization has often been perceived as the raison d'être of the GATT/WTO system, despite the more nuanced view that the WTO agreements represent a politically delicate balance of rights and responsibilities, some liberal and some intentionally illiberal, captured by the concept of "embedded liberalism" (Ruggie 1983), described in chapter 1.

What explains judicial lawmaking at the WTO—and its apparently liberalizing (i.e., market-opening) direction? In the last decade, the debate about WTO dispute settlement has been framed largely in terms of whether the system should be more politically sensitive or more highly legalized (Hudec 1999; Jackson 1990; Petersmann 1997; Weiler 2000b). Political scientists have engaged in a parallel debate about the virtues and risks of international legalization (Slaughter, Slaughter, and Mattli 1993; Goldstein and Martin 2000). The merits of the normative questions aside, there is reason to believe that an insulated, full-time judicial body, backed by the power to issue legal sanctions (such as the WTO Appellate Body) would be more likely than a system of exclusively ad hoc panels (which characterized the GATT judiciary) to engage in strategic political action (Keohane, Moravcsik, and Slaughter 2000). Permanent bodies that face a shadow of the future are more likely to think in terms of legal precedent and incremental development of law, rather than addressing merely the political problem at hand (Slaughter and Mattli 1993; Weiler 1991). Moreover, the power to enforce rulings through the authorization of sanctions may embolden a judiciary to issue rulings that would be untenable without that power.

These factors explain the possibility of judicial lawmaking and strategic action by the Appellate Body, but they do not account for constraints on judicial lawmaking. The Appellate Body's strategic space for lawmaking may be constrained by legal discourse, constitutional rules, or politics. The discursive space may be seen as nested within the constitutional space, both of which are nested in the WTO's political environment.

THE APPELLATE BODY'S DISCURSIVE SPACE: DEFERENCE VERSUS COMPLETENESS AND DYNAMISM

Under DSU Article 3.2, the Appellate Body should "clarify the existing provisions" of the covered WTO agreements "in accordance with customary rules of interpretation of public international law." In doing so, the Appellate Body, in accordance with Article 19.2, "cannot add to or diminish the rights and obligations provided in the covered agreements." In the special case of interpreting the antidumping agreement, under Article 17.6 of that agreement, where a panel "finds that a provision of the Agreement admits of more than one permissible interpretation, the panel shall find the [national] authorities' measure to be in conformity with the Agreement if it rests upon one of those permissible interpretations."

Just as there are alternative judicial approaches to statutory interpretation in the United States, the customary rules of interpretation of public international law offer alternative approaches to interpreting WTO agreements. These approaches range from those that are restrained and highly deferential to the principle of consent by members, to those that suggest more expansive judicial lawmaking in the interests of completeness and dynamic interpretation of WTO legal texts.

At the restrained end of the continuum, public international law doctrines permit international judicial bodies to be highly deferential to states when interpreting the extent of their legal obligations. Such a deferential approach is based ultimately on the positivist notion that states may be bound only through consent, strictly construed, which finds its expression in at least two doctrines. *In dubio mitius* is a well-established canon of treaty interpretation that attaches deference to state sovereignty when a rule is ambiguous. The principle dictates that if the meaning of a term is ambiguous, that meaning is to be preferred which is less onerous to the party assuming an obligation, or which interferes less with the territorial and personal supremacy of a party, or involves less general restrictions on the parties (Oppenheim 1992; Cameron and Gray 2001).

Also at the restrained end of the continuum, various customary doctrines counsel abstention in dealing with a gap in the law. Some would invoke the doctrine of *non liquet* (which means "it is not clear") if the law does not permit deciding a case one way or the other. According to that view, there are gaps in international law, and it is not the place of international courts to fill those gaps as they are not legislative organs; thus, in such cases courts should declare *non liquet*. According to another view, expressed most clearly in the *Lotus* case—a decision in 1927 that involved the application of Turkish law to foreign sailors in Turkish waters—there are no gaps in international law because whatever is not explicitly prohibited by international law is permitted; thus, there could never be a *non liquet*. Nonetheless, this view holds that "rules of law binding upon states emanate from their own will and restrictions upon the independence of states cannot therefore be presumed" (Permanent Court of International Justice 1927). Whether or not there can be a *non liquet*, international law leaves to states a wide measure of discretion, which is limited only in certain cases by prohibitive rules, without which every state remains free to behave in ways it regards best and most suitable (Weil 1997; Ford 1994).

Several policy arguments may be advanced in support of using these deferential doctrines. Those negotiating WTO agreements often intended certain provisions to be vague, or to exclude rules governing certain behavior, so that their national governments could adopt or maintain national laws that reflect any one of several possible interpretations. In such cases, they were consenting to a range of interpretations—not to a single "best interpretation." Any effort to impose a particular interpretation on such gaps or ambiguities risks contradicting state consent, the touchstone of contemporary public international law. Moreover, any effort to do so risks interpreting WTO language in ways that contradict the intent, national laws, and behavior of powerful WTO members or upsetting the delicate balance of rights and responsibilities reflected in WTO agreements. Robert Hudec suggests that the Appellate Body may have been wise to employ *in dubio mitius* in the *EC—Measures Concerning Meat and Meat Products (Hormones)* decision, because in doing so it enhanced its legitimacy by signaling its deference to national sovereignty (Hudec 1999). Finally, a deferential orientation is consistent with Article 3.2 of the DSU: "Recommendations and rulings of the DSB cannot add to or diminish the rights and obligations of Members."

At the other end of the spectrum, international law doctrine may be read to permit courts to make law by filling gaps and clarifying ambiguities to establish completeness, precision, coherence, and dynamism. The modal position among international trade law scholars is closer to this view than the deferential perspective. Some commentators argue that *non liquet* and *in dubio mitius* are impossible because the international legal system is logically or inherently complete—or should be (Weil 1997). Other commentators take a somewhat softer position, arguing that the international legal system offers primary and secondary mechanisms of interpretation that enable judges to fill gaps and clarify ambiguities in almost all circumstances (Pauwelyn 2001; Hughes 1998). Croley and Jackson have argued that customary rules of interpretation of public international law, which must guide dispute settlement panels and the Appellate Body, are aimed at resolving ambiguities in texts of international agreements—even in cases involving the Antidumping agreement, which prescribes (in Article 17.6) deference to a range of national government interpretations (Croley and Jackson 1996).

Several policy arguments support the completeness and dynamism position (Croley and Jackson 1996; Pauwelyn 2001; Howse 2002a). WTO agreements are imperfect, filled with gaps that either do not instruct how to deal with specific factual situations or with ambiguities that could plausibly be read in more than one way. In creating a legalized dispute settlement system, Uruguay Round negotiators implicitly accepted the public international law norm that demands international judicial bodies offer the best interpretation of treaty language. When faced with an appeal, the Appellate Body is required to decide the case, leaving it on one side or the other of a political dispute, even if it were to rely on a deferential doctrine. Some argue that the WTO's legislative system is so slow and culminates so infrequently in new rules that the judicial branch must engage in lawmaking if gaps and ambiguities are to be addressed and if the system is to respond in a timely manner to environmental change. Moreover, they argue that it is well established in public international law that some provisions of treaties are to be interpreted in an evolutionary fashion.

The Appellate Body has leaned toward the less deferential approach to interpretation of WTO agreements, favoring completeness and dynamism. In *Brazil—Measures Affecting Desiccated Coconut, Appellate Body Report (1997)* the Appellate Body agreed with the panel's decision not to provide a remedy on grounds that there was no applicable law, but the absence of applicable law was attributable to a temporal gap caused by the transition from the GATT to the WTO legal system—an exceptional circumstance. In another case widely mentioned as demonstrating judicial restraint, *United States—Countervailing Duties on Certain Corrosion-Resistant Carbon Steel Flat Products from Germany, Appellate Body Report (2002)*, the Appellate Body overruled a panel decision that had filled a gap with an affirmative obligation: the Appellate Body rejected the panel's inference that a de minimis standard in provisions on countervailing duty investigations had to be applied in sunset reviews. But generally, as illustrated previously, the Appellate Body has often made law by filling gaps and clarifying ambiguities. The doctrine of *non liquet* has never been invoked by either a WTO panel or the Appellate Body to permit or excuse a member's behavior.[9] *In dubio mitius* has been invoked by the Appellate Body only once, in *EC—Beef Hormones*, to reject the panel's view on a tangential question that did not stop the Appellate Body from finding the measures in question WTO-illegal. Even where the deferential standard of Article 17.6 of the antidumping agreement (which some argue is redundant in light of the *in dubio mitius* principle) must be applied, the Appellate Body has not been deferential, concluding in *U.S.—Japan Hot-Rolled Steel* that most issues under the antidumping agreement can be resolved definitively by applying customary rules of interpretation of international law, limiting the situations in which members may adopt differing interpretations of ambiguous provisions (Tarullo 2003).

The Appellate Body has implicitly emphasized completeness over deference in its approach to treaty interpretation, yet some might argue that WTO legal discourse is not without constraints on judicial lawmaking. The Vienna Convention on the Law of Treaties and the customary law it represents, which are endorsed by WTO jurisprudence, establish a set of mechanisms for treaty interpretation that require adherence to the "ordinary meaning" of a treaty's terms and resort in case of ambiguity to specified, supplementary means of interpretation. However, slight shifts of emphasis among the means of interpretation may lead to very different conclusions (McRae 2003). Moreover, while there are limits on the extent to which substantive non-WTO international law may be imported into the WTO, those limits are under considerable pressure (Marceau 1999; Trachtman 1999; Pauwelyn 2001). It is difficult to conclude that, under current practice, WTO legal discourse intrinsically constrains the extent of judicial lawmaking by the Appellate Body.

The Appellate Body's use of principles that favor completeness and dynamism through judicial lawmaking has been complemented by practice that supports stare decisis de facto. The stare decisis principle is not followed formally by international tribunals, partly because most civil law systems do not adhere to the principle. In public international law, past decisions may be persuasive, but not binding. Moreover, the WTO Appellate Body is not supposed to make definitive interpretations: Article IX:2 of the WTO agreement states that "the Ministerial Conference and General Council shall have the exclusive authority to adopt interpretations of this Agreement and the Multilateral Trade Agreements." And the Appellate Body has, on occasion, reached decisions that seem inconsistent with precedent.[10] But in general, previous decisions and doctrine are so highly persuasive in WTO jurisprudence, and their use is so central to the discourse of dispute settlement, that it may be said that the WTO observes de facto stare decisis (Bhala 1999a, 1999b, 2001). This practice is reinforced by the Appellate Body's procedure of meeting *en banc* to discuss each case and to ensure consistency across decisions, despite the decision in each case resting with a three-member division of the Appellate Body. It may even be argued that judicial lawmaking by the Appellate Body, together with the importation of public international law into WTO dispute settlement, de facto stare decisis, and the development of a legitimizing legal culture among Appellate Body members and their staff, are ratcheting WTO law forward in a way that is similar to the way common law develops (Ragosta 2002; Weiler 2000b).

Why has the Appellate Body leaned toward the end of the discursive spectrum that favors completeness and dynamism over doctrine that favors deference to sovereign states? And why does so much of its lawmaking lean in a liberalizing direction? Any answer must be speculative, but several possibilities may be suggested. Perhaps members of the Appellate Body share an ideological predisposition that favors market opening (particularly as it relates to trade remedy laws that many see as restricting trade), which may be effectuated through judicial lawmaking (Tarullo 2003). Perhaps the discourse among international trade law commentators, which tends to favor completeness and liberalization, has shaped Appellate Body members' perceptions of their duty. Or perhaps Appellate Body members are using the European Court of Justice as a historical jurisprudential model.

THE CONSTITUTIONAL SPACE

The discursive space in which the Appellate Body operates is nested in a constitutional space, which defines formal checks on and balances against the Appellate Body. Hence, an analysis of constitutional constraints is necessary for understanding the permissive conditions under which judicial lawmaking has emerged at the WTO.

The discursive shift toward expansive judicial lawmaking at the WTO was made possible by the change in constitutional checks that accompanied the move from the GATT system. In the GATT dispute settlement system, panels had to be careful about making law because any party to a dispute could block adoption of the panel report. Generally, the United States did not block adoption of panel reports that found it in contravention of GATT obligations, but it did block adoption of reports that made what it considered to be bad law (Bradley 2003).[11] GATT panels had to be somewhat deferential to disputants' interpretation of law if they wanted consent to adoption of their reports. In contrast, under the WTO system, an Appellate Body report is adopted unless there is a consensus to block its adoption, which is unlikely—and has never happened—because the prevailing party can be expected to break any consensus to block adoption. This leaves the Appellate Body with more constitutional space in which to make law than was available to GATT panels.

In theory, the WTO's legislative system could balance and correct judicial lawmaking with which the members disagree. However, as Claude Barfield has argued, legislative action in the GATT/WTO system has been neither smooth nor continuous, and the legislation of new obligations

requires a consensus among members. Hence, there is no effective legislative means of correcting judicial lawmaking. Barfield considers these two
requirements—the consensus required to block an Appellate Body report
and the consensus required to legislate—the WTO's "constitutional flaw"
(Barfield 2001).

THE POLITICAL SPACE: ENGENDERING COOPERATIVE OR
UNILATERAL POLITICAL RE-EQUILIBRATION

The WTO's legal discourse and constitutional rules are nested in politics.
Since WTO legal discourse permits the Appellate Body to engage in significant lawmaking, and WTO constitutional rules offer no meaningful
check on or balance against such lawmaking, politics imposes the ultimate
constraint. This understanding is consistent with other analyses that have
found strategic action by international judicial bodies to be tenable within
limits defined by politics (Alter 2000; Slaughter and Mattli 1993). Under
what conditions will politics operate as a constraint on WTO judicial
lawmaking?

Politically, breach and retaliation might be efficient in any single case,
or in any set of cases in which the net outcome for each member were
neutral (i.e., if each member were to "win a few and lose a few"). But the
approach would not work if it needed to be employed frequently by a
powerful member in response to judicial lawmaking that adversely and
fundamentally changed its balance of WTO rights and responsibilities. In
such a case, the aggregate shift of property rights associated with each
decision would likely engender a political reaction, for the balance of
WTO rules and responsibilities would no longer match underlying power
and interests.

Judicial lawmaking faces political constraint and correction by powerful members. First, the EC and the United States influence the extent of
judicial lawmaking through the selection of Appellate Body members. In
practice, the EC and the United States have enjoyed "special privileges"
that have enabled them to veto the selection of Appellate Body candidates
(see Raghavan 1995). This unilateral veto is used routinely by powerful
members to ensure that candidates are not exceedingly activist, biased, or
expansive lawmakers. Candidates' prior written work is read, and the
candidates are interviewed by EC and U.S. government officials before
deciding whether to support or oppose their candidacy.[12]

Second, powerful members may react to judicial lawmaking by rewrit-
ing DSU rules so as to weaken the Appellate Body. As shown before, the
EC and United States have dominated GATT/WTO decision making since
the 1960s. In much the same way that the EC and United States cooperated to dominate negotiations over the substance of the Uruguay Round
agreements, they could cooperate to change the WTO's constitutional

rules. Judicial lawmaking that fundamentally and adversely shifted the balance of rights and responsibilities of the EC and the United States could engender their cooperative action. This is not merely hypothetical, as the Appellate Body is operating in an environment in which several commentators and governments have proposed to change DSU rules.

Third, members dissatisfied with a particular decision typically signal disapproval, often through a diplomatic statement at a DSB meeting. For example, when the Appellate Body decided to permit panels, at their discretion, to consider amicus curiae briefs submitted by nonstate actors, which most developing countries had long opposed, dozens of developing-country negotiators intervened at the next WTO Council meeting to protest. Similarly, the African Group's proposal in the Doha Round DSU negotiations declares that "the panels and the Appellate Body have in several instances exceeded their mandate and fundamentally prejudiced the interests and rights of developing country Members as enshrined in the WTO Agreement" (African Group 2002). And high-ranking officials of the secretariat have met with and advised members of the Appellate Body to show restraint, when those officials perceived that the Appellate Body was tending towards an activist stance (Stoler 2002). Such statements tend to delegitimize reports of the Appellate Body and call the body to the attention of members that disapprove of instances of judicial lawmaking, conferring a sense that it may be operating near or over the edge of its strategic space.

Fourth, some have suggested that a powerful state may defy an act of supranational judicial lawmaking altogether, refusing to comply with a decision and attempting to delegitimize it (Lawrence 2004, 5). The rate of noncompliance with decisions is likely of concern to every international court.

Finally, some have suggested that the United States should exit the WTO in reaction to judicial lawmaking that is allegedly weakening U.S. trade remedy laws (Ragosta 2003). However, in the contemporary WTO context, the threat of unilateral exit has limited credibility because it would be costly (Odell and Eichengreen 1998).

3.2.6. Has the Appellate Body Exceeded the Bounds of Its Strategic Space?

The Appellate Body has perhaps demonstrated sensitivity to politics in several decisions. For example, in *European Communities—Measures Affecting Asbestos and Asbestos-Containing Products (2001)* the Appellate Body accepted a public health basis for distinguishing whether products were "like products," to conclude that cement and asbestos-containing cement were not like products within the meaning of GATT Article III. And its *U.S.—Shrimp-Turtle* and *United States—Import Prohibition of*

Certain Shrimp and Shrimp Products, Recourse to Article 21.5 by Malaysia (2001), decisions eventually enabled the United States to maintain measures banning the importation of shrimp from certain countries that do not require the use of turtle-excluder devices in shrimp-net fishing.

But at least as often, the Appellate Body has rendered decisions that run against strong political currents. For example, it ruled illegal the EC's ban on the importation of beef from hormone-treated cattle, and ruled against the U.S. system of taxing foreign sales corporations—twice: in *United States—Tax Treatment of Foreign Sales Corporations (2000),* and in *United States—Tax Treatment of Foreign Sales Corporations, Recourse to Article 21.5 of the DSU by the European Communities (2002).* The point is not that these cases were decided rightly or wrongly, or that they entailed judicial lawmaking, but they may have run contrary to a view with mass appeal or that is supported by powerful nonstate actors.

How could we know—and, more importantly, how could the Appellate Body know—that its lawmaking was exceeding the bounds of its strategic space? As suggested above, members dissatisfied with a particular decision, or judicial lawmaking in general, are likely to signal disapproval, casting the shadow of politics over the Appellate Body. The most important signals, however, come from the most powerful members—the EC and United States—for they have the power to rewrite DSU rules. The fundamental question framed above, therefore, becomes whether the Appellate Body has engaged in a pattern of judicial lawmaking that has fundamentally shifted the balance of rights and responsibilities of those powerful members.

Both the EC and the United States have won some important cases and lost some. As of December 31, 2003, in dispositive reports involving the United States as a complainant, it had been successful in 85 percent of its challenges, prevailing in seventeen cases and not prevailing in three. As of the same date, in dispositive reports involving the United States as a respondent, at least one aspect of U.S. measures had been successfully challenged in 81 percent of the cases, the complainant prevailing in twenty-two cases and the United States prevailing in five. Assuming a constant rate and scope of judicial lawmaking across these cases, it is hard to conclude that the Appellate Body has fundamentally shifted the balance of WTO rights and responsibilities against U.S. interests. Similarly, in the same period, the EC was successful in 96 percent of its challenges as a complainant, prevailing in twenty-three of twenty-four cases; and in the same period, as a respondent, at least one aspect of an EC measure was found to be WTO-inconsistent in 80 percent of dispositive reports, with the EC losing in six of eight cases. Assuming a constant rate and scope of judicial lawmaking across these cases, these data suggest that if judicial lawmaking involving the EC has shifted the balance of rights and responsibilities in any direction, it is likely in the EC's favor.[13] Many in the United

States complain about the pattern of judicial lawmaking on trade remedy laws, but the EC is generally pleased with those decisions. The EC and the United States are not cooperating to propose significant constitutional change relating to dispute settlement. This suggests that cooperative re-equilibration is unlikely anytime soon and that the Appellate Body is operating within the strategic space defined by its hardest political constraint.

Currently, the most politically important source of dissatisfaction with the Appellate Body comes from the United States. Several U.S. commentators and politicians complain about judicial "activism" at the WTO (Barfield 2001; Raustiala 2000).[14] At least one prominent U.S. commentator has shown that through clarification of ambiguities the Appellate Body has frequently found U.S. antidumping decisions and rules to be WTO-inconsistent (Tarullo 2003). And in the Trade Act of 2002, the U.S. Congress required that the executive branch transmit to Congress a report setting forward its strategy "to address concerns regarding whether dispute settlement panels and the Appellate body . . . have added to obligations or diminished rights, of the United States" (19 USCS § 3801 (2002)). The report transmitted pursuant to that mandate concluded that the disputes that have been referred to the DSB generally "have been handled expeditiously and with professionalism," and that WTO dispute settlement has "benefited a wide range of U.S. industries and their workers." However, the report adds that "the United States does not agree with the approach that WTO panels and the Appellate Body have sometimes taken in disputes," and criticizes several specific instances of judicial lawmaking in trade remedy cases. In the end, it proposes some relatively minor changes to the DSU that it claims would offer "greater Member control over the dispute settlement process" (U.S. Secretary of Commerce 2002). Judicial lawmaking at the WTO has become a political irritant in the United States, and U.S. government signals should be read to indicate that continued Appellate Body lawmaking that weakens U.S. trade remedy laws risks catalyzing unilateral political action by the United States. Nonetheless, it is difficult to conclude from the foregoing signals that the U.S. government currently perceives that judicial lawmaking has fundamentally prejudiced its interests.

3.3. Conclusion: Prospects for Continued Viability of WTO Legislative and Judicial Rules

This analysis of the WTO's legal system has shown that Europe and the United States have dominated WTO legislative bargaining and outcomes. While the WTO Appellate Body's strategic space offers substantial leeway for judicial lawmaking, it has not upset the fundamental balance of rights and responsibilities embodied in that transatlantic-dominated legislative bargaining. Hence, WTO procedural rules and processes have been operating to effectively permit powerful WTO members to strongly influence the establishment and enforcement of substantive rules, which is crucial to maintaining their political support for the organization.

Will the legislative and judicial rules remain politically functional? Is EC-U.S. dominance of the WTO legal system likely to persist? Several factors could undermine transatlantic dominance and the functionality of the rules. For example, the consensus decision-making rule could yield deadlock if WTO members' broad goals began to run orthogonal to each other—if a substantial bloc of WTO members begin disfavoring neoliberal trade, while another bloc favored it. While such a fundamental change of the regime seems unlikely in the short term, it is unclear what principles will guide the WTO in the era now following the "Washington consensus." Another possibility is that transatlantic cooperation could break down: disputes over beef hormones, U.S. taxes on foreign sales corporations, use of safeguard measures, and other trade disputes could undermine transatlantic cooperation that has been necessary for the influence of the United States and EC over the agenda-setting process in past rounds (Steinberg 1999). But in past rounds, the transatlantic powers have experienced irritants like these, and they have not been insurmountable obstacles to cooperation.

In the short term, the most plausible constraint on transatlantic domination of the WTO legislative process is increased institutionalized cooperation by the developing countries in the agenda-setting process. Sustained cooperation among developing countries until now has proven difficult: they have been easily divided by their differences and enticed into tacit cooperation with Brussels and Washington. But the developing countries are now engaged in more institutionalized cooperation efforts. Twenty-one developing countries adopted a common front on an approach to the Cancún ministerial meeting in 2003, contributing to its deadlock along North-South lines. In addition to action through established institutions, like the G-77 and UNCTAD, the developing countries are poised to reap benefits from newer institutions, such as the Advisory Centre on WTO Law (which advises developing countries on WTO legal rights and obligations) and various regional organizations like ASEAN and MERCOSUR. Moreover, for the first time in GATT/WTO history, the director-general was from a developing country. Finally, in their formal statements, developing countries have begun to employ collaborative solutions to cooperation problems, jointly staking out positions on packages of issues, an approach that will make it more difficult for the EC and the United States to split them apart. In this context, transatlantic domination of the legislative agenda-setting process could be more difficult than in the past.

Notes

1. Following on the work of Hart (1961), an international legal system is defined to include inter alia its legislative and judicial processes. The legal system, as a whole, can be understood only by evaluating the operation and interaction of both of those processes.

2. The arguments in this section are developed more fully in Steinberg 2002b.

3. This description of how EC and U.S. negotiators cooperated to close the Uruguay Round is based on interviews or conversations with several European, U.S., and GATT/WTO secretariat officials, including Julius Katz, Washington, D.C., August–December 1990 and March 1995; Horst Krenzler, Los Angeles, September 1999; and Warren Lavorel, Washington, D.C., August–December 1990 and Geneva, March 1995; and several U.S. government documents, including the following memoranda (on file with the authors): Memorandum to UR Negotiators and Coordinators, Preliminary Legal Background on Ending the Uruguay Round, From USTR General Counsel, December 1, 1989; and Memorandum for Ambassador Warren Lavorel and Ambassador Rufus Yerxa, A Single Protocol for Concluding the Round, From USTR General Counsel and Deputy General Counsel, July 20, 1990.

4. The arguments in this section are developed more fully in Steinberg 2004.

5. This description of the U.S. position in 1990 is documented in USTR, Dispute Settlement, U.S. Objectives for Brussels, in the U.S. Delegation Briefing Book for the Brussels Ministerial, December 1990 (on file with the authors).

6. Data for the 1995–2003 period is from Leitner and Lester 2004. Data from the 1948–95 period is from Busch and Reinhardt 2002.

7. Ultimately, the distinction between gap filling and ambiguity clarification may be fragile, but the distinction is respected here out of convention. See generally Hart 1961.

8. In the Uruguay Round negotiations, U.S. negotiators had refused to agree to a test that would require national authorities to quantify the relative effects of imports and other factors on domestic industry. In so refusing, the U.S. negotiators intended to enable the International Trade Commission to continue using its qualitative approach to analysis of the "substantial cause" question in safeguards cases (Reif 2002).

9. Indeed, the only reference to *non liquet* in any WTO panel report or Appellate Body decision was critical of using the principle. *India—Quantitative Restrictions on Imports of Agricultural, Textile, and Industrial Products, Report of the Panel*, WT/DS50/R, par. 3.119 (April 6, 1999).

10. Consider, for example the discussion in Part 3.2.4 of how the *U.S.— Shrimp-Turtle* case decision compares to earlier cases on the jurisdictional scope of GATT Article XX(g). An earlier example involves the interpretation of GATT Article III: The *Japan—Alcoholic Beverages*, Panel Report adopted on November 10, 1987, GATT BISD 34S/83, employed a textual approach to application of GATT Article III). Then, the *U.S.—Malt Beverages*, Report of the Panel adopted on June 19, 1992, GATT BISD 39S/206, employed an "aim and effects" approach. Finally, *Japan—Taxes on Alcoholic Beverages*, Report of the Appellate Body, WT/

DS8/AB/R, WT/DS10/AB/R, and WT/DS11/AB/R, October 4, 1996, rejected the "aim and effects" test and returned to a textual approach.

11. For example, the United States permitted the adoption of *United States Tax Legislation (DISC)*, Report of the Panel, L/4422, November 12, 1976, GATT BISD 23S/98, only in conjunction with a Contracting Parties decision, the substance of which was negotiated between the EC and the United States, interpreting various points of GATT law. And Canada agreed with parts of *Canada—Discriminatory Application of Retail Sales Tax on Gold Coins*, Report of the Panel (unadopted), February 12, 1986, and rescinded the tax, but blocked adoption of the report because it disagreed with findings relating to the MFN principle.

12. Anonymous telephone interview with current Appellate Body member (February 11, 2004); anonymous telephone interview with former senior USTR official (February 26, 2004).

13. These data are from Steinberg 2004.

14. Senator Max Baucus has claimed that WTO panels are "making up rules that the U.S. never negotiated, that Congress never approved, and I suspect, that Congress would never approve" (Bridges 2002c).

Four

Expanding Trade Rules and Conventions: Designing New Agreements at the Border

4.1. Introduction

Though world trade expanded rapidly in the years after World War II, the scope of the GATT trade regime remained modest. The Havana Charter had imagined an organization whose mandate addressed a diverse set of problems, ranging from wage levels to business practices: the GATT had a much more limited agenda. Both the articles of the GATT, which changed very little, and the successive rounds of negotiations centered on liberalization of trade barriers "at the border." In the early years, trade rounds focused on the conversion of quantitative trade barriers to tariffs, and the binding and reduction of those tariffs through negotiations. Starting in the Tokyo Round, other nontariff barriers were added to the agenda, but negotiations were still largely restricted to the reduction of explicit trade barriers in a limited set of products, primarily manufactures.

So delimited, the GATT project was a phenomenal success. Trade barriers operating at the border were reduced until they became a relatively minor impediment to international trade among industrial countries.[1] Although the increase in world trade that occurred in the postwar period was the result of many factors, the GATT should be credited with a significant role. As argued in the previous chapters, the GATT's success was a product of its adoption of rules and norms that facilitated trade negotiations, or "horse trades," among members. The rules facilitated, especially in the developed world, the mobilization of groups with interests in exporting abroad. These groups effectively countered the rent-seeking behavior of import-sensitive groups and changed the political balance among GATT contracting parties, providing support for a program of trade liberalization. The GATT's rules and norms worked particularly well for trade in manufactured items because nations could balance the impact of increased market access for exporters against the effect of concessions on import-competing industries. For sectors such as agriculture, textiles, and steel, the method was less successful, largely as a result of the extensive intervention by governments in these sectors.

By contrast, the WTO has been given a much wider remit. The WTO covers almost all categories of goods, many internationally traded services, and the trade-related aspects of intellectual property protection, and in addition puts some constraints on investment policy and government procurement. Far from dealing predominantly with border measures, the WTO rules now extend far behind the border into the realms of domestic decision-making. And rather than being concerned only with policies that have a clear impact on trade, the WTO's agenda now includes policies traditionally thought of as primarily domestic regulatory issues.

This chapter and the next examine these changes in the purview of the trade regime, and explore the implications for the economics and politics of the system. This chapter begins with a review of the significance of the Uruguay Round agenda in facilitating these changes and suggests a framework for consideration of their impact. It then looks at the success of the trade system in incorporating rules for those sectors that, though nominally within the trade system, had lagged behind the manufacturing sector in moving towards a liberal regime. Two new agreements, covering textiles and agriculture, aimed to reintegrate the rules and practices covering these sectors with those that governed goods in the manufacturing sector. The chapter also considers the consolidation of the rules for trade remedies (antidumping provisions and countervailing duties), and those for subsidies: this consolidation can also be considered as a part of the completion of the original GATT trade agenda. Chapter 5, by contrast, examines the expansion of the trade rules to areas not in the GATT, including services and intellectual property protection, as well as the inclusion of other "new" regulatory issues that were placed on the WTO agenda.

4.2. The Uruguay Round Tasks

The shift in the trade regime's focus from a code of conduct on manufacturing trade to a comprehensive agreement on essentially all trade-related issues was the major accomplishment of the Uruguay Round. The eighth round of GATT trade negotiations was charged by governments with three distinct tasks. The first was to bring more fully into the GATT system some important areas of commerce that had been overlooked, or that had proved difficult to incorporate in the past. Among those areas were agricultural products and trade in textiles and clothing.[2] These negotiations represented the completion of the "traditional" trade liberalization agenda through the inclusion of sectors that had seemingly escaped the regime's discipline. Trade in these commodities had proved difficult to liberalize because of the domestic interests involved; they did not in general pose fundamental administrative problems or raise new legal or political issues. The issues that were at play in these "laggard" sectors were familiar to participants. In the case of textiles, the trade issues involved primarily the aggressive use of border instruments (mainly quantitative restrictions) to protect domestic industry from imports. In agriculture, the issues revolved around the impact of domestic farm policies. But the trade effect of domestic subsidies had long been recognized as a legitimate area of regulation in the GATT articles. The problem of applying these rules to domestic farm programs was more political than conceptual.

The second task of the Uruguay Round was organizational: to consolidate the Tokyo Round codes into a single document, to increase the number of nations agreeing to be bound by the codes, and to establish a common set of rules and institutional arrangements to deal with violations. By the close of the round, all but four of the codes had been integrated into the WTO, subjecting them to multilateral application.[3] The new integrated agreements revised the subsidies and the antidumping codes, as well as redefining the Standards Code to distinguish between risk-based regulations and those concerned with technical standards. Since all members of the WTO undertook to implement these rules as a "single undertaking," this increased the chance of rule violations. Legal discipline was therefore to be better enforced through reforming the dispute settlement process.

Though requiring considerable negotiating skill, these code modifications, reformed and presented as a unified document, were still within the traditional orbit of international trade rules. Rules on domestic subsidies were needed because of the potential impact of such subsidies on trade patterns. The abuse of national technical standards and health regulations as protectionist devices had also been recognized for some time. The logic of the codes on antidumping and countervailing duty policies was based on a common understanding of how the unrestrained actions of importing nations could lead to the disruption of world markets. Both clearly involve trade policy objectives in that they constrain the regulations introduced to assist sectors "hurt" by the expansion of trade.

The third task of the Uruguay Round was the incorporation into the multilateral trade regime of new categories of trade, in particular trade in services and in products that embody intellectual property that had not previously been considered in the purview of the GATT regime. The regulations that influence these aspects of the economy are not necessarily part of traditional trade policy and involve regulatory instruments normally thought of as in the realm of domestic policymaking.[4] In some cases, the border is still the locus of operation of the instruments that regulate these issues, but in the area of trade in services almost all the measures that impede trade operate behind the border. The extension of trade rules to these new areas of policy was a more radical departure for the trade system than consolidating trade remedy rules and incorporating laggard sectors. Policy regulation in these areas raised issues of the applicability of the principles of the GATT and questioned standard notions about what constitutes "free trade" and "protection." By contrast, with the partial exception of the regulation of domestic agricultural subsidies, the extension of trade rules into areas of domestic regulation was not a central part of the incorporation of the laggard sectors or the regulation of trade remedy laws.

These tasks were linked in a way that was crucial to the political acceptability of the round. The lack of enforceable rules for agriculture and the reliance on trade-restrictive quotas in the case of textiles was a serious handicap to developing countries wishing to expand their trade into developed country markets. Yet it was not easy to find a compromise between the United States and the EC with respect to agriculture. Developed-country suppliers of services and goods that required intellectual property protection wanted to get freer access to developing-country markets. Although there were also important bargains within the developed world, the overarching political bargain that launched and to a certain extent sustained the Uruguay Round over its seven and a half years of negotiations was that of access to rich-country markets for agricultural products and textiles in exchange for access to emerging markets for services and adherence to basic intellectual property protection in developing countries. On the whole, however, many of the concessions made by the developing world took effect early, while the benefits in opening developed-nation markets such as the textile market took effect only after a rather long-term phasing-in. Disillusionment with the final bargain and the way this bargain has evolved in the years subsequent to the round has added to the tensions already mentioned and set the scene for the current trade negotiations.

4.3. Extension of Scope of Trade System

Although this chapter deals with the issues "at the border," it is useful to begin by distinguishing between the two trends mentioned previously, and exploring the implications of the expansion of the scope of international agreement. One trend is the tendency to move from the focus on border measures to include in trade rules government activity that is "behind the border." The other is to expand the scope of international rules to include areas of responsibility that are normally considered to reside firmly in the domain of domestic regulations. Superimposing the two dimensions of instrumentality and objectives gives a framework for considering the extent and implications of these changes in the scope of trade rules (table 4.1).

The table categorizes the set of typical government instruments or policy measures that have a significant and definable impact on trade flows.[5] The category of policies operated in support of a direct trade objective includes tariffs and quotas operated at the border, along with export subsidies and trade remedies. These are the traditional province of the GATT.

TABLE 4.1.
Schema for Categorizing the Extension of International Trade Rules

	Instruments with Trade Policy Objectives	*Instruments with Domestic Policy Objectives*
Instruments operated at the border (primarily goods)	Tariffs Quotas Export subsidies Antidumping duties Countervailing duties Safeguard actions	Import restrictions for human health Import restrictions for plant and animal health Immigration controls Currency export rules
Instruments operated behind the border (both goods and services)	Domestic subsidies Skills qualifications for migrants Rights of establishment for foreign firms Reserve requirements for foreign banks Trade-related requirements for inward investment	Industrial standards Intellectual property protection Competition policies Investment restrictions Government purchasing Environmental regulations Labor regulations

But it also includes measures such as domestic subsidies applied within the border and those regulations that have the potential effect of discriminating against foreign suppliers of services and investors. These were not fully incorporated into trade rules until the Uruguay Round, though they were addressed partially in the Tokyo Round codes. This category also includes measures that are targeted at trade impacts of investment rules, such as export requirements and regulations designed to stimulate the use of domestic goods and services. These issues were addressed in the Trade-Related Investment Measures (TRIMS) agreement in the Uruguay Round. Discriminatory subsidy policies designed to give domestic firms a competitive edge are also included under this heading.

The trade rules that operate in this domain are aimed primarily at removing barriers to trade; encouraging the exploitation of cost differences to enhance efficiency, for the importing country as well as for the trade system; and allowing consumers a wider choice of goods and services. The intellectual underpinning (see chapter 1) of such rules is the notion that healthy competition among firms in contestable markets benefits all participants. The principles of nondiscrimination and national treatment are a manifestation of this view.

The main political tensions in this context are shown in table 4.2—they are with domestic interests that would be adversely affected by freer trade. The classic confrontation is between rent-seeking producers who benefit

TABLE 4.2.
The Politics of Different Trade Restraints

	Instruments with Trade Policy Objectives	Instruments with Domestic Policy Objectives
Instruments operated at the border (primarily goods)	Traditional rent-seeking Protection of employment National competitiveness	Traditional rent-seeking Collective preferences Cultural differences Consumer protection
Instruments operated behind the border (both goods and services)	Traditional rent-seeking Concerns over foreign investment National competitiveness Protection of employees	Traditional rent-seeking Regulatory politics Employment and labor politics Industrial policy (including intellectual property issues)

from protection and consumers and overseas suppliers who gain from the removal of protection within or at the border. The politics are thus familiar, and the definition of what constitutes liberal trade is not, in general, controversial. One can fit infant industry protection and concerns about protecting employment into this framework. For instruments operated behind the border, there are additional questions of whether domestically owned business should be favored at the expense of foreign-owned business, which some argue, is less likely to be supportive of labor rights or of desires to bring in and develop technology within a nation. Although there are enormous practical differences between trade policy instruments that can be operated at the border and those operated behind the border, their objectives are usually clear-cut.

More fundamental is the distinction between those instruments with trade policy objectives and those with domestic policy objectives. This category of trade-related policies, those with a predominantly domestic objective, includes many that are operated at the border, such as measures introduced for purposes such as public health and safety, protection of the natural environment from invasive species, control of animal and plant diseases, and immigration controls.[6] But this category also includes instruments designed to address domestic objectives that operate within the border. Such instruments primarily affect domestic firms and markets, and only incidentally influence trade. Examples of such instruments would be rules for worker protection, competition policy, and the protection of rights from artistic or innovative endeavor. Many of these instruments can be considered as stimulating the provision of public goods, including the public good of a competitive and well-governed domestic economy. But they can have a markedly discriminatory effect on the activities of foreign firms and individuals and thus become the focus of trade rules. The fundamental issue for the trade system is that it is by no means clear that these public goods can always be produced in an efficient way without having some spillover impact on trade.

Not only is the economic rationale different, but the politics of such domestic policies are distinct. The stakeholders and interest groups are markedly different. Rather than emerging from tension between rent-seekers and consumers, as in the case of "traditional" trade policies, trade-related domestic regulations reflect the societal balance between individual and collective responsibility (although rent seeking is likely to be often present). Such regulations, for example, may focus on the level of consumer or environmental protection, or on the extent to which invention should be encouraged through intellectual property at the expense of short-term higher prices. Efficient provision of these policy goals still requires attention to the interface of the economy with the rest of the world. Regulations may need to be designed with the aim of avoiding the creation of negative externalities, and the existence of trade may bring some additional challenges to the regulator. But trade itself will also change the set of options available and open up new regulatory possibilities. Trade rules thus can be considered an adjunct to domestic policies, helping to make them more efficient. The prime objective is therefore the improvement of the operation of domestic regulations defined in terms of meeting their objectives. Whether a domestic regulation is efficient or inefficient may not be definable in terms of its trade impact. Thus, different criteria for success may have to be devised for trade rules in this area. Trade policy should be helping to improve the quality of domestic policy rather than impeding it with counterproductive constraints. For this, new guiding precepts may be needed.

Why do these two extensions of the scope of trade rules, behind the border and into the realm of domestic objectives, cause problems for the legitimacy of the trade system? Traditional trade policies relate largely to government actions aimed at benefiting domestic constituents. Extending the reach of rules and investigations to instruments that operate within the borders (of both importers and exporters) clearly has the effect of bringing more actors into the picture. The difficulties in negotiating trade-opening agreements in the area of agriculture and textiles illustrate some aspects of this problem, as does the issue of defining acceptable industrial subsidies. But the extension into the realm of domestic regulations brings a whole new set of problems to the fore. Not only are there likely to be many more actors involved, but the viewpoint of those actors can be strikingly different. Those that have a trade "focus" will cast the issues as the impact of domestic regulations on trade. Those that have a domestic or regulatory "focus" will cast the same issues as the restricting effect of trade on the ability of governments to pursue their objectives.[7] One group sees domestic instruments as a potential constraint on the achievement of trade objectives. The other sees trade instruments as a way to pursue domestic objectives. Hence tensions exist, just as import-competing producers and consumers struggle for influence over the more traditional trade policy agenda. These tensions are likely to be especially strong in the upper-right-hand quadrant, where, in comparison with the more technical political debates of the lower-right-hand-quadrant, specific consumer preferences and cultural concerns are most dominant.

4.4. Incorporating the "Laggard" Sectors

The decision of countries to negotiate over the "laggard" sectors was driven predominantly by traditional exporters who considered that the trade regime was ignoring their particular interests. In the period up to the Uruguay Round, the two most glaring exceptions to GATT rules were trade in textiles and clothing and in agriculture. Both had moved rather slowly along the path of trade liberalization and had not yielded to the market-opening techniques of the successive trade rounds. Growth in exports in those sectors that had escaped GATT discipline lagged behind those in mainstream manufactures. Powerful protectionist interests had been able to devise strategies that insulated them from the broader trade policy trends, and the reform of these sectors was spurred by an alliance among the countries whose producers were hardest hit by their inability to gain access to GATT member markets. The countries that pushed for the inclusion of textiles and clothing were predominantly the developing countries that faced difficulties expanding an industry that seemed to offer a way to develop. In the case of agriculture, a loose alliance of small agricultural exporters (the Cairns Group) and the United States kept this issue high on the agenda.

Although the interests of these exporters were comprehensively addressed in the round, the result was only modest liberalization of trade. Instead of pushing for trade openness as the only acceptable goal, negotiators pursued the same strategy that had characterized trade negotiations since 1947: first establish rules of behavior and bind countries to transparent, if high, tariff levels and worry later about lowering those levels. In terms of this more modest goal, the talks were highly successful, and the nature of the regulation at the border for these sectors is now much closer to that in other areas of goods trade. Whether or not nations can now agree to embark upon significantly lowering barriers to imports is an open question, and one actively being tested in the Doha Round.

4.4.1. Trade in Textiles and Clothing

The multiple and complex barriers to trade in textiles and clothing were a major irritant in the years leading up to the Uruguay Round. Successive tariff-cutting rounds had failed to reduce protection in this sector. Developing countries, in particular, considered that the developed markets were restricted in one of the few sectors of light manufacturing in which they could develop export capacity. Textile interests in developed countries, in particular in the United States and the EU, were well aware of the potential for expansion of exports from these countries, and exerted considerable pressure on politicians to maintain trade barriers. Employment in textile industries has traditionally been concentrated in a few regions in developed countries, and protection was seen as a way of preserving jobs in otherwise backward regions. As a consequence, a succession of illiberal textile agreements kept this sector out of the mainstream of the GATT. Trade was quota-constrained, and the quotas increased at a pace inadequate to liberalize the market. Reflecting the changing balance of membership in the GATT, members undertook in the Uruguay Round to end the special treatment of textiles. It was hoped that this could be achieved by incorporating the decision in a total package that would include gains in other areas and hence provide incentives to reach an agreement despite domestic opposition from textile lobbies in textile importing countries.

The gradual separation of textile trade rules from those for other manufacturing products began in the 1950s, with the introduction of "voluntary" export restraints (VERs) initially by Japan on exports to the United States (at the time of Japan's accession to the GATT in 1955) and by Hong Kong, India, and Pakistan on their exports to the United Kingdom (in 1956). The first multilateral attempt to regulate trade in textiles in the postwar period dates back to the lead-up to the Kennedy Round: such a move had been a condition of support for the round by U.S. textile interests. A Short-Term Agreement on Cotton Textiles was negotiated in 1961 in order to allow developed countries to control the import of cotton textiles from countries such as Japan that were deemed to be actual or potential sources of market disruption. This was replaced by a Long-Term Arrangement Regarding International Trade in Cotton Textiles (LTA) in 1962, and the agreement was renewed in 1967 and 1970 (Cable 1987; Keesing and Wolf 1980). Thus the textile regime of managed trade represented a marked departure from the normal practices of the GATT. The LTA covered textile and clothing products made predominantly of cotton. Controls could be placed on imports when markets were disrupted, and quotas could be either imposed unilaterally (Article 3) or negotiated bilaterally (Article 4). Quota volumes had to rise by at least 5 percent each year.[8] The LTA was replaced in 1974 by the Multi-Fiber Arrangement

(MFA), once again as a way of gaining the support of the U.S. textile industry for a broader trade round, and the new agreement extended its coverage to all textiles and clothing, of wool, cotton, or synthetic fibers. A somewhat faster quota growth rate (6 percent) was allowed, and there was a provision for small and new suppliers. A Textile Surveillance Board was created to monitor the arrangement (Cable 1987). The MFA was renewed in 1977, in 1981, and again in 1986. By this time there were fifty-four signatories to the MFA, which was held together by the considerable value of the quota rents in the major markets and the fear of a return to more protectionist unilateral trade restrictions if it failed.

By the start of the Uruguay Round, developing countries had begun to press for the return of textiles and clothing to the principles and practices of the GATT. Textiles represented a major share of OECD imports from developing countries (up to 45 percent in the early 1980s), and, as Hoekman and Kostecki point out, "it was the MFA and not MFN that was the cornerstone of the institutional framework for North-South trade" (2001, 227). The International Textiles and Clothing Bureau (ITCB) began to promote such a move on behalf of developing-country members, and changes in the MFA began to be seen as a part of the "bargain" with those countries attempting to expand the agenda for the Uruguay Round. After considerable debate as to how to incorporate textiles into the GATT rules and liberalize market access, the basis of an agreement was on the table by the time of the abortive GATT ministerial in Brussels in December 1990, and was incorporated into the Dunkel Draft in 1991 that laid out the framework for the eventual Uruguay Round agreement.

The Agreement on Textiles and Clothing (ATC) that emerged from the Uruguay Round replaced the MFA. (The major provisions of the ATC are summarized in table 4.3.) The ATC was clearly a success in terms of the objective of corralling a laggard sector into the mainstream of the GATT. It is an agreement with the explicit mission of ending the exceptional treatment of textiles and clothing. Quotas were to be increased and more of the trade brought under GATT rules in four steps until, at the end of 2004, the quotas were eliminated and textile trade should conform to the "tariffs only" standard of the GATT/WTO. At this point the ATC would cease to exist.

Although the ATC changed the form of trade barriers, it did little to reduce the level of tariff protection in this sector, which remains high.[9] The agreement that brings textile trade under GATT rules is strongly "backloaded," with almost one-half of the trade escaping such disciplines until the final step (see table 4.4). The chief potential beneficiaries of the agreement, developing countries, have cited this agreement as one of a number of examples of their limited satisfaction with the operation of the WTO.

TABLE 4.3.
Major Principles and Provisions of the Agreement on Textiles and Clothing (ATC)

Subject	Comments
Article 2. Integration process	Four steps over 10 years
Article 3. Treatment of non-MFA restrictions	
Article 4. Administration restrictions	
Article 5. Rules on circumvention of the quotas	
Article 6. Special safeguard	Deals with new cases of serious damage or threat to domestic producers during transition period
Article 7. Commitments undertaken in all areas of the UR as they related to textiles and clothing	
Article 8. Textiles Monitoring Body	
Annex Product coverage	Encompasses yarns, fabrics, made-up textile products, and clothing

Source: WTO 1995.

Though the obligations of developing countries have increased, many have yet to see concrete benefits from the agreement. While they could potentially gain from the ATC, such benefits were uncertain given the dominant competitive position that China holds in textiles trade. The developing world feared that the United States (and possibly the EU and Japan) may not be able to deliver the large dose of liberalization that began at the end of 2004 in the face of domestic pressure from textile firms and unions.[10]

The story of trade in textiles is easily explained in domestic policy terms. Powerful lobbies in the developed countries have successfully kept the full discipline of the GATT trade rules from operating. Quotas, rearguarded with high tariffs, have prevented the efficient operation of the international market. The resulting higher prices have put consumer interests at loggerheads with those of producers. But a constant supply of new producers has constrained the rents that the textile industry can extract. Indeed, besides protecting the domestic industry, the main impact of textile protectionism may have been to redistribute the rental value of the quotas among different supplying nations. The abolition of quotas will convert the quota rents into tariff revenue, to the advantage of the treasuries of the importing countries. This in itself may not, however, expand trade in this sector to the extent anticipated by developing countries. The full benefit of more liberal trade in textiles will only be realized when tariffs fall to lower levels.

TABLE 4.4.
Steps in Incorporation of Clothing and Textiles in GATT/WTO

Step	Percentage of Products to be Brought under GATT	How Fast Remaining Quotas Should Open Up
Step 1: January 1, 1995 to December 31, 1997	16% (minimum, taking 1990 imports as base)	6.96% per year
Step 2: January 1, 1998 to December 31, 2001	17%	8.7% per year
Step 3: January 1, 2002 to December 31, 2004	18%	11.05% per year
Step 4: January 1, 2005	49% (maximum)	No quotas left
Step 5: Full integration into GATT (and final elimination of quotas) ATC terminates		

Source: WTO 1995.

4.4.2. The Incorporation of Agriculture

Agriculture has been an even more contentious area of trade than textiles and clothing. The GATT did not ignore agriculture: it just treated it differently by exempting it from certain basic disciplines (Josling, Tangermann, and Warley 1996). The main "exceptions" that sheltered agricultural goods from the full force of the GATT disciplines were incorporated in Article XI, which allowed quantitative trade restrictions to persist under certain circumstances; Article XVI, which tolerated export subsidies for primary products; and Article XX, which recognized the right of countries to use trade restriction in support of health and safety standards.[11] Each of these exemptions has caused its own set of problems for those that were keen to see a consistent and comprehensive liberal trade system: in each case, the exclusion was a response to domestic political pressures in the major countries.

The provision in the GATT (Article XI) that disallowed quantitative restrictions on imports in general specified, however, that they could be used in support of quantitative controls on domestic production. Such domestic quotas or supply-control programs were common in the industrial countries as instruments to balance domestic markets. The logic appeared unassailable: to have domestic supply control and yet allow imports to enter without quantitative restriction would undermine the effectiveness of domestic policy. And yet the problem was that it became relatively easy to set up a domestic supply-control program, whether effective or not, as a way of justifying quantitative controls on imports, in many cases the primary means of keeping up domestic prices. Thus the economic case for a GATT exemption became the political cover for further protection.

A similar "capture" of the GATT rules took place in the area of export subsidies. For nonagricultural goods it was recognized that export subsidies were among the most restrictive of trade policies. But for agriculture, such subsidies had been used to dispose of periodic surpluses that had undermined domestic prices. The provision that condoned subsidies on exports of primary products (in Article XVI) was therefore designed to allow such subsidies to be used in the stabilization (and support) of domestic prices. The problem in this case was that it was not possible to separate the policies that were designed for price stabilization from those whose main objective was to support domestic production and dispose of structural surpluses on the world market, at the expense of more efficient suppliers. Article XVI, and subsequently the Subsidies Code (see below) attempted to restrain those policies that gained exporters a "more than equitable share" of world trade. Dispute panels in the 1980s tried in vain to make this principle operationable (Josling and Tangermann, 2003).

The basic principle that appeared to guide governments was that trade rules could not be allowed to get in the way of the management of domestic markets: Articles XI and XVI of the GATT were designed to ensure that agricultural policy was relieved of some of the disciplines applied in the market for other traded goods. The root of the problem was that, to be effective, domestic farm support policies usually needed the border protection afforded by quantitative restrictions and the boost to demand given by export subsidies. But even the weakened rules in these articles were not firmly enforced. The United States was granted a waiver from the application of Article XI in 1955, further removing agriculture from effective discipline.[12] The EU chose for its main instrument of border protection the "variable levy," which remained undefined in the GATT for thirty years.[13] Thus the two agricultural "superpowers" had effectively removed the scrutiny of agricultural policies from the GATT.[14]

The Uruguay Round Agreement on Agriculture (URAA) corrected many of these "exceptions." Nontariff barriers were replaced by bound tariffs, and the supply-control clause of Article XI ceased to be applicable. The U.S. waiver was withdrawn. The variable levy is specifically proscribed in the URAA, and export subsidies have been limited. The URAA established new rules that radically improved the agro-food trade system. More specifically, the agreement

- converted nontariff border measures to tariffs and bound all tariffs (i.e., they cannot be increased without negotiation with other countries);

- reduced tariffs by 36 percent (on average) over six years from a 1986–88 base, with a minimum reduction of 15 percent per tariff line (with a 24 percent reduction over ten years for developing countries);

- established rules for the application of additional (safeguard) duties (up to one-third of normal duties) if imports surge or if world prices fall below preset trigger price levels for goods subject to tariffication;

- created minimum access commitments as a share of domestic consumption for products subject to tariffication;

- reduced domestic support—as measured by the total Aggregate Measure of Support (AMS) from a 1986–88 base—by 20 percent over six years (domestic support considered minimally trade distorting not included; direct payment for production-limiting program not included in AMS reductions under certain conditions);

- banned new export subsidies and introduced constraints on existing subsidies (budget expenditures for export subsidies reduced by 36 percent, and volume by 21 percent, over the six-year implementation period).

Developing countries were subject to only two-thirds of the cuts in tariffs, domestic support, and export subsidies and over a period of ten years.

One political price extracted by those who were concerned about this partial reentry of agriculture into the mainstream of the GATT/WTO rule system was to exclude for a period of nine years the full impact of the subsidies agreement (the Agreement on Subsidies and Countervailing Measures, described below) on agricultural (domestic and export) subsidies. Article 13 of the URAA (known as the Peace Clause) gave considerable shelter until 2004 to such farm subsidies, which might otherwise be challenged under the agreement.[15] On the other hand, those countries that were keen to pursue the long-range goal of integration of agricultural trade rules with those of manufactured goods were able to insert a clause in the URAA (Article 20) that committed members to a continuation of the reform process and to further negotiations to begin by the end of the transition period (i.e., by the year 2000).[16] But, to illustrate the balance achieved between different viewpoints, Article 20 also recognizes the need to take into account "non-trade concerns," a concept introduced by countries such as Japan that were worried about the impact of trade liberalization on the social significance of agricultural production and the risks to security of excessive reliance on imported foodstuffs.

Two other aspects of the URAA are significant in the broader context of the trade system. The inclusion of significant aspects of special and differential treatment in the provisions of the URAA (both in the rules and in the schedules for trade liberalization) was necessary to gain support from developing countries concerned that rules adopted largely to curb the excesses of farm policies in the rich countries could impinge on their own development strategies. But such a weakening of the provisions of the URAA in favor of developing countries has also had a less desirable impact, as their own border protection levels have stayed high and the scope for trade diversion in this sector in regional agreements among developing countries has not been reduced. The establishment of a Committee on Agriculture in the WTO has also been significant, giving countries the possibility for challenges of each other's policy notifications and enabling the preparation for the current negotiations to continue in a relatively informal setting.

As with the ATC and the textiles sector, the Agreement on Agriculture brought the rules governing agricultural trade more into line with other products. But just as textile tariffs are still high, the Agreement on Agriculture did little to liberalize trade in agricultural products and improve market access. Agricultural tariffs for all products and countries average 61 percent (see figure 4.1).[17] Tariffs on agricultural goods are still on average about five times as high as on manufactured goods and hence continue to distort trade patterns.[18] The process of "tariffication" of nontariff border measures has produced a number of tariffs bound at such high levels (megatariffs) that it is difficult to see how they can be reduced by conventional tariff-reduction techniques.[19] Where tariff rate quotas were negotiated to prize open agricultural markets, the prospect of quota rents has led governments to develop a network of bilateral deals and private sector actors to resist their expansion. This has, in turn, exacerbated the problem of competition between state trading enterprises and the private trade.

Perhaps the most significant agricultural "exception" is that export subsidies still exist, and are in effect legitimized by their incorporation in country schedules. Such subsidies still dominate the market for dairy products and sugar and have depressing effects on cereals prices. Removal of these export subsidies, predominantly used by the EU, has become a major goal of other exporters of temperate-zone farm products, actively endorsed by developing countries, in the Doha Round. Expenditure on domestic support for agriculture is on the rise in many countries, though arguably paid in less trade-distorting ways.[20] In short, the domestic farm policies of the major industrial countries have been required to make only relatively minor changes to bring them into conformity with the agreement, and markets are marginally more open than at the start of the Uruguay Round.[21]

Why, then, have we not seen the more rapid emergence of a liberal trade system for agricultural products since the inception of the WTO? Farm programs are difficult to change in many developed countries, and the notion that they are constrained by trade agreements does not sit well

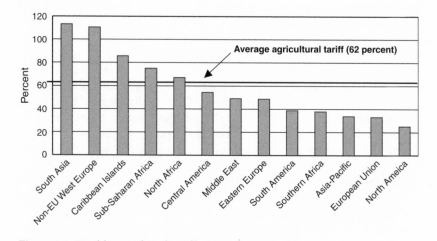

Figure 4.1. World agricultural tariffs, averages by region

with domestic politicians and interest groups.[22] But over time there has been a significant extension of trade rules to incorporate restraints on the behavior of governments in this area of policy. In essence, the efforts of the negotiators in the Uruguay Round went into the crafting of the trade rules for agriculture and not the reduction of trade barriers. The reduction of import tariffs and domestic and export subsidies is the task of the current round of agricultural trade negotiations that began in March 2000 and was later incorporated as part of the Doha Development Agenda. The success in establishing new rules for agricultural trade will ultimately be judged by the extent to which countries follow up by opening markets. Much of the political struggle between liberal trade advocates and rural protectionists lies ahead.

One clear, if limited, measure of the successes in agricultural trade reform following the Uruguay Round is the way in which countries have implemented their obligations. Tariff ceilings have not been breached, tariff-rate quotas have been made available, if not always filled, export subsidies have come down on schedule despite very weak world markets, and domestic support in most countries is well below allowable limits. The process of notification and monitoring has been thorough, and the information now available on agricultural trade policies and practices represents a significant increase in transparency. Discussions within the WTO Committee on Agriculture have created a basis for understanding among governments that is already smoothing the way for further negotiations. The adoption of the Agreement on Agriculture has also, apparently, restrained trade conflicts over the external effects of farm support policies. Instead, most trade conflicts have festered over food safety and environmental issues peripheral to agricultural protection, such as regulations on genetically modified organisms.

Failures in the agricultural area have come from the inherent conflicts between those countries that see open markets as a solution to problems facing domestic agriculture and those that see such markets as a threat to the desired development of the sector. Trade policy will always entail a compromise between those who seek overseas outlets and those who wish to protect their markets from others. Progress toward trade liberalization is slow in agriculture for the obvious reason that many groups oppose such progress. All the WTO can do is to set rules that restrain this conflict and attempt to move countries over time toward a trade system that satisfies the needs of its member countries.

This dynamic frames the current agricultural trade talks. One group of countries is determined to see the trade system for agricultural products move rapidly and decisively in the direction of that which is in place for manufactured goods. The Cairns Group, of medium-sized agricultural exporters, argues for the substantial reduction of tariff barriers by a formula that would in particular cut "megatariffs," eliminate export subsidies, further discipline domestic support, and remove rules such as the "special" safeguard in place for agriculture in some countries.[23] At the other extreme, Japan and Korea are strongly against any major cuts in high tariffs and will resist pressures to cut domestic support, on the grounds that agriculture plays an important societal role. Newly emerging on the negotiating scene is a loose coalition of developing countries, known as the G-20 that have united with the twin aims of pressuring the United States and the EU (and Japan) to reduce protection and to deflect attention from the desire of the developed countries to see rapid liberalization in G-20's own import markets.

The positions of the United States and the EU, somewhat surprisingly, are not so far apart from each other as in previous negotiations. Both are committed to tariff reductions, though the United States will push for deeper cuts in higher levels of tariffs: both will be constrained by domestic pressures in opening up sensitive markets, such as sugar and milk products. There is also agreement that export subsidies must be further restrained, but the EU has put a price on its agreement to reduce and possibly eliminate export subsidies: the United States will have to rein in its export credit programs and its food aid disbursements. On domestic support, both are looking for ways to redefine permissible domestic policies in such a way that their own emerging programs can be sheltered from challenge. In the case of the EU, these programs include rural development, environmental subsidies, animal welfare measures, and regional aid schemes. In the United States, the allowable policies must include conservation, rural development, income insurance, and countercyclical measures, as embodied in the 2002 farm bill. When their trading partners, in August 2003, suggested that the United States and the EU settle on a joint approach to the agricultural negotiations, they were able to respond. But the resulting joint proposal was met with criticism: other countries feared that any relaxation of the disciplines on domestic support would allow the United States and the EU to avoid once again painful cuts in domestic programs. One week later Brazil, India, South Africa, China, and sixteen other developing countries presented their version of the framework for the agricultural modalities in response to that of the EU and the United States, calling for much stronger constraints on domestic farm programs.[24] In August 2004, a Framework Agreement was reached that attempted to reconcile positions on domestice support.

4.5. Consolidating the Codes

Along with the expansion of free trade obligations in the Uruguay Round talks, members also readdressed the question of what constitutes a legitimate exception to a policy of open trade and the range of legal remedies open to governments to provide protection to ailing sectors. The trade rules included in the original GATT agreement of 1947 specify conditions under which a country can be excused from an obligation it had previously made to open up its market to foreign goods.[25] Just as negotiating over the liberalization of the agricultural and textile sectors was possible for GATT members, so too was the clarification of legitimate exceptions to these agreements. Unlike the issues of trade in services and the obligation to incorporate intellectual property protection, the bargaining process for trade remedies was predictable and the mandate universally recognized as well within that authorized to negotiators.

One should not be surprised at the time and attention the liberal trade regime has paid to the question of exceptions. Trade liberalization typically leads to a distributional shift among domestic producers. In response to the negative impact on some groups of open trade borders, nations have created a set of domestic policy instruments to shield such groups from market forces. By the start of the Tokyo Round, these nontariff border measures had become as visible a constraint to trade as traditional tariffs. The means chosen to regulate state behavior inconsistent with GATT rules and norms was the enactment of "plurilateral" codes. Nine such codes were agreed to by groups of GATT members, covering antidumping, standards, import licensing, customs valuation, government procurement, civil aircraft, and subsidies and countervailing measures, as well as dairy trade and trade in bovine meat.[26] These Tokyo Round codes had two important attributes: they were binding on only the GATT contracting parties who chose to participate, and they had generally weak enforcement procedures.

A major task of the Uruguay Round was to consolidate the various agreements that had been negotiated in the Tokyo Round and incorporate them fully into the GATT legal structure. While the old rules were binding only on signatories, the incorporation of these agreements into the GATT structure meant that many nations were undertaking a significant increase in their legal obligations. As explained in chapter 3, joining the new WTO was a "single undertaking," that is, members accepted all the multilateral agreements concluded in the Uruguay Round.[27] For most members, the bundle of benefits of WTO membership represented a significant increase in their level of obligations. In addition, many members found that the new rules strayed into tools they traditionally used to meet domestic policy goals. Thus the consolidation of the codes was a major step in the construction of the multilateral trade system.

The Uruguay Round in particular provided the opportunity to consolidate and revise the rules on trade remedies. Trade remedies are national reactions to changes in imports that threaten the viability of domestic industries. In general, these reactions include quotas or additional tariffs, but can also be in the form of subsidies given to the industry concerned or to workers that are displaced. Among the most contentious discussions on the codes were those that addressed the issue of how governments could react to import surges and to the threat or actuality of injury to domestic firms. These discussions resulted in new multilateral agreements on safeguards, antidumping, and permissible subsidies and countervailing duties. The main characteristic of these three agreements, from the point of view of the extension of the reach of trade rules, is that each requires information to be gathered behind the border (in importing and where appropriate exporting countries) and assessed in a transparent process. The new agreements in this area provide detailed guidelines for such evidence, the procedures to be followed by governments in their application of these policies, and the backstopping of the integrated dispute settlement mechanism for obliging countries to follow the rules.

4.5.1. The Safeguards Agreement

U.S. congressional support for the original GATT 1947 hinged on the inclusion of a safeguard provision, allowing the United States to "escape" from a trade treaty obligation, if necessary, to protect domestic sectors threatened by imports. The American-supported Article XIX of the GATT allowed nations to raise duties if domestic industries suffered a loss. The countries suffering from the import surge had significant latitude in mak-

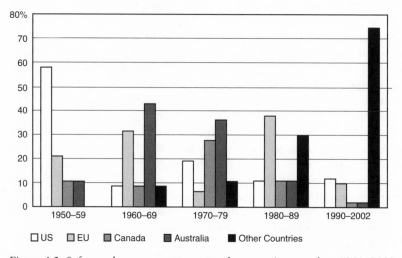

Figure 4.2. Safeguard measures: percentage by reporting member, 1950–2002

ing the case for a safeguard action. The degree of loss, the list of acceptable causes of the loss that could trigger safeguards, and the redress expected of the exporting nation were purposefully left underdefined in the original legal text, giving GATT members limited freedom to choose their own domestic assessment mechanism. Thus in early cases it was determined that injury could occur even when unassociated with the application of a trade agreement. Further, injury could be the result of a relative increase in imports, perhaps reflecting economic changes having little to do with international trade. However, even with this open-ended interpretation, the article was rarely invoked, in good part because of the nondiscrimination element of the remedy—the tariff increase needed to be applied to all members of the GATT. Instead, nations increasingly used other, more targeted remedies, notably voluntary export restraints (VERs) and antidumping actions, as a means to deal with import surges.

Over time the country using the safeguard has changed (see figure 4.2). Initially, a high proportion of the actions were taken by the United States. In the 1960s and 1970s safeguard action was favored by Australia, while the EU dominated such action in the 1980s. Now the use of the safeguard by the major trading countries has diminished in significance.

Although negotiators in the Uruguay Round had no single view on how to reform safeguard measures, all agreed that Article XIX was an ineffective safety valve. Developing nations argued that the use of VERs had undermined the trade discipline of the developed nations; the developed nations wanted a measure that could be selectively applied; and all parties felt that a lack of oversight had led to a misuse of the remedy. Even given this disagreement over the use of the instrument, participants did not reject the original premise of the safety mechanism: some safeguard measure was necessary to assure domestic political support for open trade.

In addressing reform, negotiators were confronted with three central problems. First, the legal safeguard measure for temporary problems due to import pressures contained in Article XIX had to be made more attractive relative to other measures such as the VER (Croome 1995, 53). Bringing safeguards back into the GATT system was a prerequisite for any safeguard agreement. Second, there was a significant difference in opinion on the question of coverage and selectivity. The developing world wanted to be exempt from safeguard actions; the developed world, especially the EC, wanted to be able to place restrictions selectively on countries contributing to the import surge. The notion of selectivity evoked considerable discussion, as the idea was counter to the central MFN norm of the trade regime. Members of the prestigious Leutwiler Group of trade experts, as well as most of the developing world, argued against the notion.[28] Furthermore, most developing-country negotiators argued against the use of retaliation. Countries argued that some safeguard actions should lead to neither compensation nor retaliation, though this approach would have been a shift in the ideological basis of the GATT system. Lastly, there was a question of who should monitor and assess whether or not a particular safeguard action was legitimate. The locus of power to decide what constituted a serious injury, the length of time needed as remedy, and the breadth of relief lay within member states but could, and many suggested should, be delegated to a standing committee. This discussion of the criteria for injury was buttressed on one side by Pacific Rim countries that wanted strict conditions and on the other by the EC, which argued that if conditions for use were too harsh, countries would return to gray-area remedies.

The final agreement was based on a compromise proposal made by the EC in 1989. The EC suggested that under particular conditions, countries could use quantitative restrictions as well as, or instead of, tariffs as a safeguard action. These restrictions could be set to reflect trade flows, allowing some selectivity in the restrictions. In addition, the EC offered a theoretical argument for having different criteria for short- and long-term safeguards. The former would not be subject to compensation or retaliation, while the latter would be permissible only with committee approval and as a means for more fundamental sectoral adjustment. The EC also argued that developing countries that contributed small amounts of exports to a particular country should be exempt from the additional tariff or quota imposed under the safeguards agreement.

Under the new rules established in the WTO Agreement on Safeguards, all VERs were to be eliminated, although countries were allowed to maintain one VER through the end of 1999. Safeguards were classified into two types—short term and more structural measures. When evoking the former, for absolute increases in imports, according to the criteria negotiators agreed to, countries are not subject to compensation or retaliation. After three years, however, the continued invocation of the safeguard requires compensation or faces the threat of retaliation. Developing countries are exempt if they hold less than 3 percent of the market (and all developing countries combined have less than 9 percent). Developing countries could use a safeguard measure for two years longer than the normal eight and could reintroduce them if necessary. Although oversight for the use of long-term safeguards moved to the WTO, nations themselves still made the individual assessments of whether or not a particular industry was injured.

The controversy that greeted the U.S. invocation of the safeguard provision in 2001 for certain steel products suggests that underlying questions of the legitimacy of this remedy remain unanswered. The agreed rules specify that only if an investigation showed that imports had led to serious injury would a safeguard action be undertaken and be legitimate. The United States announced that it was invoking a "legitimate" safeguard provision and that it owed no compensation for three years because there had been an absolute increase in imports. The EC immediately denied the validity of the action, arguing that there had been no absolute increase in steel imports. Within weeks, the EU threatened retaliation, and moved for the creation of a dispute panel. The panel and the Appellate Body both ruled that that U.S. safeguards violated WTO obligations in *United States—Definitive Safeguard Measures on Imports of Certain Steel Products (2003)*. Shortly thereafter, the United States terminated the measures, with its announcement relying not on the WTO decision but on a new International Trade Commission report that found little or no benefit in the continuation of the safeguards.

The case is illustrative of an underlying and unresolved problem with the agreement: the tension between a system that allows domestic governments to determine whether or not a particular industry has been harmed and the delegation of oversight on the validity of that decision to a multilateral organization. This tension should not be interpreted as evidence that the system is unworkable. No international organization will be able to stop rent-seeking producers from getting aid from their governments, even when it is unjustified. The rules, however, can constrain the range of behavior that policymakers use in response to industries affected by imports. Further, the threat of retaliation, such as the EU's publication of a list in 2002 of possible products for retaliation in the case of steel, designed to target U.S. goods from states important politically to the Republican Party, may actually cause political leaders to rethink domestic support for the increase in the duty. Underlying all this rather theatrical use of additional duties and counterduties is a political reality—if there were no legitimate response to producers trade problems within the system, leaders might well abort the entire WTO project. Although they must be interpreted so as to leave politicians a way to invoke safeguards in appropriate cases (Sykes 2003b), underspecified and amorphous rules may be a functional necessity, especially as more WTO members turn to democratic electoral forms of governance.

4.5.2. The Antidumping Agreement

The GATT 1947 recognized that nations needed safeguards other than those provided by Article XIX against the potential ill- effects of market aberrations. By the time GATT contracting parties began to negotiate a trade regime on these matters, U.S. domestic law already specified a set of "legitimate" rules for foreign commerce. Those rules, oriented toward both foreign governments and corporations, suggested a relationship between government and producer that was far more distant than that found in many other countries. Although the original rules in the GATT, for both antidumping and subsidies, were extremely vague, the legal basis of the argument for their use has been influenced, over time, by the U.S. view on appropriate commercial conduct. The antidumping agreements that regulate the pricing policies of private corporations have been influenced by the very broad definition of dumping in U.S. law, while the GATT rules on countervailing duties have responded to the push by the United States for a very broad interpretation of illegitimate government subsidies. As under U.S. law, the GATT trade regime considers "unfair" intervention in the market, when causing injury to a producer, to be a legitimate cause for an increase in trade barriers.

The basis for antidumping rules was given by Article VI of the GATT. Modeled on a 1921 U.S. law aimed at practices of pricing imported products at less than "fair value," the Article allowed countries to break their tariff bindings and violate their nondiscrimination obligation by putting on a targeted duty to offset the presumed impact of a dumped product.[29] Beginning in the Kennedy Round, negotiators attempted to address more specific aspects of the use of such measures. Continuing dissention on the interpretation of both parts of the law, that is, on whether there is dumping (i.e., below-cost pricing in the importing market) and whether there is injury from it, fueled the push for reform. The result has been an increasingly detailed account of the circumstances by which countries can respond to producer injury resulting from sales at "less than normal value." The Tokyo Round replaced the original antidumping agreement

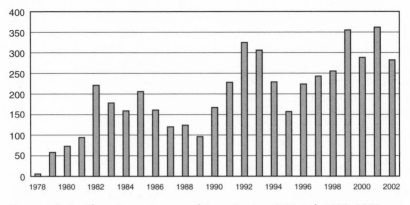

Figure 4.3. Antidumping actions: total investigations initiated, 1978–2002

with a more detailed code, and this was in turn incorporated into the Agreement on the Implementation of Article VI of the GATT 1994 concluded in the Uruguay Round.

Figure 4.3 shows the trend in the use of antidumping actions over time. Among the major trading countries, the United States is both a common target and a frequent user of the antidumping rules. The use of antidumping protection by the developed world against imports, especially from the newly developed economies, explains much of the acrimony that developed over the antidumping rules during the Uruguay Round. While one group of countries wanted the rules to allow the minimum amount of discretion and the maximum transparency, others wanted to retain more flexibility in dealing with trading practices (Croome 1995, 68). The former position was argued by exporting nations, such as Korea and Japan, which wanted predictable and tight standards. The alternative position was advocated by the United States and EC, the latter advocating a response to the "new reality" in which countries had moved to circumscribe these laws in new ways.

Antidumping negotiations became progressively more difficult over the course of the round as differences in fundamental interests were revealed. Exporting nations in Asia argued that antidumping rules hampered free trade and that sanctions should be allowed only under the most extreme circumstances. The United States and Europe had a far more liberal interpretation of the rule and understood that domestic circumstance mandated a flexible interpretation of when a duty could be imposed. Although all sides participated in often tedious negotiations over particular aspects of the rules, for example how to set price, profit, and injury conditions, the parties could not finesse the underlying problem of disagreement over the legitimacy of the rule itself. Was dumping part of normal price compe-

tition, as argued by Japan and Hong Kong (Croome 1995, 178)? Or, as
the United States repeatedly claimed, did export targeting in the home
market give the importers' government the right to construct a "legitimate" price, including a profit of 8 percent, in order to protect its producers against predatory pricing? Although work continued for months on a
compromise, the fourteen-delegation working group could not come to
an agreement. Instead, positions became so polarized that GATT director-
general Dunkel asked four country delegates not involved in the talks to
offer a solution to the impasse.[30]

Antidumping issues were emblematic of the complexity of the problems
facing GATT members during the round. Nearly fifteen hundred cases
had been initiated during the 1980s, suggesting a significant increase in
the use of the rules (Croome 1995, 264). Figures 4.4a and 4.4b show the
initiating and the target countries, respectively, over this time. The EC
refusal to adhere to a 1990 panel decision, that they were not justified in
an antidumping action against Japan, did not surprise observers. The EC
argued that the rules themselves were faulty, as Japan had in effect circum-
vented the rule. The final antidumping agreement included a strong provision against such circumvention, but also tightened up the procedures for
investigating dumping charges and calculating dumping margins. Thus
the agreement in effect finessed competing interests: the carefully worded
final document represented less a compromise than a form of arbitration
among parties (Croome 1995, 265). The text of the Tokyo Round code
had been expanded to include elements that the opposing sides wanted—
a mixture of more detail on the definition of dumping and injury with an
expansion of legitimate grounds for use of the duty.[31]

THE SUBSIDIES AND COUNTERVAILING MEASURES AGREEMENT

In contrast to antidumping measures that are oriented toward private
corporate practices, the subsidy code attempts to discipline subsidies
given by governments. The Tokyo Round developed a code elaborating
on the interpretation of Articles VI, XIV, and XXIII of the GATT (the
Subsidies Code), where the conditions for using subsidies and imposing
countervailing duties were spelled out. The Uruguay Round in turn elaborated on the Subsidies Code and incorporated it into the single undertaking of the WTO.

Subsidy negotiations were less difficult than were the antidumping talks,
in part because of different coalition among countries. The intent of the
Uruguay Round review of subsidies was both to increase the range of
policies subject to GATT disciplines and to clarify the conditions under
which a countervailing duty was legitimate in the face of an inconsistent
actions by a member. The United States was most interested in the former

a.

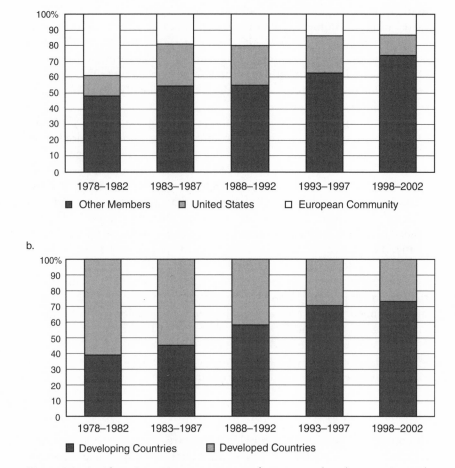

b.

Figure 4.4. Antidumping actions: percentage of measures taken, by reporting and by targeted member respectively, 1978–2002

aspect of the negotiations: U.S. negotiators wanted the regime to prohibit as many forms of government subsidies as possible, except where they were part of technology or environmental programs. Given the U.S. position on countervailing duties, almost all other countries wanted to address the second of these issues, that is, the legitimate conditions for punishment. (See figure 4.5 for the use of countervailing duties over time and figures 4.6a and 4.6b for their incidence by initiating and targeted country).

In contrast to the breakdown in negotiations that occurred in antidumping talks, an early secretariat suggestion for a distinction among types of subsidies, following ideas put forward by the United States and

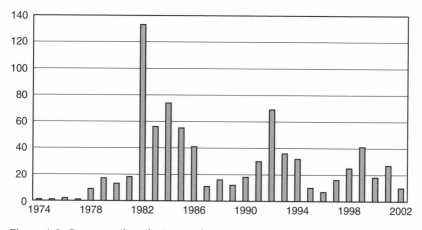

Figure 4.5. Countervailing duties: total investigations initiated, 1974–2002

Switzerland, became a focal point for talks. A three-part framework, known as the "traffic light" approach, was adopted. The framework divided subsidies into categories: prohibited (red), actionable (amber), and nonactionable (green) (Croome 1995, 62–63, 171–73). While countries could disagree on what policies fell in each category (e.g., the United States thought almost nothing was green except for research and environmental policies), the framework created a common language and purpose for negotiations. Over the course of the talks, the categories came to be defined by the degree to which an action distorted trade. Agricultural subsidies, an issue that the EC maintained was a matter for the agricultural working group, were not to be included initially, but became covered upon expiry of the Peace Clause in 2004.[32]

The Agreement on Subsidies and Countervailing Measures (SCM agreement) was more specific on the issue of subsidies than were the earlier documents. The agreement, defines the prohibited category to include subsidies conditioned on export performance or on use of domestic products over imported products; this provision, of course, excludes agricultural products. For subsidies within the actionable category, countervailing duties are legitimate only when a subsidy leads to serious injury and when the product was subsidized by more than 5 percent. The concept of de minimis was defined as less than 1 percent of imports for the developed world and less than 2 or 3 percent, depending upon income, for other countries. The permitted, nonactionable subsidies include some of those oriented not only towards research and the environment, but towards regional development. And by use of the concept that the agreement restricted only subsidies "specific" to an industry or group of enterprises, the agreement effectively excluded general subsidies that cover many industries such as those for health care, income support, or public educa-

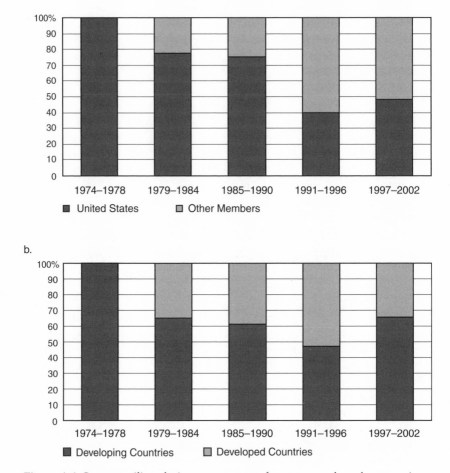

Figure 4.6 Countervailing duties: percentage of measures taken, by reporting member and by targeted member respectively, 1974–2002

tion. The developing economies received special treatment, although only those countries whose per capita incomes were under one thousand dollars a year were free to use export subsidies without fear of retaliation. Other developing nations had to phase out such subsidies within eight years. The importance of this rule was little appreciated because the decision occurred without knowledge of the institutional changes that would mandate a "single undertaking." The result was less dissent than would have been expected from the affected parties.[33]

4.6. The Unfinished Business

The Uruguay Round did not manage to tidy up all the loose ends from the GATT. Two of the Tokyo Round codes, in particular, proved impossible to convert into general obligations under the WTO. These two codes, covering government procurement and trade in civil aircraft, reflected particular political difficulties and the reality of the market. The codes had not in themselves solved the inherent problems in these areas of trade. The rules on government procurement, for example, were biased in favor of home producers in the signatory nations, and trade in civil aircraft was characterized by protectionist barriers for a small number of aircraft manufacturers.

An Agreement on Government Procurement was negotiated in the Tokyo Round and came into force in 1981. The code has only twenty-five signatories and covers bidding procedures for certain government procurements. The aim of the agreement is to encourage countries to open up procurement to suppliers from other countries. Principles of nondiscrimination and national treatment were incorporated, but the effect on trade flows is limited by the fact that the agreement only applies to sectors that are included in schedules of national commitments.[34] This "positive list" approach, employed also in the GATS commitments, has the obvious weakness of making noninclusion the "default." Interests that wish to get a sector included have a more difficult time. "Negative list" processes put the burden on the sector arguing for its exclusion. Some success in expanding the scope of the commitments was achieved in the Uruguay Round, and the new agreement came into operation in 1996. However, countries still have a long way to go in opening up this significant area of international commerce.

The reasons for the sensitivity in this area of trade are clear. There is unlikely to be a broad constituency for increased openness in government procurement. Countries that feel themselves to be competitive in supplying goods have an incentive to improve market access, but few countries appear willing to give up the ability to discriminate in favor of either domestic providers or regional partners. This is not a case where the multilateral regime has great hope of success, though efficiency might be improved by the purchase by all governments of goods and services from the cheapest source. But where the internal market is itself not free, it is fanciful to assume the development of free global access. This is, however, an area where regional agreements may be picking up the slack. Eventually there could be a constituency for the coordination of such plurilateral agreements on government purchasing. At the global level, the most that can be expected at present is some emphasis on transparency in government procurement, and that was indeed the topic chosen at Doha for possible inclusion in the round.

The Agreement on Trade in Civil Aircraft was negotiated in the Tokyo Round and entered into force in 1980. It currently has twenty-four signatories. The agreement eliminates tariffs on nonmilitary aircraft and parts. It includes disciplines on government purchasing of aircraft and financial support for the production of civil aircraft. However, the actual number of countries that produce civil aircraft is much smaller, and trade disputes, both between the EU and the United States over subsidies to Boeing and Airbus Industrie and between Canada and Brazil over smaller passenger planes, have been long and contentious. The structure of the industry and the small numbers of countries involved combine to make this a low priority for global regulation.

4.7. Conclusion

The extension of GATT rules in the Uruguay Round to include the laggard sectors of agriculture and textiles was largely successful. There was no intrinsic reason why textiles and agriculture as sectors should have been treated differently from the manufacturing sector in terms of trade rules. The reasons had more to do with the domestic significance of producers' interests and the distribution of export capacity in the world. Both sectors proved difficult to integrate with the GATT process of successive rounds of tariff negotiations. The Uruguay Round completed the task that had been left unfinished by bringing these sectors under the rubric of the rules system for border protection. In the case of agriculture, the URAA went further to include restraints on domestic subsidies in some respects more constraining than for other sectors. On the other hand, the ATC was deliberately designed to terminate with the full integration of that sector in the WTO rules. But in both cases the task of trade liberalization has only just begun. Therefore the question that faces the trade system is whether the appropriate balance can be found to allow both importing and exporting countries to agree to a major shift in protection and to accept the prospect of a significant shift in production patterns in these areas.

Textiles policy is still sensitive in the developed countries, and the politics may not be in place for a major liberalization in the near future. In agriculture, signals are mixed on the prospects for more progress, with the United States agreeing to a major increase in payments to farmers that other countries fear may exacerbate weak world prices. However, reform has not stopped entirely, and agricultural markets could be liberalized significantly in the current round. This may depend on the involvement of groups other than the traditional farm interests to push policies toward those that are more consistent with an open trade system. On the other hand, the drift in farm policies toward stimulating rural development and encouraging environmentally friendly farming practices promises further trade tensions as the distinction between domestic and trade objectives becomes blurred.

The importance of agriculture to developing countries may be enough to tilt the balance in the direction of liberalization. These countries have expressed disappointment at the small gains in market access that have materialized in agricultural products since the Uruguay Round. Agriculture has thus been included as one of the "implementation issues" identified in the Doha agenda that need to be addressed as talks progress on new trade topics. Moreover, developing countries are aware of the relatively modest success in reducing domestic support in the OECD countries and contrast that with the changes in their own policies that are expected to be required by the outcome of a new round.

The success of the Uruguay Round in consolidating the trade remedy rules is evident by the fact that they are not central to the agenda of the Doha Round. The one significant issue is the operation of the antidumping agreement, considered by several countries, including Japan and Korea, to be operating in a way that is contrary to their interests. As discussed above, this is the continuation of a long-running debate on the scope and depth of this agreement. What may be changing is the proliferation of such regulations in developing countries. Eventually, the United States and the EU may find it in their interest to constrain antidumping actions as they become more often the targets of trade remedies. The Doha Round has promised a clarification and interpretation of certain aspects of the antidumping agreement. Thus the "grand bargain" that will be necessary to conclude the Doha Round will likely include at least a modest rebalancing of the obligations and concessions reached in the Uruguay Round a decade ago.

Notes

1. Though industrial country tariffs are now low, at about 4 percent on average, many developing countries still maintain higher tariffs against manufactured goods.

2. A number of other traded products, such as minerals, petroleum, and steel, had also evaded effective multilateral rules, but no attempt was made in the Uruguay Round (or since) to incorporate these sectors. Though generally covered by GATT/WTO regulations, most of the international discussions of trade in these products take place outside the realm of the multilateral trade system.

3. Of the four Tokyo Round codes that were not incorporated into the WTO, two (the dairy and bovine meat agreements) were terminated in 1997 and the Agreement on Trade in Civil Aircraft and the Agreement on Government Procurement remain plurilateral in nature.

4. The binary distinction between "trade" and "domestic" policies and objectives is adopted for convenience. In reality there is a continuum of objectives, with room for considerable differences of opinion as to what constitutes each category.

5. Clearly a large set of government measures have only a general or indirect impact on trade, such as education and health policies and national defense. By way of an example, educational services have been included in the schedules of some countries that specify their commitment to open up to foreign competition. Over time more of these policies may migrate to the category of trade-relevant domestic policies, though one would expect considerable resistance.

6. One could also include currency controls in this category, as they are related to domestic objectives of macroeconomic stability.

7. This difference shows up in terminology. Trade experts talk of the "trade and . . ." agenda (trade and labor or trade and environment): others are more likely to refer to these issues as "the environment and trade," or "labor standards and trade."

8. The LTA was seen as an alternative to using Article XIX safeguards in cases of serious injury to domestic firms as a result of import surges. The LTA required the weaker test of "market disruption" but did not allow retaliation.

9. The United States, in particular, maintains high tariffs on many textile and clothing imports, ranging from 25 percent for woven wool fabrics up to 79 percent for raw cotton products. EU tariffs are mostly in the range of 9–12 percent. For details of textile tariffs see Schott 1994, 58.

10. The United States refused at the Doha ministerial to agree to a faster phaseout of the textile quotas that had been requested by developing countries. However, the administration was able to resist pressures that emerged during the House debate over trade promotion authority (TPA) to extend the MFA beyond 2004.

11. The issue of health and safety regulations is considered in the next chapter, as relating to domestic policy objectives rather than with trade issues as such. Davis (2003) discusses the more general question of the structure of trade negotiations in agriculture and over health issues such as the use of hormones in beef.

12. In effect, the United States could operate quantitative restrictions on imports in support of domestic policies even if there were not effective quantitative controls on domestic production. Section 22 of the Agricultural Adjustment Act (as amended) mandated such protection, and the United States had little choice but to ask its trading partners for a waiver.

13. The variable levy for cereals and other agricultural imports was an import duty that rose when world prices were low and fell when they were high. It was never clear whether this levy was a tariff that happened to move often, or a quantitative restriction (as an importer had to apply for a license on which the applicable rate of duty was stamped), or a measure that had somehow evaded the scrutiny of the drafters of the GATT. It joined other trade barriers, such as voluntary export restraints, as "gray area measures."

14. The attempts to resolve some of these trade disputes through the GATT dispute settlement process proved a source of frustration. This led to trade wars and unilateral action and in the end contributed greatly to the pressure for firmer rules for dispute panels in the Uruguay Round (Josling and Tangermann 2003). Among these the oilseed dispute had the most impact, and indeed was settled only as a part of the package that ended the Uruguay Round negotiations.

15. For a full discussion of the Peace Clause and the possible impact of its expiry, see Steinberg and Josling 2003.

16. Thus agriculture became part of the "built-in agenda" that included continued negotiations in services (see chapter 5). These negotiations did indeed begin in 2000 but have now been folded in to the Doha Development Agenda.

17. See Gibson et al. 2001 for more details on the level of tariffs in agricultural products, including averages by commodity, and Josling 1998 for the linkages between the WTO rules and farm policy reform.

18. The gap for industrial countries is even greater, where the ratio of agricultural to industrial tariffs is closer to ten to one.

19. See Josling and Rae 2003 for a discussion of alternative tariff reduction formulas and their implications.

20. The OECD reports annually a "total support estimate" (TSE) representing the monetary value of transfers to agriculture, including transfers from consumers through higher prices and transfers from taxpayers through budgetary expenditure. The TSE stood at $302 billion in 1986–88, at the start of the Uruguay Round, and rose slightly to $318 billion by 2002 (OECD 2003). However, the most trade-distorting elements of this transfer (market price support) declined from $186 billion to $149 billion over this period. As a share of GDP, the TSE declined from 2.3 percent to 1.2 percent over the same period.

21. The current market access, export subsidy, and domestic support conditions are described in International Agricultural Trade Resarch Consortium 2001, along with a discussion of the situation in the area of "product attributes."

22. Note that the economic benefit of subsidies and price controls may have been capitalized in, for example, the value of farmland, so that reducing the subsidies sharply harms existing farmers who may have paid for or borrowed against land valued at an artificially high level. See Tullock 1975. (This point was suggested by an anonymous reviewer, to whom we are grateful.)

23. The Cairns Group includes small to medium-sized agricultural exporting countries that maintain relatively little agricultural protection. The current members of the Cairns Group are Australia, Argentina, Bolivia, Brazil, Canada, Chile, Colombia, Costa Rica, Fiji, Guatemala, Indonesia, Malaysia, New Zealand, Paraguay, Philippines, South Africa, Thailand, and Uruguay.

24. Many of the Cairns Group countries associated themselves with the proposal, as did several non–Cairns Group WTO members. The group originally numbered twenty countries, but three other countries associated themselves with the group (and one country left) giving rise to the alternative name of G-22. Since Cancún at least three countries have distanced themselves from the group, and the name "G-20" is now said to refer to the date (August 20) on which their original proposal was tabled.

25. Trade safeguards can be broadly classified as "temporary" or "permanent" (see Hoekman and Kostecki 2002, 303). Permanent exemptions include those for national security (Articles XXI and XIV bis) and the general exemptions for health and moral reasons in Article XX. Temporary exemptions can be triggered either by economy-wide problems, such as balance-of-payments imbalances (Articles XII and XVIII (b)), or by the situation in particular industries. In this latter category fall predefined circumstances either related to the "unfair" practices of foreign private or state actors (Article VI) or not related to any such practice (Article XIX). In addition, the agricultural and textiles agreements have their own safeguards provisions, and if all else fails, countries can request waivers of their obligations (Article IX) or renegotiate their concessions to reflect new realities (Article XXVIII). In this section the main focus will be on Article VI and XIX provisions.

26. The Standards Code was the only one of the seven that addressed the trade effect of domestic regulations, as opposed to the practices employed by governments at the border to alleviate pressure on domestic markets. As such, it raises many of the same issues of domestic regulation as does trade in services. It is therefore discussed in the next chapter, even though it predates the Uruguay Round. The weak codes covering dairy and bovine meat trade were a relic of the attempts to negotiate international commodity agreements, and played little role in the development of the GATT.

27. There were four exceptions to the single undertaking: the plurilateral agreements regarding government procurement, civil aviation, and bovine meat and dairy products. The latter two plurilaterals have been discontinued subsequent to the Uruguay Round.

28. A 1985 report by the Leutwiler Group, set up to advise on GATT issues, argued: "Time and again the negotiation of VERs with one supplier has been followed by a proliferation of bilateral deals with all efficient suppliers who are not in a position to refuse. . . . It is therefore untrue that selective action helps to limit the extent of disruption of trade. Moreover, the process of discrimination against the most efficient suppliers contravenes the principle of comparative advantage and maximizes the cost to the world economy of the protection granted to the inefficient" (Croome 1995, 55).

29. The GATT/WTO system does not in general attempt to regulate the behavior of firms. Thus the object of the antidumping rules is confined to the activities of governments in countering dumping.

30. Although the four delegates (from New Zealand, Australia, Mexico and Switzerland) produced a text, neither the United States nor the EC supported their modest proposals (Croome, 1995, pp. 180–181).

31. For further information on antidumping, see Finger 1993; Prusa 1999; and Lindsey and Ikenson 2002.

32. The agricultural agreement also made explicit the extent to which farm subsidies were to be treated differently from those granted to the nonfarm sector. In that agreement there are no "red" (prohibited) subsidies.

33. For further information, see Sykes (2003a).

34. Attempts to use positive lists for trade liberalization in regional trade agreements have almost always led to slower progress that those that choose the negative list approach.

Five

Extending Trade Rules to Domestic Regulations: Developing "Behind the Border" Instruments

5.1. Introduction

The narrow focus and limitations of the rules of the multilateral trade system embodied in the GATT were becoming clear by the mid-1970s, as the first effects of globalization began to be felt. Freer trade, coupled with open capital markets, encouraged businesses to rethink their production structures and strategies. For many, the location of production became increasingly divorced from the location of the market. Foreign direct investment boomed, facilitated by the emergence of a capital market without borders. Outsourcing became a way to take advantage of the diversity of production costs and conditions. But firms that had expanded beyond the borders of individual states also began to take an interest in the issue of disparities in regulations that they faced. A coalition of public and private interests began to take aim at the restrictive aspects of regulatory differences, grouping them under the general heading of "nontariff barriers." Those that were directly linked to trade policy, such as the trade remedies increasingly used by countries to offset injury from import surges and subsidized exports, were eventually covered by the conversion of the plurilateral Tokyo Round codes into multilateral agreements, as discussed in the previous chapter. Those trade barriers that were a side effect of differing domestic regulations posed more fundamental challenges for the design of trade rules.

The more formidable task of the Uruguay Round was to bring trade disciplines to areas of trade that had so far escaped attention. The most radical departure of the Uruguay Round from GATT practice was its success in incorporating two new aspects of international trade into the framework of the multilateral system. This included the establishment of rules to govern trade in services, in recognition of their growing role in the trade system, and of the protection of intellectual property, that had been covered by some plurilateral codes outside the realm of the GATT but had not been backed up by any dispute settlement process.[1] Both services and intellectual property were actively being integrated into the internal trade rules of the EEC. Experience in that endeavor gave confidence to negotiators that rules were feasible in these new areas of trade policy. The United States–Canada Free Trade Agreement had also experimented in the extension of trade rules in these directions. The General Agreement on Trade in Services (GATS) and the Agreement on Trade-Related Aspects of Intellectual Property Rights (TRIPS) took their place along with the GATT as major legislative instruments of the trade system. Unlike the GATT and GATS, however, TRIPS extends the obligation of governments beyond the fashioning of rules to facilitate trade and into an area previously considered to be an aspect of purely domestic policy.

Multilateral rules in these new areas are not necessarily welfare-enhancing. As indicated in chapter 1, there are powerful theoretical reasons to believe that *goods trade* liberalization enhances welfare in each country that engages in it; that expectation is backed by empirical evidence. By contrast, rules in some of the new areas, such as global protection of intellectual property rights, may be rent seeking (Barton 2001), and liberalization in other new areas, such as telecommunications, may be efficient but have serious distributive consequences between countries.

Domestic policies related to health and safety standards had also largely escaped the discipline of the trade rules even when they had a major impact on trade. A new Agreement on Sanitary and Phytosanitary Measures attempted to put constraints on domestic policies in this area, in particular by obliging the use of risk assessment backed up by scientific evidence. An improved Standards Code, the Agreement on Technical Barriers to Trade, addressed technical measures that operated behind-the-border in an attempt to discipline the use of such regulations for covert protection of domestic producers.

In incorporating "new" areas, in particular services and intellectual property rights, and detailing multilateral rules to govern other behind-the-border topics such as human health and safety, the trade system changed its nature in highly significant ways. First, as shown in table 4.2, the negotiation and conclusion of agreements on these new issues have changed the composition and character of the domestic political coalitions that have traditionally driven trade policy. For most of the GATT era, trade policy in Europe and the United States was driven by a tension between efficient export-oriented goods producers and inefficient import-competing goods producers joined by organized labor. Global negotiations on the new issues have brought new nonstate actors—such as services producers and consumers, consumer watchdog groups, and environmentalists—into the domestic politics of trade policymaking. Moreover, as summarized in table 5.1, the new issues demanded new principles of global regulation. In several contexts, trade negotiators started to draft new agreements based on the old principles of most-favored nation (MFN) and national treatment, but learned that negotiations on that basis

TABLE 5.1.
Legal Tool Kit for Different Trade Restraints

	Instruments with Trade Policy Objectives	Instruments with Domestic Policy Objectives
Instruments operated at the border (primarily goods)	Tariff reductions Quota liberalizations MFN	National treatment Mutual recognition Presumptions favoring international, least-trade-restrictive, or scientifically based standards
Instruments operated behind the border (both goods and services)	Rights of establishment National treatment Investment incentives Subsidies	Harmonization or approximation of standards Transparency of standard making Effective enforcement requirements

would fail. Hence, they developed new principles to guide agreement in the new areas.

Why did the trade system expand its scope to cover these other aspects of trade? How did it adapt the rules for goods trade to cover other areas of international commerce? What "principles" were behind the new rulesets? And how has this "mission creep" changed the nature of domestic and international trade politics? These questions are the focus of this chapter.

5.2. Bringing in Services: Negotiation of the GATS

The conclusion of an agreement on trade in services within the rules of the trade system was probably the most innovative aspect of the Uruguay Round. While global trade in goods had reached $10.4 trillion by 1995, the value of service trade had been rising rapidly and reached $2.28 trillion by that same year (World Bank 1997). Moreover, a large share of foreign direct investment is in service-providing sectors. The incorporation of services into trade rules involved, for the first time, rule making on aspects of labor movement and the right of establishment of business entities in other countries, as these are intrinsically linked to service provision across borders. Service trade had remained outside the GATT, and its significance in international economic relations was generally underplayed.[2] Services do not cross boundaries in the same way that goods do, with remote buyers and sellers sending products across a border. Services are essentially nonstorable: the act of production and consumption are in essence simultaneous. For this reason the service provider and the buyer have to be in contact. This poses significant problems of asymmetric information, as the buyer often has limited recourse if the service is substandard. Governments have generally taken a strong regulatory stance in service markets, usually by regulating the seller and the process of service provision. This method of regulation itself is de facto more difficult in the case of cross-border services. But it also makes relatively easy the discrimination against foreign suppliers. Thus the main challenge for the incorporation of services in the trade system is to identify which domestic actions are in fact trade barriers and which regulations are necessary and prudent.

Moreover, agreement to liberalize service trade could not be reached merely by applying the old rules on nondiscrimination to scheduled sectors. Based on the success of that formula in forty years of GATT trade rounds, services negotiators began with a framework that required all parties to offer unconditional MFN treatment to the service sectors of other parties and to affirmatively schedule service subsectors that would be subject to the national treatment principle. This approach was a complete failure because asymmetry in openness meant that countries with closed services subsectors could simply catch a free ride on the economies with open services: the closed economies offered to affirmatively schedule virtually none of their closed subsectors and expected that the framework would assure continued access to the open economies by virtue of the MFN guarantee. As a result, at the end of the Uruguay Round, the United States effectively changed the rules of the negotiations, taking derogations from the MFN requirement in important subsectors of services. That move created a credible threat to close those subsectors to services trade from noncooperative countries and resulted in serious offers by those countries to liberalize important subsectors. Altogether, about eighty countries put on the table offers of access to service markets, and these were agreed and placed in country schedules.

Hence, the Uruguay Round was successful in generating accord on a General Agreement on Trade in Services (GATS). The GATS includes general principles that govern policies affecting trade in services (including unconditional MFN and national treatment of scheduled sectors), country schedules detailing the extent to which each country agrees to provide access to service sectors, annexes that contain detail about particular services (and to which other service agreements can, and have, been added), and two major subsector-specific agreements, covering basic telecommunications and financial services. The Council for Trade in Services was set up to administer the agreement. Where bilateral service access agreements existed, the GATS required that they be opened up for negotiation by other members and that they be notified to the WTO. Two more sets of negotiations have so far achieved minimal results, in the areas of maritime transport and the conditions for movement of temporary service workers (movement of natural persons), as discussed below.

The GATS distinguishes among four "modes" of delivery of a service: direct cross-border sales (such as services rendered over a telephone line or the Internet); consumption abroad (as in the case of tourism); the establishment of a commercial presence (setting up a branch of a bank); and temporary entrance of service providers (nonnationals on consultancy or specialized construction tasks). Of these delivery modes, the one most like goods trade is direct sales across borders. But as no physical good crosses the border in the case of service trade, trade restrictions will be almost entirely "within the border." In fact the only "footprint" may often be the financial transaction that accompanies the service. If regulation is undertaken at the point of production, that point will often be in the jurisdiction of the exporter (i.e., subject to home-country controls). Hence importer governments may have difficulty in providing adequate oversight of such transactions.

The GATS is still in its infancy. Many service sectors are not covered, and many aspects of service trade still have to be negotiated. This includes the issues of subsidies paid to service providers, government procurement of services, safeguards against import surges, technical standards as barriers to service trade, qualifications of service providers, and the process of securing licenses for foreign service providers. Though the regulation of service providers from abroad and the control of service establishments in other countries take trade policy well inside borders, the emphasis is still on aspects of regulation that relate to trade. Services that are not traded, and those that are only incidental to trade, are not covered.

Nevertheless, it should be noted that the GATS has a number of important and immediate implications, even in areas where special agreements have not been negotiated. It imposes a requirement of "transparency," meaning that regulations affecting trade have to be published and available to trading partners. And the members must have judicial or quasi-judicial procedures such as administrative tribunals for reviewing administrative decisions affecting trade in services. Moreover, the way that nations regulate monopolies (such as those for telecommunications services) is restricted in order to ensure that these monopolies do not discriminate against foreign suppliers. Thus, this agreement is a major step toward a set of world standards requiring legal styles of administration similar to those typical in the United States and Europe, and less typical of Asia or of the poorer developing nations.

Though the commercial and political conditions surrounding traded services are somewhat specific to the type of service, a brief discussion of four of the most important sectors among traded goods will give an indication of both the extent of the trade commitment and the difficulties of incorporating such activities into trade rules.

5.2.1. Telecommunications Services

The telecommunications (telecoms) sector has played a major role in the development of the modern, "global" economy, through the increasingly rapid transmission of information among individuals and businesses. Incorporating this sector into the GATS was both desirable and contentious. If there were benefits to be had from liberalization of services, then the sector was a prime candidate for such a move. But, as public utilities in many countries, basic telecommunications services were considered to be a domestic prerogative. The GATS annex on telecoms specifies that foreign service suppliers be given access to the basic infrastructure of public telecommunication networks without discrimination. While several countries included some of the value-added telecom services in their schedules, subjecting those services to the nondiscrimination rules of the annex, the Uruguay Round ended with no specific commitments on the liberalization of basic telecommunications services, such as voice telephony.

An agreement that included commitments on liberalization of basic telecommunications was negotiated shortly after the conclusion of the round. Failure to reach the agreement during the round was probably more a matter of misjudgment than of fundamental bargaining differences. And after the round, two things combined to facilitate agreement. First, the United States brought its market power to bear on the post–Uruguay Round basic telecommunications negotiations. As the round concluded, GATT/WTO negotiators agreed to continue negotiating on basic telecoms. At the same time, the United States took a derogation on its MFN commitment for basic telecommunications, suggesting a threat to discriminate against telecoms providers from countries that were not forthcoming in the negotiations (Steinberg 1994). Second, consumers of basic telecommunications services organized in several countries to demand liberalization so that they could become more productive by taking advantage of the efficiencies of the unfolding information technology revolution. This shifted trade politics in those countries, pitting consumers against the previously almighty postal, telegraph, and telephone (PTT) monopolies (Borrus and Cohen 1997). Conclusion of the agreement to liberalize basic telecommunications was then catalyzed by the Federal Communications Commission decision in late 1996 to impose a price cap on what U.S. carriers could pay foreign countries on accounting rates, a unilateral regulatory measure that drove down the level of accounting rates dramatically (Cowhey and Sherman 1998).

Hence, the negotiations concluded successfully in February 1997 with an Agreement on Basic Telecommunications that effectively regulates the national regulators—the former PTT monopolies. In many countries, developing countries in particular, this has enabled foreign telecommunications service providers to greatly diminish the market share, size, and control of PTT monopolies. Some speculate that the new national regulations in some countries might be favoring the establishment of private telecommunications monopolies or oligopolies, replacing the PTTs with private rent-seekers.

5.2.2. Financial Services

Another sector fundamental to the smooth working of the global economy is the financial services sector. The inclusion of financial services in the GATS was in itself a major accomplishment on the road to opening up an important part of the economy. But the extent to which rules of nondiscrimination can apply in this area is circumscribed. Responsibility for prudential oversight was reserved for governments, along with the instruments needed for the control of monetary policy.

As with basic telecoms, specific commitments on the liberalization of financial services eluded the negotiators in the Uruguay Round. And as with basic telecoms, the impetus for a post–Uruguay Round agreement was a last-minute shift in the legal principles that were to apply to the sector. In the closing days of the Uruguay Round, the United States negotiated language that permitted it to take an MFN derogation for financial services beginning six months after the GATS entered into force. When by July 1995 the post–Uruguay Round negotiations failed to yield a package with a "critical mass" of signatories, the United States exercised its right to take a derogation, effectively raising the ante by an implicit threat to discriminate against financial service providers from recalcitrant countries. The resulting pressure yielded an agreement on financial services in December 1997.

5.2.3. Movement of Natural Persons

Services are often provided by the temporary entry of workers, often with particular skills, into a country requiring the service. Work permits and visas restrict such access and raise the cost of the service. Discrimination among such temporary residents is also a potential problem for the service provider. The Uruguay Round concluded an annex on "the movement of natural persons" (i.e., as opposed to corporate entities) for the provision of services. Negotiations on the offers of liberalization, however, were also prolonged after the Uruguay Round had been signed, and a limited agreement on such provisions was finally reached in 1996. Negotiators were careful to separate the treatment of temporary workers from the conditions for the entry of people to look for or accept permanent employment, as well as from issues of citizenship and naturalization rights.[3]

Though cautious in scope, this aspect of the GATS does represent a major qualitative "advance" for trade rules. In treating this particular aspect of labor movement as an issue that is subject to agreed rules and enforceable constraints on the actions of sovereign governments, the door has been opened a crack for other immigration issues to be introduced if countries believed that doing so would be appropriate. The distinction between tradable goods and services is weakening: this, in turn, makes less distinct the notion that trade and factor movements should forever be treated by different rules.

5.2.4. Maritime Transport

Mention should be made of the one major failure of the GATS agenda for liberalization commitments, the inability of countries to agree on schedules for the opening up of maritime transport sectors. Negotiations were always likely to be difficult. Countries commonly have regulations that favor transport, in particular cabotage, in their own vessels. The motivations range from support for the shipbuilding industry to the advantages for military capabilities of having a domestic merchant marine fleet. The United States was in no position to take the lead, declining to put the Jones Act, a preferential scheme for restricting access to foreign vessels for carrying cargo within coastal waters, on the table. Additional complications arose from the existence of liner conferences that restrict ocean shipping in certain areas to control competition.[4] Talks on commitments in this area were planned to end in June 1996 but reached no conclusion. Continued negotiations in the context of the "built-in agenda" have not so far shown any breakthrough in this area.[5]

5.2.5. Future Negotiations on Services

The GATS, recognizing the range of service sectors that could be covered by agreed disciplines and stimulated by further liberalization, obligated countries to continue the process of negotiation, both broadening its scope and including more sectors. As a result, the process of negotiation on extending the services agreement has been continuing. Along with agriculture and a small number of other issues, it constituted the post–Uruguay Round "built-in agenda" that was not dependent on the launching of a new round. But the uncertainty created by the failed ministerial in Seattle slowed progress somewhat, and it took the launch of a new round at Doha to breath life into the services negotiation. The failure to reach agreement at Cancún two years later raises questions about the future of these negotiations, of course.

5.2.6. Principles behind Service Trade Rules

How well do the GATT nondiscrimination principles of MFN and national treatment apply to trade in services? In political terms, the answer is not very well. The GATT nondiscrimination principles of MFN and national treatment worked well when applied to trade in goods because tariff rates in the early GATT years were uniformly high. With market closure across all countries as a starting point for negotiations, nondiscrimination principles could work in conjunction with a norm of reciprocity to liberalize goods trade without substantial free-riding. In contrast, the starting point for negotiations on liberalization of services trade had a different structure: some markets (such as that of the United States) were open, while others were closed. Simple replication of the old GATT nondiscrimination principles in a draft GATS agreement created an incentive for closed countries to free ride by relying on the MFN principle to maintain access to open countries without offering to open their own markets to services trade. As illustrated by the basic telecommunications and financial services negotiations, liberalization could be achieved only after the world's largest open market—the United States—took a derogation on MFN treatment.

In terms of formal effectiveness, the applicability of GATT principles in the service context depends crucially on the mode of delivery of the service. How should one define MFN and national treatment in the case of cross-border service transactions? Regulations covering the provision of a service from abroad will tend to be discriminatory among suppliers if the conditions in the exporting and importing markets differ, and may also discriminate between domestic and foreign services merely as a function of the nature of the risks being faced. Essentially, the problem often comes down to the willingness of the government in the importing country to accept the ability of the exporting country government to provide the desired regulation of the service supplier. This points more toward mutual recognition of administrative capacities than traditional MFN or national treatment as a guideline for policy.

In the case of "consumption abroad" services, the principles of nondiscrimination apply much more directly. Few countries now restrict the private consumption patterns of tourists and others prepared to travel to consume services on the basis of their national origin, though consumption of public services may indeed be severely restricted. This mode of service provision is the least contentious and probably the one with the least tendency to discriminate.

By contrast, the third mode of service delivery identified in the GATS, foreign establishment, raises much more contentious questions as to the operation of domestic regulations. One can argue that it is appropriate to ensure that there is no discrimination between WTO members, or discrimination in favor of domestic concerns. All foreign firms and individuals should be able to have the same rights to set up service-providing establishments in competition with domestic businesses, but in practice such discrimination is very hard to avoid. Matters of nationality, security concerns, regional preferences, and ethnic and cultural considerations all play a role in the active discrimination among service suppliers. In contrast to cross-border service provisions, commercial presence usually implies "host-country control." The importing country will be responsible for the fiduciary regulations and the certification of professional service providers. The task of making this conform to nondiscrimination principles is likely to be a challenge for the trade system for many years to come. Regional and bilateral agreements among countries may be the favored way to increase competition in domestic service sectors.

The fourth mode, the presence of temporary service workers, also poses significant challenges for nondiscrimination. All countries have discriminatory immigration and visa policies, and so are unlikely to agree to a policy of nondiscrimination. Indeed the concept of nationality and citizenship is itself rooted in the notion of discrimination, though often with the ability for immigrants to assume the obligations and derive the benefits from discrimination in favor of citizens. Temporary service workers do not often get equal treatment in the provision of social services. To domestic workers, such discrimination may seem reasonable, but it undoubtedly has an impact on the provision of traded services by foreigners. Although it is consistent with the logic of a free global market to allow service providers to travel freely to find customers (and in some parts of the world such travel is widely practiced to the advantage of consumers and the workers themselves), the clash with political reality is obvious. The trade system may have to settle for less than utopian rules on the "movement of natural persons."

The GATS itself reflects these problems. National treatment is offered only selectively in country schedules. The fact that countries can offer liberalization in some modes of delivery but not others reinforces this imbalance. It will take many rounds of negotiations before service providers can decide where and with whom to do business without the complexity of differing national regulations.[6]

5.3. Health, Agricultural Regulations, and Industrial Standards

The first Agreement on Technical Barriers to Trade (often called the Standards Code) emerged from the Tokyo Round as a plurilateral agreement that interprets the conditions under which countries could restrict imports through technical regulations. Its limited number of signatories made it of marginal use in controlling the tendency for countries to favor domestic industries in technical regulations. The Standards Code covered, among other aspects of trade policy, technical regulations and standards relating to food safety and animal and plant health measures (Stanton 1999). The Standards Code restated the principle that such measures should not "create unnecessary obstacles to trade." However, neither the original GATT Article XX nor the Standards Code was able to stem disruptions of trade caused by a proliferation of technical restrictions.

Four flaws in the pre–Uruguay Round legal infrastructure blunted the effectiveness of disciplines on technical barriers: gaps and ambiguities in the GATT and the Standards Code; the lack of a single integrated rule system; the GATT's consensus-based dispute settlement process; and the exemption of production and process standards from the disciplines of the Standards Code. As with many international agreements, the Standards Code contained several rules that were vague, in many cases because ambiguity bridged differences between negotiators. These ambiguities made it difficult to determine, ex ante and ex post, whether a particular national regulation contravened GATT rules. Moreover, not all GATT contracting parties signed the Standards Code, or other Tokyo Round Codes, giving rise to a system sometimes referred to as "GATT à la carte." This effectively precluded a number of standards-related disputes from being brought before a GATT panel for resolution. But even where two countries had signed the Standards Code, a consensus-based GATT dispute settlement process allowed either the petitioner or the respondent to block a panel report, or even to deny a request to convene a panel. Finally, the Standards Code itself only disciplined measures that "lay down characteristics of a product such as levels of quality, performance, safety or dimensions," thereby omitting any explicit reference to production and process methods.

To remedy these defects, multilateral disciplines on the use of technical barriers were revised, expanded, and strengthened in the 1986–94 Uruguay Round. The Standards Code was rewritten to remedy some of the defects, and more significantly, a separate agreement was negotiated to cover sanitary and phytosanitary measures. The new Agreement on Technical Barriers to Trade (TBT agreement) and the Agreement on Sanitary and Phytosanitary Measures (SPS agreement) entered into force on January 1, 1995. The SPS agreement featured disciplines that were designed to prevent the disingenuous use of health and safety regulations as a nontransparent means of providing protection for domestic producers.[7] The new TBT agreement stipulated legally binding rules for "related processes and production methods," closing the loophole in the Standards Code that had frustrated the application of the code to many domestic regulations (Josling, Roberts, and Orden 2004).[8]

5.3.1. Health and Safety Regulations and the SPS Agreement

The need to allow countries to impose trade restrictions to support their domestic health and safety standards was recognized in the GATT 1947. The right to use trade restrictions for this purpose, as well as constraints on their use, was encapsulated in Article XX of the GATT, which states in relevant part:

> Subject to the requirement that such measures are not applied in a manner which would constitute a means of arbitrary or unjustifiable discrimination between countries where the same conditions prevail, or a disguised restriction on international trade, . . . nothing in this [GATT] Agreement shall be construed to prevent the adoption or enforcement by any contracting party of measures . . . necessary to protect human, animal or plant life or health.

Though clear in intent, the provisions of Article XX were somewhat difficult to implement. Consequently, the contracting parties to the GATT agreed to negotiate disciplines on the preparation, adoption, and application of these measures beginning in the 1973–79 Tokyo Round. The Standards Code was the result of these negotiations, but this did not stem the proliferation of such restrictions, especially in the agricultural area. Hence, Uruguay Round negotiators concluded the SPS agreement, which was designed to require somewhat higher standards than the TBT agreement in the health and safety area. In addition, Uruguay Round negotiators concluded new rules for dispute settlement that would be critical to the effectiveness of both of these WTO agreements.

The negotiation of the SPS agreement had significant legal implications. It became clear to negotiators by 1990 that the protectionist use of technical barriers to trade could not be disciplined effectively by simply applying old GATT principles to agricultural safety measures that were the topic of the SPS agreement, and that additional rules were needed. Neither MFN nor national treatment precluded the use of food safety measures that were facially neutral yet had a discriminatory impact and lacked any scientific basis. For example, since the 1980s, the European Community has banned the internal sale of beef from cattle treated with growth hormones. Similarly, since the late 1990s, the EC has banned the internal sale of products containing genetically modified organisms (GMOs). In both cases, European producers would be free to continue selling their products, because their ranchers do not use growth hormones and their farmers do not use GMOs, and U.S. producers are effectively shut out of the market, because their ranchers and farmers do. Moreover, in neither case has the EC been able to offer a scientific study showing that the use of growth hormones or GMOs threatens human, animal, or plant life or health. Hence, the EC's technical measures in these areas have effectively discriminated against U.S. producers, even though they are facially neutral and lack any scientific basis. Therefore, U.S. negotiators insisted that the SPS agreement include a new rule: if a WTO member maintains an SPS measure that is more stringent than a multilaterally recognized standard, then that measure must not be maintained without sufficient scientific basis. The absence of a scientific basis for the EC's beef hormones directive was key to the 1998 Appellate Body decision that the directive is WTO-illegal (WTO 1998a).

5.3.2. The TBT Agreement

Regulation that aims at protecting people, animals, or plants from direct and definable health risks, such as the spread of disease, potentially allergic reactions, or pest infestations, is covered by the SPS agreement. All other technical regulations (i.e., those not aimed at reducing sanitary and phytosanitary risks) are covered by the separate TBT agreement.[9] Like the SPS agreement, the TBT agreement aims to distinguish measures necessary for achieving some regulatory objective from disguised trade protection.[10] Specifically, the TBT agreement extends the GATT principles of national treatment and MFN obligations, stating,

> Members shall ensure that in respect of technical regulations, products imported from the territory of any Member shall be accorded treatment no less favorable than that accorded to like products of national origin and to like products originating in any other country. (Article 2.1)

As under the SPS agreement, the TBT agreement also stipulates that countries avoid unnecessary trade impediments:

> Members shall ensure that technical regulations are not prepared, adopted or applied with a view to or with the effect of creating unnecessary obstacles to international trade. For this purpose, technical regulations shall not be more trade-restrictive than necessary to fulfill a legitimate objective, taking account of the risks non-fulfillment would create. (Article 2.2)

Beyond these general trade-promoting provisions, the TBT agreement is on the face of it quite permissive. The agreement does not limit a government's right to impose domestic trade restrictions when pursuing a legitimate goal in a nonprotectionist way. The key provisions of the TBT agreement define the basic concepts of "legitimate goals" and "non-protectionist actions" related to technical regulations promulgated by central government bodies. Other provisions deal with standards and conformity assessments and with the actions of other (subfederal and local) government agencies (Josling, Roberts, and Orden 2004).

A partial list of legitimate objectives for technical barriers is given in the TBT agreement, as well as an indication of the types of evidence that can be used to judge whether the instruments used are meeting those objectives:

> Such legitimate objectives are, *inter alia:* national security requirements; the prevention of deceptive practices; protection of human health or safety, animal or plant life or health [except as covered by the SPS agreement], or the environment. In assessing such risks, relevant elements of consideration are, *inter alia:* available scientific and technical information, related processing technology or intended end-uses of products.

According to these provisions, an import regulation has to meet two conditions: first, that the regulation aims to fulfill a legitimate objective; and, second, that there is no other measure less restrictive of trade available to fulfill the legitimate objective. The combination of "legitimate objective" and "least trade restrictive" conditions forms the core of the disciplines on domestic regulations imposed by the TBT agreement. The SPS agreement clearly requires a sufficient scientific basis for the measure in question, allowing for national standards to be higher than those required by international norms, provided they are scientifically based, and also permitting nations to take scientific uncertainties into account. In contrast, the TBT agreement appears to set less strict standards and allows more discretion. However, technical regulations that refer in their objective to issues of a scientific nature would presumably be subject to evaluation based on the scientific knowledge available (Heumiller and Josling 2001).

5.3.3. Safety Standards, Trade Rules, and Domestic Politics

Health and safety regulations do not fit in very well with the traditional principles of the GATT. This was implicit in the need to add the "scientific basis" standard to the SPS agreement. More broadly, discrimination is inherent in the application of trade restrictions based on the incidence of disease in the exporting country. As many of these regulations are applied within the borders, national treatment is not a major problem. Reciprocity does not work well in the case of health and safety standards, and there is little with which to "bargain" concessions. In addition, the notion of allowing imports in as a "concession" to other countries is fundamentally inconsistent with the notion of sensible and scientifically based import protocols. As important is the practical impact of trade rules in this area. Extending the scope of WTO rules (in the SPS and TBT agreements) to include "production and processing methods" immediately opens up the possibility that countries need to know how products are produced in the exporting country. No longer can the standards be enforced at the border. This in itself poses a challenge to the traditional concept of trade agreements. As a consequence, the concepts underlying the trade rules on safety standards are inherently problematic.

From a political perspective, the negotiation of rules in the food safety area catalyzed the involvement of new domestic actors in trade politics. For example, the new rules did not include "animal welfare" as a basis for restricting imports. This exclusion led to the mobilization of animal welfare advocates, who have since demanded to participate in trade policymaking processes and criticized the WTO's rules and mission. Similarly, the rules do not recognize "consumer preference" or "fear" as a basis for restricting imports. The negotiators' rationale was that individual consumers exercise preferences whenever they purchase a product; while the state has an interest in restricting imports that have a social cost (e.g., where imports are shown scientifically to pose a risk to human health), they have no interest in restricting the importation of goods based on consumer preferences alone. Nonetheless, the absence of consumer "preference" or "fear" as a basis for governmental import restrictions has led to mobilization of consumer interest groups who also challenge WTO rules. In short, conclusion of the SPS and TBT agreements has changed the composition of the domestic coalitions that have traditionally run this area of national trade policymaking.

5.4. Intellectual Property Protection and the Trading System

Many countries protect intellectual property (IP) rights, including copyrights and other related rights for literary and artistic works, patents for the protection of some industrial property, trademarks, and trade secrets. However, coverage is not universal, and the scope and duration of IP protection differs widely. This led some prominent sectors of the U.S. and European economies in the early 1980s to consider the possibility of incorporating in the trade rules a requirement for at least a minimum degree of IP protection. As major exporters of such goods as pharmaceuticals, software, movies, music, and trademarked luxury goods, they wanted protection against copying. Moreover, the growth of cross-national production networks had become contingent on effective licensing arrangements, which demanded reliable intellectual property protection (Borrus and Zysman 1997). These IP-producing sectors had been dissatisfied with their ability to strengthen intellectual property rules through action in the World Intellectual Property Organization (WIPO), the relevant special-purpose international organization. During the 1980s, the United States also began to unilaterally threaten trade sanctions as a way to encourage nations to strengthen their intellectual property systems.

The introduction of intellectual property protection into the rules of the trade system was a major source of North-South contention in the lead-up to the Uruguay Round. Developing countries, led by India and Brazil, argued that such an extension would inhibit their development and compel them to discipline their nascent software and pharmaceutical industries in the interest of protecting patents owned by firms in the OECD countries. More broadly, IP protection establishes a monopoly for the right-holder and there is little reason to believe that it stimulates research and development by industries in the world's poorer countries (Barton 2001). Therefore, from the perspective of most developing countries, global expansion of the IP rights of industries in the North looked more like a cynical act of rent seeking than a liberal act of mutual welfare enhancement. These nations did not want to go beyond the plurilateral agreements that already existed, in particular the WIPO-administered efforts that aimed at developing model statutes for adoption by countries, the Paris Convention for the Protection of Industrial Property (patents, trademarks, etc.) and the Berne Convention for the Protection of Literary and Artistic Works (copyright). Nonetheless, as described in chapter 3, the EC and United States successfully drafted an intellectual property agreement in the context of the Uruguay Round and imposed it on developing countries. The Agreement on Trade-Related Aspects of Intellectual Property Rights (TRIPS) became effective in 1995 at the inception of the WTO. It not only set higher substantive standards for national legislation, but also required adequate means of enforcement of those substantive rights within each member country, and made the standards and enforcement requirements subject to WTO dispute settlement.

Conclusion of the TRIPS agreement has had important legal and political implications. As a legal matter, it has taken the GATT/WTO system into uncharted territory, covering not merely border measures, but also mandating threshold national regulatory standards and means of enforcing those standards. Politically, it has placed WTO rules and negotiations into the center of domestic political battles over the appropriate scope of

IP protection, and has been responsible more than any other issue area for exacerbating North-South acrimony in Geneva. Particularly severe have been the disputes over the effects of TRIPS and patents generally on access to medicines in the developing world.[11] These disputes will be reviewed in the next chapter.

5.4.1. The TRIPS Agreement

Rules on service trade took the WTO into new areas of cross-border commerce, but at least some of the original GATT principles remain at the core of the GATS. The same claim is harder to sustain in the case of the TRIPS agreement. The agreement does include obligations based on MFN and national treatment. But the scope and duration of intellectual property protection, which are now addressed in the TRIPS agreement, had been essentially an issue for domestic regulation. Whether intellectual property is embodied in a product that crosses a border may not be directly relevant to the decision as to whether and for how long to grant protection. The domestic and trade aspects become entwined mainly if a protected, imported product has been priced lower in another country, or if a product that has been subject to intellectual property protection competes in a market with goods not subject to that protection. In the first case, "parallel" imports undercut the desired pricing in the domestic market and third-country markets, and in the second case unauthorized copies will tend to sell at a lower cost and reduce markets for patent and copyright holders. Thus, the domestic policy issue is how to make sure that domestic regulations are not undercut, and the trade policy issue is whether and how to ensure that all products and services benefiting from the same patent or copyright are covered by the same regulations. In that limited sense, nondiscrimination is implied. But it is less clear that a uniform level of protection of intellectual property (or indeed any level of protection) is in itself desirable as an objective. So a case could be made for discrimination by intellectual property jurisdictions to ensure equal treatment of the intellectual property within those jurisdictions (including trade in goods embodying the IP), but not necessarily between them where competition could apply.

The clearest motivation for the TRIPS agreement was to reduce competition from unauthorized "pirating" of valuable items of IP such as software and pharmaceuticals. Its guiding principle is that each country should establish a minimum protection system for intellectual property, agree to implement it along particular lines, and provide adequate means for enforcement of IP rights. Coverage across types of intellectual property is made more uniform (Maskus 2000). The introduction of such a framework for domestic policy is unequivocally distinct from the principle of nondiscrimination among sources of foreign goods or services or the equitable treatment of those goods and services in the home market.

5.4.2. TRIPS, Domestic Policy, and Politics

This is not, of course, to say that trade may not in certain cases be facilitated by the harmonization of coverage or that the efficiency of the world trade system is not enhanced by the protection of IP. But the TRIPS is inherently different from most of the other parts of the WTO in that, in two respects, it is not primarily a trade agreement.

First, as in the case of the SPS agreement, TRIPS requires domestic regulations to be adjusted. But it goes even further than that agreement in that it obliges countries to provide minimum levels of protection where such protection may not be in the interests of that country. In effect, the result is to oblige countries to institute policies that "lock in" innovation rents and first-mover advantages that accrue to foreign nationals and companies. IP protection, at least in the area of industrial property, is usually justified as providing a temporary "monopoly" position to the patent holder or designer as a way of encouraging innovation. Competition has therefore to be controlled, as trade threatens to undermine the stream of rents to the inventor. As viewed by proponents, TRIPS prohibits nations from "free riding" by acquiring at low cost the products developed in other nations, and thus not paying the higher prices that allow for recovery of the research or development cost. As seen by critics, it threatens development by slowing the spread of technology, hampering the ability of developing countries to compete in markets where the industrial world already has an advantage, and failing to stimulate innovation in the world's poorer countries. But both agree that the main effect of the agreement is to protect rents in profitable activities. The thrust of the TRIPS is therefore very different from the notion of "driving out" rents by the steady reduction of protection at the border.

Second, the TRIPS agreement requires means of effective enforcement of intellectual property rights in all WTO member countries. Such a requirement demands the development of national institutions that can protect intellectual property rights and their enforcement—the establishment of a patent office, education of lawyers and judges about the nature of IP rights, constraints on the corruption of judges and other officials who administer and adjudicate IP rights and enforcement. Ultimately, TRIPS mandates rule of law, which history has proven difficult to achieve in most of the world.

The TRIPS agreement is perhaps best seen, from the perspective of the rules of the trade system, as a part of an emerging global infrastructure for commerce. Those who argue for its legitimacy in the WTO see the universal adoption of IP protection as necessary to allow businesses to invest in research, establish cross-national production networks, and sell into foreign markets without fear of being undercut by competitors that have not had the same product development costs. It is part of the projection of national regulations onto the global market. It is not aimed primarily at government action against imports. One could argue that a decision not to protect a particular form of intellectual property is an indirect subsidy to domestic firms. In any event, it moves the trade system away from the notion that trade rules do not dictate to countries what they should do at home but merely encourage them to pursue their objectives in ways that least distort trade. The principle of mutual benefits from trade by exploiting comparative advantage is not applicable. To the extent there is a parallel principle, it is that the costs to the consumer of developing such goods as pharmaceuticals and movies should be allocated across the entire world in order to ensure the development of an adequate quantity of such goods and (more problematically) the equitable division of their cost of development.[12]

5.5. The Newest Problems: New Tools, Actors, and Coalitions?

The first WTO ministerial after the Marrakesh meeting that established the organization was held in Singapore in 1996. In many ways a high point of the new trade system, the Singapore ministerial set the WTO on an even more ambitious path. Far from consolidating the expanded agenda inherited from the Uruguay Round, trade ministers and their officials began to explore new areas for trade rules. Though it was clear that these new areas would take time to negotiate, working groups were set up to consider the options and the modalities for formulating rules on these topics. The three key working groups were to study trade and investment, trade and competition, and transparency in government procurement. In addition, the Goods Council was asked to consider the possibilities for further negotiations on trade facilitation.

The second WTO ministerial took place in Seattle, where delegations were met with demonstrations and riots that nearly collapsed the meeting. Much of the concern, both inside and outside the Conference Hall at Seattle, did not revolve around these "Singapore issues." The two topics that defined the meeting for NGOs in the streets, as well as the tensions between developed and developing countries in the negotiating chamber, were the role of the WTO in the areas of the environment and labor. The blue-green alliance that emerged in opposition to the ratification of the NAFTA and WTO in the U.S. Congress stayed together and peaked in the impressive show of street theater in Seattle. But despite similarities in some of the issues, the coalition has had difficulties in maintaining a united front, and the issues are now separated again in the WTO agenda. Environmental discussions were discussed at the Fifth Ministerial held in Cancún in September 2003. While the labor issue is not formally included in the present WTO agenda, the WTO secretariat coordinates with the International Labour Organization (ILO), conveniently located also in Geneva.

What brought these new issues—investment, competition, environment, and labor—onto the trade agenda? An idiosyncratic story might be told for each topic, but there is a common thread. Each may be considered a "spillover" from past rounds of trade liberalization. As integration has deepened, as trade barriers have fallen, each of these issues has become increasingly salient to particular nonstate actors in Europe and the United States. Freer movement of goods has made it increasingly efficient for producers to establish cross-border production networks—arm's-length contractual relationships between enterprises in different countries to perform some subset of the functions required for product research, design, building, and distribution. But freer movement of goods has also created demand by producers to establish their own foreign enterprises to perform those functions; that economic demand for foreign direct investment has translated into political demands by firms in Europe and the United States to assure free and unfettered investment rules in other countries. Similarly, as government-imposed border measures have diminished, monopolistic and oligopolistic practices have emerged as salient barriers to distribution in certain markets, particularly in Asia. As trade barriers have fallen, environmentalists have become concerned that "dirty" products may be imported into their country, and that investment will move to countries with lower environmental standards, engendering a "race to the bottom" in national environmental standards. And as trade barriers fall, organized labor fears that businesses are shifting investment and production to countries with less stringent labor standards, and engendering a "race to the bottom" in labor standards.

To address concerns raised in each of these new areas, simple application of the old GATT principles will not suffice. The issues go beyond mere discrimination and border measures. In all four areas, the stringency, enforcement, and style of national regulatory systems is at stake. For example, should WTO rules require a high level of environmental protection? Should effective enforcement of those rules be somehow guaranteed? And should the rules be advanced through a market-based incentive system or a top-down command-and-control regulatory system?

The emergence of these problems, and their solutions, imply new coalitions of nonstate actors in domestic trade politics. For example, successful

attempts to address environmental concerns would likely bring environmentalists into coalition with import-competing producers in Europe and
the United States to support the WTO, while engendering opposition to
the WTO by businesses in developing countries. In contrast, continued
failure to address environmental concerns will likely harden European
and U.S. environmentalists' opposition to the WTO and its mission. Similar dynamics might be at play on the labor issue, but some analysts have
suggested that no policies consistent with trade liberalization will ever
bring European or U.S. organized labor to support the WTO. Investment
liberalization has been supported by business groups and trade associations in the North, but has simultaneously catalyzed opposition from environmentalists and organized labor in the North, and from populists and
protected sectors in the South. Efforts in the WTO to address policies on
competition have been supported by European and U.S. export-oriented
producers who want increased and reliable access to Asian markets with
closed distribution networks, but they have been met with less enthusiasm
by import-competing producers who fear that the efforts could weaken
antidumping laws that they claim protect them against predatory prices
by foreign cartels.

5.5.1. Trade and Investment

The Uruguay Round Agreement on Trade-Related Investment Measures
(TRIMS) was far less significant for business and less controversial than
the TRIPS agreement, but it broke new ground nonetheless. This
agreement also deals with domestic policy choices rather than explicitly
focusing on border policies. Investment policy is at the heart of development strategy but is also important to businesses aiming to establish a
presence overseas. The TRIMS agreement does not require MFN or national treatment of foreign investors, but rules that tie investments to trade
performance and thereby deny national treatment of goods are limited by
the TRIMS agreement.[13] An illustrative list of such impermissible investment performance requirements is appended to the agreement, and includes, for example, domestic content requirements, that is, requirements
that factories in a nation obtain specified portions of their inputs locally.
    As with the TRIPS agreement, the TRIMS agreement is in essence an
infrastructural project for the global marketplace. However, unlike the
TRIPS agreement, it focuses on trade-distorting national policies. In particular, trade distortions are to be removed by constraining policies that,
for example, make inward investment conditional on domestic input purchases (local content requirements) or export targets (trade-balancing requirements). But there is an unspoken implication in the TRIMS agree-

ment that the intention is to limit the control that developing countries have over their own development policy. Insofar as they are restrained from pursuing unwise policies, this could be defended. But it still represents a significant intrusion on domestic economic sovereignty.

Principles of nondiscrimination are only weakly relevant to the TRIMS agreement: countries can still decide to favor domestic over foreign investment, and from which countries to accept investment. Similarly, while U.S. industry would like the agreement to require national treatment on the right to establish a business enterprise and on other matters, so there would be no distinction between foreign and domestic investment regulations, the agreement does not go that far (Graham 1998). Reciprocity of obligations and concessions also has had little meaning when negotiating on matters of foreign direct investment (FDI). The principle that guides supporters of the TRIMS agreement could be expressed as "unrestricted ability to invest" in foreign countries without the conditions that the host country would like to impose. Although the prohibition against domestic content requirements certainly helps remove a barrier to trade, the agreement is another departure from the notion of restricting the actions of countries at the border and preventing "externalities" associated with domestic policies.

Negotiation on improved rules governing trade and investment has been agreed for consideration in the Doha Round, though the outcome of the Cancún ministerial has shown that such negotiations are not without controversy. Although some firms in other developed nations are also supporters, the main pressure for such an initiative came from the EU, which considered that this was a desirable extension of the trade rules. But experience with strong opposition by environmentalists and organized labor to the Multilateral Agreement on Investment (MAI) negotiations, discussed in, and then abandoned by, the OECD, has made countries wary about expanding the TRIMS agreement, with its limited scope of trade-related measures, to a more general set of provisions on investment.

5.5.2. Trade and Competition Policy (Antitrust)

Perhaps the most logical extension of trade rules (besides linking trade with international financial rules) is in the direction of competition. Trade liberalization removes many conditions necessary for the use of monopoly power within countries, but the international market may need to be monitored for collusive behavior and exploitation of consumers. Some established GATT/WTO principles do not obviously apply to global regulation of competition policy: a requirement of nondiscrimination among suppliers and reciprocity would not be relevant, though national treatment has some meaning in the application of competition law. Competition rules could be based on three principles: establishment of competition regulations in all trading countries (as in the TRIPS agreement), enforcement of those rules, and cooperation among competition authorities to facilitate antitrust enforcement. For some, the movement of competition policy issues into the WTO is a way to improve economic efficiency and to counterbalance the TRIPS agreement; for others it is a threat to local or state-owned monopolies, to industrial structure itself, or to such long-standing trade provisions as antidumping law (OECD 1996b; Graham and Richardson 1997).

5.5.3. Trade and the Environment

The GATT 1947 was drafted in the era before "environmental" topics had reached the radar screens of politicians and trade officials. References to environmental programs that might have trade impacts are scarce in the GATT articles. GATT Article XX(b) permits many otherwise illegal trade restrictions that are "necessary to protect human, animal, or plant life or health," and Article XX(g) permits many otherwise illegal trade restrictions "relating to the conservation of exhaustible natural resources if such measures are made effective in conjunction with restrictions on domestic production or consumption."

The trade and the environment movement was catalyzed in the early 1990s by a series of decisions interpreting Article XX(g). In the most publicized of these decisions, a GATT dispute settlement panel held that a trade restriction could be justified under Article XX(g) only if the natural resources in question were located within the jurisdiction of the country maintaining the trade measure. This limitation on invocation of Article XX(g) led to a panel's conclusion that application of the U.S. Marine Mammals Protection Act was contravening the GATT. Specifically, two panels held that the United States could not continue to prohibit the importation of tuna from countries that were using fishing techniques that led to the widespread drowning of porpoises. In the most authoritative of these cases, the panel reasoned that the United States import ban was part of an effort to conserve exhaustible natural resources *outside* its jurisdiction. These cases (*United States—Restrictions on Imports of Tuna (1991)* and *United States—Restrictions on Imports of Tuna (1994)*) suggested to some the possibility that multilateral environmental agreements (MEAs) that require trade restrictions for enforcement (such as the Convention on International Trade of Endangered Species) would be deemed to contravene the GATT (WTO 1994).

Although there are several schools of thought on the issue, WTO jurisprudence seems to have weakened the precedential value of the *U.S.—*

Tuna-Dolphin cases. In the early WTO years, several countries challenged a U.S. ban on the importation of shrimp from countries that permitted shrimp-net fishing without requiring the use of a turtle-excluder device. The failure to use such a device was leading to the drowning of sea turtles. The Appellate Body did not expressly address the jurisdictional scope of Article XX(g), noting that sea turtles were migratory animals that exist in U.S. waters and so the natural resources in question were located within U.S. jurisdiction. The Appellate Body nevertheless made it clear that certain import measures of the type at issue in the case could be consistent with Article XX. To this extent it significantly undercut the *U.S.—Tuna-Dolphin* cases (Howse 2002a). At the same time, it went on to find the U.S. measures not excepted by Article XX(g) for other reasons. The U.S. complied with the *U.S.—Shrimp-Turtle* ruling and with the GATT exception by slightly modifying its measures and still maintaining the import ban (WTO 1998b, 2001). Nonetheless, environmentalists saw this as another example of ways in which the GATT/WTO system is undermining environmental protection (Grunbaum 2002).

More broadly, environmentalists have been most concerned about two issues. First, they worry that WTO members might not be able to restrict imports that could harm their own environment. Second, they fear that a WTO member might not be able to restrict imports the production or processing of which harms the environment outside that member's territory—as in the *U.S.—Tuna-Dolphin* and *U.S.—Shrimp-Turtle* cases. They are particularly concerned that trade provisions of MEAs might be ruled WTO-illegal. And they speculate that the illegality of trade measures aimed at extrajurisdictional activity will encourage investment flight from greener jurisdictions and favor a "race to the bottom" in environmental standards. (Steinberg 2002).

Though the objectives of sustainable development and environmental protection were included in the WTO preamble, the WTO agreement contains little that addresses these concerns. The debate as to how deeply the WTO should get involved in environmental issues has intensified in the period following the Uruguay Round. The issue of trade and environment is discussed in greater detail in chapter 7.

5.5.4. Trade and Labor Standards

Labor standards are not currently addressed in the WTO, though they are indirectly referenced in some of the agreements. The closest the GATT comes to directly addressing the issue is Article XX(e), which permits most otherwise illegal trade restrictions "relating to the products of prison labour." To incorporate labor standards and hence use the dispute settlement process for adjudication would be a major step. The pressure comes from a different source than the support for further restraints on investment, health and safety policy, and intellectual property protection. But the effect would be the same: to move even further "behind the border" in the application of trade rules.

Some organized labor activists in Europe and the United States flatly oppose trade liberalization on the ground that it will shift production and jobs to lower-wage economies. As was described in chapter 1, economic theory has a reply to that concern: job creation will more than compensate job losses in a freely trading economy.

Better-reasoned arguments for WTO regulation of labor standards fall into two categories. First, some argue that core labor standards (such as free association and collective bargaining) are human rights, and that the WTO system should protect those human rights. Second, some argue that if labor standards are not brought into the WTO, there may be a "race to the bottom." Just as the argument for national child labor laws in the United States early in the last century was that individual states that enacted such laws would find it impossible to compete with states that had not enacted them, the argument is that global standards are now needed to protect nations that attempt to protect their workers (Cleveland 2003).

The objection to the incorporation of labor standards is that it gives a handle to those that wish to restrict trade to ratchet up standards to levels that developing countries cannot reach. Moreover, trade restrictions that depend on a foreign country's labor standards seem counter to the MFN principle, whereby all potential suppliers should have equal access to a given market. And it is not easy to see how countries can trade concessions and grant reciprocity in the area of labor standards. The principle behind proposals for WTO rules on labor seems to be a level global playing field or a trade-sanctioned race to the top. The issue of trade and labor is discussed in greater detail in chapter 7.

5.6. The Search for New Principles and New Coalitions

In chapter 1, we asked how political support for the multilateral trade system has remained intact as it has emerged in the postwar period. This chapter has attempted to cast light on whether the expansion of the scope of the rule-based system has changed the nature of this political support. The trade system faces legal and political challenges as it expands its scope to include issues related to domestic regulation.

The new areas of trade rules, most notably the TRIPS agreement, pose a challenge to the underlying principles of the trade system. Not only is it more difficult to frame trade rules in these areas based on the "old" principles, but there often appears to be a clash between desirable domestic regulation and the demands of the trade system.

The legal principles that guided the GATT in its fifty-year regime may not be sufficient for the current agenda, especially those aspects that overlap with domestic policies. International constraints on these domestic policies may need to be based on premises different from those that guided the approach to border measures. The concept of MFN treatment among suppliers, for instance, may have to take on a new meaning. Rather than nondiscrimination, the emphasis of domestic regulatory policy may have to shift to justified discrimination. The task of the multilateral institution may be to demand that justification for such discrimination be made transparent and challengeable—and to conceptualize legitimate bases for discrimination. The concept of national treatment, so useful to prevent discrimination once goods and services enter the domestic market, may also need to change. It may need to be complemented by recognition of a principle of national sovereignty to affirm the ultimate responsibility of countries for the health and welfare of their own citizens. Discrimination between domestic and imported products may play a crucial role in providing domestic regulations that safeguard consumers against service providers. Much intellectual property law is premised on a high degree of discrimination between those that have property rights in a particular market and those that do not. At the least, MFN and national treatment may have to be redefined in cases such as these.

Would modification of the core principles of the GATT, suggested above, be sufficient for regulation of today's trade system? When the issue is trade regulation at the border, nondiscrimination has been relevant to help liberalize trade in agriculture, textiles, and many services. Where the target is domestic regulations—as in some service modes, health and safety regulations, intellectual property protection, and labor and environmental standards—these principles are not likely sufficient. Instead, such principles as universality, uniformity, and transparency seem more useful. In some of these areas, commitments to uniformity imply global agreement on the appropriate standards, as for intellectual property or environmental protection, and a concern about the appropriate allocation among different nations of the costs of meeting these standards. And in many countries and on many issues (such as intellectual property and environmental and labor protection), substantive legal change will not be enough: national institutions will need to be created to ensure adequate enforcement of regulatory measures.

The attempt to devise principles for coordinating domestic regulation and avoiding clashes with trade policy objectives has a history in the development of regional integration. In particular, the EC had faced many of these problems in its own "internal market" program of 1985–92.

Some of the concepts found useful in that case might be appropriate to the development of multilateral trade rules. These include the principles of sovereignty and subsidiarity, which attempt to define the reach of the supranational rules; mutual recognition of the regulations, testing, or certification of other countries; framework agreements that do not specify precise legislative actions but agree on a template for national action; and approximation of regulations to reduce conflict arising from different standards in different countries without demanding the more politically difficult universality implied by complete harmonization.

Table 5.1 suggested the contents of the legal tool kit that might be used as trade issues shift from the older liberalization issues to the newer integration issues that require behind-the-border measures. MFN and national treatment were well suited to addressing the older issues; principles of harmonization and approximation, transparency, and effective enforcement may be more appropriate for guiding WTO law on behind-the-border issues. Such shifts take the trade system away from the regulation of commerce towards the establishment of a global market with predictable and trade-friendly domestic policies. How far countries are prepared to go in this direction is still an open question, but the extent of success or failure will turn partly on how global rules in these new areas shape the domestic political coalitions engaging in trade policymaking, particularly in the WTO's most powerful members. The new issues have brought new players (such as environmentalists and service providers) to the domestic bargaining table and have increased the GATT/WTO's salience to other players (such as IP producers and organized labor). Addressing or failing to address issues of salience to these groups will determine the extent to which they support or oppose the WTO and its mission. Given North-South differences over environment, labor, services, intellectual property, and other matters, it is hard to see all of these issues being addressed to the satisfaction of EU and U.S. interest groups in the short term. And democratization in developing countries will not make the task any easier.

Notes

1. The Havana Charter had envisaged rules for service trade, but these rules had become a casualty of the abandonment of the ITO, discussed in chapter 2.

2. Services were regarded as "nontradables" in many economic models of international trade until the late 1980s.

3. This is an area where temporary migration for specific jobs, and even the right to look for work in other countries, is likely to advance more rapidly within the context of regional trade agreements. Some of the "deeper" regional agreements already include the right to move to seek work (the EU and the CER

agreement between Australia and New Zealand), while others are moving in that direction in the case of skilled workers (Caribbean Community, CARICOM). However, increased concerns over security and immigration will hinder the rapid liberalization of rules on access to labor market.

4. The UNCTAD has also made attempts over the years to regulate these conferences, to little avail.

5. This may also be one area where heightened security precautions in several countries could militate against a relaxation of national preferences and discrimination among suppliers.

6. For further information on the services issue, see Sauvé and Stern 2000.

7. Annex A of the SPS agreement states that it applies to any measure intended (*a*) to protect animal or plant life or health within the territory of the member from risks arising from the entry, establishment, or spread of pests, diseases, disease-carrying organisms, or disease-causing organisms; (*b*) to protect human or animal life or health within the territory of the member from risks arising from additives, contaminants, toxins, or disease-causing organisms in foods, beverages, or feedstuffs; (*c*) to protect human life or health within the territory of the member from risks arising from diseases carried by animals, plants, or products thereof, or from the entry, establishment, or spread of pests; or (*d*) to prevent or limit other damage within the territory of the member from the entry, establishment, or spread of pests. Sanitary or phytosanitary measures include all relevant laws, decrees, regulations, requirements, and procedures including, inter alia, end product criteria; processes and production methods; testing, inspection, certification, and approval procedures; quarantine treatments including relevant requirements associated with the transport of animals or plants, or with the materials necessary for their survival during transport; provisions on relevant statistical methods, sampling procedures, and methods of risk assessment; and packaging and labeling requirements directly related to food safety.

8. Note that these rules attempt to prevent the use of production standards in ways that unnecessarily discriminate against imports; they do not deal with the question of whether products made by different processes are the same product. The latter is an important issue in the environmental context, where the fact of similarity in the final product has been used by WTO panels to reject rules saying that only products made by certain environmentally approved processes may be imported.

9. Article 1.5 of the TBT agreement states that "the provisions of this Agreement do not apply to sanitary and phytosanitary measures as defined in Annex A of the Agreement on the Application of Sanitary and Phytosanitary Measures."

10. For a more detailed discussion of the TBT agreement see Heumiller and Josling 2001 and Roberts et al. 2001. The relationship between the TBT agreement and labeling schemes will be discussed in chapters 6 and 7.

11. See, e.g., U.K. Commission on Intellectual Property Rights 2002, especially chapter 2, and the proceedings of the World Health Organization/World Trade Organization Workshop on Differential Pricing and Financing of Essential Drugs at Hosbjor, Norway in April 2001.

12. For more information, see Gervais 1998; Maskus 2000; and Matthews 2002.

13. TRIMS applies only to trade in goods and not trade in services.

Six

Expansion of GATT/WTO Membership and the Proliferation of Regional Groups

6.1. Introduction

The trade system reflects its "membership," the national actors that participate in decisions and are subject to its rules. Changes in the system can be brought about by shifts in the composition and behavior of the membership. This chapter focuses on two such shifts: the increased number of countries participating actively in the institutions of the multilateral trade system, and the expansion in the number of regional trade agreements that appear to provide some "insurance" for their membership but may undermine the multilateral system.

Among the most significant changes in the GATT/WTO system has been its expansion in membership. The regime has grown from its original 22 founding members to over 140 at the turn of the century. The addition of new nations is important, in part because of challenges that derive from the management of a larger organization. The enlargement has led to a fundamental change in the character of the regime. In the early years the GATT was perceived of as a "rich nations' club," focusing on the needs of the developed nations, though some of the more prominent developing nations such as Brazil and India played a role.[1] By the year 2000, the WTO included a majority of developing nations, many of which are among the poorest countries in the world. Further, with the inclusion of China and the expectation of Russian accession, the WTO community includes all the major nations of the world, even those that were previously uninterested in open trade and thus stayed outside the trade regime.[2] Not coincidently, the membership chose an experienced politician from Thailand, Supachai Panitchpakdi, to be its director-general from September 2002, the first developing-country leader of the GATT/WTO trade system.

Another significant change in the way in which national actors have participated in the regulation of the trade system has been the result of the growth of preferential trade agreements (PTAs) that involve developing as well as developed countries, including free trade areas, customs unions, bilateral trade pacts, and nonreciprocal trade agreements tied to development programs.[3] In fact, almost every member participates in at least one such discriminatory trade accord, and many are members of more than one such agreement, making the current trade system a combination of discriminatory and nondiscriminatory rules.[4]

The main question addressed in this chapter is how the changing nature of state actor participation, both the proliferation of membership and the increasing use of discriminatory trade agreements, has changed the nature of the GATT/WTO trade system. After describing the process of accession to the GATT/WTO, this chapter explores the effects of these changes in membership, with particular attention to the emerging role of developing nations in the GATT/WTO, and to the implications of China's membership. This expansion has led to a fundamental shift in the agenda of the contemporary WTO with little compensating change in the decision-making system. Political control, once vested squarely in the Quad nations, has devolved in a manner that results in greater complexity and poses a challenge to the effective operation of the system. We suggest below that the growth in regional arrangements also derives in part from the expansion of the number of regime members, and associated changes in underlying power relations. The extent to which the regional agreements may have helped to "resolve" the problems of political support for free trade in a democratically acceptable way is an important aspect of the trade system.

6.2. GATT/WTO Membership Conditions

The procedure by which a country enters the trade regime is outlined only in very general terms in GATT and WTO documents. Over time, however, the regime has developed a set of complex procedures for accession. For the initial members, accession was governed by a Protocol of Provisional Application, under which the applicant merely agreed not to enact new legislation inconsistent with GATT. In essence, existing trade-restrictive legislation was grandfathered into the agreement until, at some later point, it could be negotiated away. Other countries could signal their willingness to apply the GATT and become contracting parties under the provisions of Article XXXIII. Many of the newly independent developing nations were able to join by way of a simpler procedure, under GATT Article XXVI:5(c), that required only that a contracting party certify that the new country had assumed "full autonomy" to conduct its own "external commercial relations." But there also emerged three categories of countries that were participants in the GATT without being contracting parties in the formal sense. First, the colonial powers usually accepted on behalf of their colonies and territories the obligations of the General Agreement.[5] Second, at the time of independence, several countries chose a de facto membership in advance of taking a decision on joining. And third, some acceding countries were awarded provisional membership pending the outcome of the accession process. Japan was able to join in 1955 on a provisional basis that allowed it to delay undertaking certain MFN commitments,[6] and Switzerland was a provisional member from 1958 to 1966.

The current process of admission for new nations involves a far more intrusive liberalization program. This is accomplished with the aid of a working party, comprised of interested trading partners, that orchestrates the application and extracts a set of promises from the applicant on how its trade policies will be made consistent with previous WTO agreements. The applicant must provide data on its relevant legislation, in itself a very substantial amount of information now that the WTO framework covers intellectual property and services as well as traditional trade barriers. WTO members respond to this offer, and may request further commitments and legislative changes to ensure that the entering nation opens its economy to an extent that reflects "the general benefits the Applicant will enjoy upon membership."[7] Moreover, GATT Article XXXV and WTO Agreement Article XIII, which permit a member to refuse to apply the GATT/WTO to a new member on accession, effectively forces acceding territories to provide concessions that please all of the larger trading states.[8] The process is arduous and complex, and amounts to a full-scale trade negotiation in which applicants must provide benefits to other nations, in return for membership, comparable to those they might have provided in the trade rounds in which they did not participate. Finally, a positive decision for accession requires a two-thirds vote of the parties to the existing agreement (GATT Article XXXIII; WTO Agreement Article XII).[9]

The complexity of the application process has clearly not been a deterrent to potential new members. But the negotiations surrounding new applications are themselves of some significance in opening up trade. Membership is now seen as a necessary condition for inbound investment, and those who are not members have little recourse in trade disputes. So as the GATT/WTO system increases its scope, the benefits of membership become greater, and the cost of exclusion more noticeable.[10] In order to avoid the marginalization of the poorest countries, a new and simpler accession process was approved for the least-developed countries in December 2002.

Negotiations for China's entry into the WTO were particularly extensive, lasting sixteen years. The process included agreements on accepting the various WTO agreements, specific reduction schedules for agricultural and industrial tariffs, and detailed market-opening and regulatory commitments in such services areas as telecommunications, banking, insurance, and professional services, including accounting and architecture. The working group's negotiations were paralleled by separate bilateral talks with such key trading partners as the United States and the European Union. At the political level the negotiations were linked to debates over issues not directly connected to the WTO negotiations, such as China's human rights record and the status of Taiwan (Chinese Taipei). As a measure of the complexity of the negotiations, the final report of the working party contained 343 numbered paragraphs and a large number of annexes. But politics eventually triumphed over administrative complexity, and China was admitted to membership at the Doha ministerial in November 2001.[11]

6.2.1. The Accession of China: A Special Case?

The accession of China to the WTO poses issues that are in many respects unique.[12] It may technically be a developing nation, but its political-economic structure is unique and it is so economically and politically significant that its entry is certain to produce substantial change in the WTO. Its accession expands the territorial scope of the WTO and the level of trade that it governs; it also helps to "lock in" the impressive steps China has taken towards economic liberalization over the last two decades. These changes will be difficult to institutionalize, especially for a government that still adheres to many of the elements of a centrally controlled economy. The main changes to which China agreed on accession are summarized in box 6.1.

China is fundamentally different from other WTO members, partly because of its size, but also because of its particular political-economic structure. Some of these features of the Chinese type of market economy could undermine or complicate basic WTO commitments: a continuing large role for state enterprises; a lack of transparency of some domestic rules and rule-making processes; a lack of meaningful competition policy rules; weak regulatory systems, especially pertaining to the environment; and an absence of democratic guarantees. And some other features of the Chinese system raise doubts about its ability to keep its commitments: a judicial system that, on commercial matters, is in the early stages of development and is not always perceived as independent of politics; considerable corruption in some regions; and relatively weak central government authority over commercial matters.[13] These issues are not dealt with well under current WTO rules but had to be faced in the negotiations associated with China's entry. Some of them paralleled the strong trade tensions between the United States and Japan during the 1980s. And the issues are not simply ones for China's trading partners; they also affect China, which will be expected to create many new institutions and to increase the role of transparency and of markets, even when such changes may affect its political traditions.

Box 6.1 China's Responsibilities under the WTO Accession Agreement

- Tariff reductions
  - Industrial tariffs of greatest importance to U.S. business will be reduced from 25 percent to 7 percent.
  - Agricultural tariffs of greatest importance to U.S. farmers will be reduced from 31 percent to 14 percent.

- Service commitments
  - Substantial opening of a broad range of service sectors, including important U.S. sectors such as banking, insurance, telecommunications, and professional services.

- Systemic reforms
  - Broad reforms in the areas of transparency, notice and comment, uniform application of laws, and judicial review will help to address barriers to foreign companies doing business in China.

- Adherence to existing WTO agreement.

- China-specific trade-liberalizing provisions
  - Rights to import from and export to customers in China directly within three years.
  - Right to engage in distribution of all products in China within three years of accession (except that chemical fertilizers, crude oil, and refined petroleum can be distributed at the wholesale level five years after accession).
  - Investment and import approvals no longer subject to trade-distorting requirements such as technology transfer, foreign exchange balancing, export performance, and local content requirements.
  - Right to export to China without establishing an investment presence there.
  - Phase-out of nontariff measures (NTMs) with all WTO-inconsistent NTMs eliminated by January 1, 2005.
  - Elimination of state-trading import monopolies for agricultural and industrial products.
  - Requirement that state-owned enterprises must make purchases and sales based solely on commercial considerations.
  - Elimination of export subsidies on agricultural goods and elimination of import substitution and export subsidies on industrial goods.

- Safeguard mechanism
  - WTO members can continue to use special nonmarket economy methodology for measuring dumping in antidumping cases against China for 15 years.
  - Under a China-specific safeguard mechanism, WTO members can restrain imports from China that disrupt their markets for 12 years.

(Source: James P. Zumwalt, Economic Minister Counselor, United States Embassy, Beijing, "How WTO Membership Affects China," January 9, 2002).

Concern about these differences in form is exacerbated, in the case of China, by scale and geo-military context. Many current WTO members have domestic political-economic systems that are sufficiently different in form from a typical Western, liberal model to generate tension with other members. But China's economy is much bigger than that of any of those members (Cohen 1998). Moreover, the resulting friction will be experienced in a context in which China is perceived as a military rival of some important WTO members. Thus, the political friction associated with China's entry into the world trading system is explained by the fact that China is different along three dimensions: its political-economic form, the scale of its economic strength, and the strategic-military context in which it has acceded.

According to even the most generous estimates of the extent to which China's market has liberalized, at least 30 percent of Chinese gross domestic product is still produced by state-invested enterprises.[14] Action by state-invested enterprises has the potential to undermine all four cornerstones of the GATT. For the most part, the GATT assumes that economic decisions are made by commercial firms and by intermediate or final consumers based largely on price and quality, but state-invested enterprises do not always make decisions based on these commercial criteria. For example, it is not difficult to imagine state-invested enterprises that consume computer chips deciding to purchase all of their computer chips from state-invested chip manufacturers. This could effectively undermine the GATT's Article III national treatment provision. Similar arguments can be made about how state-invested enterprises may engage in behavior that would undermine the Article I MFN commitment, the Article II commitment to a schedule of concessions, and the Article XI commitment against maintaining quantitative restrictions.[15] And these arguments would seem to apply with equal force in the case of local government influence over township-village enterprises (TVEs). GATT Article XVII was intended to discipline activity by state enterprises but the drafters could never have anticipated that this article would sufficiently address problems created by the accession of a country as big as China with such a big role for the state. The primary requirement of Article XVII is that state enterprises shall make purchases or sales "solely in accordance with commercial considerations." But this discipline cannot be effective where the reason for purchases or sales by state enterprises is not transparent.

Second, more broadly, the GATT system assumes that members' laws, regulations, and administrative and legislative processes are transparent. This transparency is crucial to the effectiveness of the GATT's main principles. For example, true national treatment (Article I) requires that both domestic and foreign producers know the rules of the game. Similarly, a lack of transparency about rules or regulations affecting imports could have the same effect as a quantitative restriction (Article XI). The formulation of rules also demands a transparent process so that foreign interests can be represented to ensure that the rule is not discriminatory in its effect. And, as suggested in the preceding paragraph, any meaningful discipline on state enterprises entails transparency. GATT Article X requires the publication of trade regulations prior to their application, but this discipline may not be broad enough to cover all of the kinds of nontransparencies encountered in China. The WTO has requirements of procedural transparency in the context of establishing and modifying technical, sanitary, and phytosanitary regulations; standards; and conformity assessment procedures, but relatively few requirements of procedural transparency in other important contexts. More problematic, transparency is difficult to monitor since, by definition, governments do not broadcast nontransparent directives or "administrative guidance." In short, it is often very difficult to know whether a pattern of behavior or outcomes constituted a GATT Article X violation.

Third, China lacks any meaningful competition policy and the WTO system does not require a member to have a competition policy (although such a requirement may evolve in the course of a future round). While there are few complaints at this time about anticompetitive activities in the private sector in China, it does not take great imagination to see that such problems could arise in the future. For example, to the extent that China continues to reduce the role of state-owned enterprises, government authorities could decide to give a legal monopoly to certain currently state-owned enterprises, particularly in the early phases of privatization. This is a pattern that has been followed in some other Asian countries and in eastern Europe. Monopolistic or monopsonistic behavior is the private sector analogue to discriminatory behavior by state-invested enterprises and can eviscerate the effectiveness and meaningfulness of the GATT's four cornerstones just as effectively.

Fourth, China's accession may raise in a more immediate way the link between trade rules and human rights. GATT rules do not provide an exception from general GATT obligations for trade actions taken in response to gross human rights violations: Article XX(e), which permits trade restrictions relating to the products of prison labor, is about as far as GATT goes. The extent to which China embraces human rights and democracy may have no direct international economic impact, but it has an international political importance because it bears on the extent of U.S. satisfaction with an institution based on unconditional MFN.[16] Many in the United States and elsewhere believe that there should be some linkage between U.S.-China trade relations and Chinese progress on human rights and democratization, more generally.[17]

In summary, the entry of China is likely to lead to trade tensions and to pressure for new WTO rules in several areas. The absence of strong rules in these areas may be understood as a relic of the WTO's history: the institution was never expected to intermediate trade relations between Western laissez-faire democracies and a large political economic system like that of China's, which is changing from a centrally planned, Communist system to something as of yet not fully defined. All these issues were in the minds of the negotiators involved in China's entry. It remains to be seen how well their solutions will work in the reality of China and in the decision making of WTO.

6.3. Increasing Involvement of Developing Countries

In its early days, the GATT focused primarily on the lowering of trade barriers among developed nations. Developing nations were, at best, beneficiaries of lowered tariffs and of the relaxation of nontariff barriers. There was some concern in the early years that developing nations might need to retain tariffs to protect infant industries; this, along with developing-nation concerns over trade balances, was reflected in changes to the GATT articles in 1955.[18] At the time, developing-nation exports consisted primarily of commodities, and it was recognized in the Haberler Report, commissioned by the GATT in 1958, that it would be beneficial to developing nations for developed nations to lower their tariffs on agricultural imports. It was also thought at that time necessary to develop schemes to reduce fluctuations in commodity prices (GATT 1958). Lowering import barriers was feasible for some tropical products, where processors in the industrial countries had an incentive to obtain low-priced raw materials, but for others, such as sugar, that competed with temperate-zone production, strong lobbies in the United States and Europe resisted such liberalization. Efforts to stabilize commodity prices, negotiated largely within the orbit of the United Nations Conference on Trade and Development (UNCTAD), also failed to deliver their promise.

In 1965 the GATT made its first substantial response to the demands of developing nations by adding three new articles, as Part IV of the agreement. These articles declared the importance of enabling developing nations to increase exports of primary, processed, and manufactured products, and contained hortatory commitments by the developed nations to give priority to improving market access. The new provisions were quite general and abstract, and not nearly as binding as the rest of the GATT. But they did include the statement that the developed nations did not expect reciprocity for their own commitments to remove tariffs and other barriers to the exports of the developing countries. This was interpreted, by footnote, to mean that in trade negotiations, the less-developed countries "should not be expected . . . to make contributions which are inconsistent with their individual development, financial, and trade needs, taking into consideration past trade developments." Though clearly designed to benefit developing countries, the provision had the result of removing developing countries even further from the essential bargains that had to be struck in tariff-cutting rounds.

The initial surge in the number of GATT contracting parties reached a plateau of around eighty countries in the 1970s, reflecting both the completion of the granting of independence to nations in Africa and the inclusion of most of the Latin American states. This latter group played a more active role in the organization than did the former, reflecting the more extensive participation in international trade and the lower reliance on preferential access to Europe of the Latin American countries. It may also have been stimulated by that continent's intellectual leadership in the rethinking of international economic relations in the 1970s. The new ideas, based on the political theory of dependence (*dependencia*) and the economic observation of declining terms of trade for primary product exports, held that the international economic system was fundamentally biased against developing nations. It followed that it was essential to make fundamental changes in that system, to redress the balance.

Among the arguments and concerns put forward from this perspective were the following:

- The prices of the commodity exports of the developing nations would never increase as fast as those of their industrial imports, so that their economies would always face declining terms of trade.[19]

- The developed nations would protect the manufacture of their low-wage sectors, such as shoes and textiles, through quotas and tariff escalation, and this would make it impossible for developing nations to enter such markets, which had been the introductory steps in the development of an advanced economy.[20]

- The developed nations would charge unfairly high prices for the technology embodied in the products (e.g., pharmaceuticals) and in the manufacturing plants supplied to developing nations through direct investment by leading European and American companies.

- As a consequence, these countries were facing a "trade gap," under which they were not able to export enough to pay for the things they needed to import for their economy and economic development.

As a result of this analysis, these countries pushed, in a variety of forums, for a New International Economic Order (NIEO). Among its key components were a call for international funds to stabilize commodity prices (by restricting production and by buying stocks when prices were low and selling the stocks when prices were high), preferential tariff arrangements designed to benefit developing nations, and restrictions on international technology-licensing contracts designed to prohibit ways in which the developed-world licensors might take advantage of the developing-nation licensees. One of the key exponents of the new order was Raúl Prebisch, the first secretary general of UNCTAD, created in 1964. Under his leadership, UNCTAD became the institution that developed and elaborated a developing-nation position in trade matters. At the same time, the G-77, a group of developing nations, operating under the intellectual leadership of Brazil and India, emerged as a lobbying bloc to reflect developing-nation positions in forums such as the GATT and the United Nations.[21] A few years later, the success of the Organization for Petroleum Exporting Countries (OPEC) in forming a cartel to raise the price of petroleum gave further impetus to the ideas presented in the New International Economic Order.[22] The developing countries had arrived on the international scene, if not as equal partners then at least with ideas of their own.

The emergence of the demands from developing countries for preferential treatment posed some challenges for the GATT. But the logic of differential treatment was not alien to the GATT. The trade regime, from its earliest incarnation in talks on the ITO, had specified that countries could form regional supplements to the multilateral regime. In Europe, such regional trade areas were accepted as part of the economic landscape. Developing countries began to look on such agreements as an "insurance policy" for smaller nations who feared that specialization of their economies could leave them vulnerable to shifts in the policies of their larger trading partners. In 1960 most of the Latin American countries formed the Latin American Free Trade Area (LAFTA), aimed at rationalizing production in the region.[23] In 1969, a new regional trade group, the Andean Pact, was formed by several South American nations to create a united bloc in negotiating terms of investment from developed-world firms, with the hope that this would improve the terms of access; its key innovation was Decision 24, a common standard regulating the terms of access to technology and requiring national participation in ownership of foreign investments. In 1963, the European Union created the Yaounde Convention (revised in 1975 as the Lomé Convention and in 2000 as the Cotonou Agreement), an agreement with more than seventy of its members' former colonies, especially in Africa and the Caribbean, that included provisions to offer these nations access to European markets tariff-free, though on a nonreciprocal basis.

While regional trade was a means to improve market share on a preferential basis, within the supposedly nondiscriminatory GATT several important accommodations to developing-nation concerns also were made in this period. The most important, granted in 1971 (at the instigation of UNCTAD), was a waiver from GATT nondiscrimination principles with the creation of the Generalized System of Preferences (GSP). Under this arrangement, a developed nation is authorized to offer a developing nation a lower tariff than that offered to other developed nations. Such discrimination, in the absence of the waiver, would clearly be a violation of the most-favored nation principle. Effectively, the nation offering the preferential tariff is favoring the industry of the developing-nation beneficiary at the expense of a (possibly more efficient) industry in a developed-nation trading partner. Yet, in the name of economic development, the exception was widely accepted, and most developed nations have offered various forms of GSP preference to developing nations ever since. These have, of course, become less important as the general level of tariffs and trade barriers has fallen.

This arrangement was extended through the "enabling clause" in 1979, a decision on "differential and more favourable treatment" for developing nations.[24] This decision was designed not only to authorize preferences but also to restate the earlier position that developed countries would not expect reciprocity for tariff concessions made to developing countries, and that they would exercise "the utmost restraint" in seeking concessions or contributions inconsistent with the special financial and trade needs of the developing countries. But the most important accommodation was implicit in the concept of à la carte agreements incorporated into the Tokyo Round package, as discussed in chapter 4. Acquiescence to these agreements was voluntary, and they typically applied only to trade among signatories. Since developed nations were more likely to accept these agreements, the GATT became a "multispeed" institution, in which developed nations accepted more severe restrictions than did developing nations. In some respects, this positive discrimination fitted with the development philosophy of the day, under which developing nations thought that the best path to development involved significant protection for, and governmental participation in, national industries designed to provide substitutes for imports.[25] But this "GATT à la carte" masked an effective discrimination based on the subject matter being negotiated. It left developing countries with little leverage to demand liberalization in the sectors that were of most export interest, such as agriculture, textiles, and clothing.

While discriminatory trade rules were at the top of the trade agenda for those who subscribed to a *dependencia* view of the world, they became less important in the 1980s and 1990s as an alternative ideology, known as the Washington consensus, came to dominate development thinking and practice. The new economic logic stressed that governmental intervention in national economies usually hurt, that it was important to allow markets to set prices, and that free trade was more likely to assist economic development than would autarchic import substitution. This completely reversed the trade policy paradigm and led to a very different stance on economic development and international trade.

Several factors underlay this philosophical swing. Probably the most immediate was the debt crisis that began in Mexico in 1982, when its export earnings (especially those from oil) fell and, at the same time, world interest rates rose, making it harder for that nation (and many others) to meet their debt obligations. High interest rates exacerbated the "debt problem" in the region, and debt servicing began to take an increasing proportion of export earnings. This made it impossible to continue a policy of government financial support to national semipublic firms by borrowing on international capital markets, a policy that had been the basis for much of the public-sector-led development efforts of the 1970s. Further, the Washington consensus appeared to be supported by the evidence. The East Asian "tigers," that is, Hong Kong, South Korea, Singapore, and Taiwan, which relied heavily on exports, really were more successful in their development than more autarchic nations. Later in the period, the bankruptcy of Communist-style government-managed development suggested more evidence of the benefits of liberal economic policies.

The economic weakness of the developing nations as a result of the debt overhang also encouraged them to accept the Washington consensus, for it was the economic orthodoxy held strongly by the World Bank and the International Monetary Fund. The nations had to turn to these institutions for help, and these institutions would generally require policies consistent with the Washington consensus as a condition for granting that help. These international institutions—and many others—were buttressed in their orthodoxy by the rise to power of Ronald Reagan in Washington and Margaret Thatcher in London, whose administrations espoused conservative economic principles and applied them in their international politics.

In this new pattern, nations opened themselves to international trade, both because such a policy was required by the international financial institutions as a condition of loans and because they expected that such opening would enable them to obtain access to investment by firms in the developed world. Thus, many developing nations opened their markets to developed-world goods, not in a reciprocal deal at the GATT, but as a condition of receiving IMF or World Bank funding. Developed-world firms now invested, not just to serve the local market but also to serve the global market and establish cross-national production networks. The comparative advantages of such offshore production often rested on the low wages of the nationals employed. During the later part of the period, there emerged a new generation of regional arrangements such as the North American Free Trade Agreement (NAFTA), in which developing nations entered preferential trading arrangements to gain duty-free access to a specific developed-world market, such as that of the United States.

These trends can be seen very clearly in the economic journey of Mexico, which had, in the earlier era, been one of the middle-income nations most protected, autarchic, and centered on government agencies. As the country's leaders sought to open up its economic system, they attempted to make this opening irreversible by entering into international commitments. Thus, Mexico joined GATT in 1986, a decision that reflected a sharp break with the nation's past policies. And then, in 1990, the leadership decided to negotiate a free trade treaty with the United States, the North American Free Trade Agreement (NAFTA). Among the basic compromises exemplified in NAFTA were coordinated schedules to open the Mexican commodity agricultural sector to U.S. competition while encouraging U.S. foreign direct investment in manufacture to grow at a rate that would, if all went as planned, create employment to absorb those displaced economically from the countryside by agricultural imports. There were also expected to be specialty agriculture exports to the United States, displacing traditional growers in California and Florida. And in the process, Mexico privatized many of its public-sector banking, telecommunications, and transportation corporations, some of which were in large part acquired by U.S. firms. The result has been a major change in the nation's economic system, followed later by an equally dramatic opening of its political system.

At about the same time, the United States, joined by the nations of Europe, began a program to encourage the global acceptance of intellectual property rights. It was these nations whose industries had much to lose from the generic production of pharmaceuticals, as in India, where patents covered only the production processes for pharmaceuticals and not the pharmaceuticals themselves, and from global copying of movies and software, as was the norm in much of the world. Under pressure from Congress, the United States began a program in the 1980s of using its Section 301 trade authority to require developing nations to raise their intellectual property standards under the threat of losing access to its market. Thus trade sanctions were imposed or considered against a variety of nations with respect particularly to their failure to provide the kinds of intellectual property protection the United States desired for computer software, pharmaceuticals, and musical and cinematic recordings. Added to this new intellectual property pressure was the pressure of the same developed nations to extend GATT into services—for many in the developing world, this meant that national banks, insurance, and telecommunications entities (usually government controlled) would be subject to competition and takeover by developed-world firms. This was frequently the ultimate result, although in many cases the global firms also brought substantial improvements in efficiency and quality of service and thus benefited the economy of their hosts.

The agenda for the Uruguay Round emphasized a large number of issues that could especially impact developing nations. In particular, developing nations strongly opposed the expansion of the GATT process into areas such as intellectual property, services, and investment. There were, of course, also other issues, some extremely divisive within the developed world—the most important was probably agriculture, in which U.S.-European differences held up the round for a time. Indeed, the placement of agriculture on the agenda was generally viewed as valuable to the developing world, and the round saw the emergence of the Cairns Group of agricultural exporters, which included both traditional developed-nation exporters such as Australia and Canada and developing-world exporters such as Argentina. In the case of textiles, most developing countries favored the phaseout of the Multi-Fiber Arrangement, though some of the less efficient suppliers of textiles undoubtedly gained from the existence of the quota system.

Although already in the majority, the developing world was effectively left out of key negotiations on many of the controversial areas. Regime members were forced to accept the extralegal "Green Room" process in which an inner group of nations met to make the crucial cross-sector compromises. Clearly, some such arrangement was essential in order to make the negotiations feasible, and various forms of inner-group consultations had been in existence since the 1970s, with greater or less developing-nation participation. But as the number of members expanded regularly, more nations felt excluded. Through the "single undertaking" described in chapter 3, the developing world was effectively presented with a fait accompli, even as its numerical position increased.

Even though a small number of developing nations had "voice," the outcome of talks continued to reflect, in many cases, the interests of developed countries. While the agreements entered into in the Uruguay Round were sometimes "front-weighted" in their favor, what the developing world had to concede, in many cases, took effect within a few years— for example, the commitments with respect to services and many of the requirements of TRIPS. Much of what it received in return was either ambiguous in value, for example, the benefit from the changes in U.S. and European agricultural protectionism, or delayed. For example, as explained more fully in chapter 4, the most beneficial concession, from the viewpoint of their exports, was the phasing out of the Multi-Fiber Arrangement under which U.S. and European textile and clothing industries were protected—with the phaseout occuring in 2005, and high tariffs on such goods remaining.[26] The developing nations were given little opportunity, save for some transition periods, for special and differential treatment in areas like TRIPS. There were also important issues as to who benefited from the round as a whole. According to studies conducted at the time of the Uruguay Round, some of the nations of sub-Sahara Africa may well have been harmed by the restrictions on agricultural export subsidies that had benefited them, though other developing nations probably benefited substantially from these restrictions (Michalopoulos 2000). However, at least one more recent analysis suggests that the economic result as a whole may have been unfavorable to the developing nations (Finger and Nogués 2001).

Perhaps most important, the leading nations decided that the "two-speed" system embodied in the Tokyo Round was no longer in their interest. After all, many of the key concessions would now be made by the developing nations in areas such as intellectual property and services; if they could simply refuse to accept the new codes in these areas, the basic intended balance of the negotiations would be lost. Therefore, adherence to the various Uruguay Round codes was no longer made optional. This was part of the "single undertaking" concept described more fully in chapter 3. The formal legal device was for the leading economic nations to withdraw from the original GATT agreement, and then to enter a new agreement to create the WTO. In order to enter the WTO, one had to accept *all* the new GATT provisions and the new agreements as a requirement. The developing nations were economically compelled to accept all these agreements in order to retain MFN access to developed-world markets.[27] But the inclusion of the new issues such as intellectual property and services, the loss of the ability to reject certain agreements, and the general negotiating pattern left many in developing nations bitter about the Uruguay Round.

Although the riots at the Seattle meeting of the WTO ministers demonstrated that a new era had come, there had been prior premonitions. The most visible warnings and concerns were those associated with the environment and with labor standards. The NAFTA and the Uruguay Round both clearly envisioned that substantial manufacturing capability would emerge in the developing world and would compete with the low-wage manufacturing sectors of the developed world. And in 1991, a GATT panel issued a first decision stating that the United States could not exclude tuna caught in a way that did not protect dolphins (see chapter 5). Although this decision was formally irrelevant, as Mexico withdrew its underlying complaint against the United States in order to reduce the political complications of negotiating the NAFTA, along with several later decisions it indicated that it would be difficult, under GATT rules, to exclude products on the basis that the process by which they were made

was environmentally unsound. This led developed-world environmentalists to turn against the GATT out of fear that new manufacturing centers
would not honor appropriate environmental standards. Later, the 1998
beef hormone decision, holding that a European restriction on beef grown
with the assistance of certain hormones was WTO-incompatible because
the regulation was not scientifically justified, led to a parallel European
environmentalist reaction against the WTO. There has been some European concern that similar logic would be applied by a panel considering
EU regulations limiting imports of genetically modified foods. The labor
community, which felt that it had much to lose from the emergence of
low-wage competitors, joined in the opposition, and managed to get special labor and environmental supplements to the NAFTA, and to place
labor and environmental concerns on the political, if not the formal
agenda, of the WTO. Developing nations opposed the inclusion of either
subject, fearing that either could be used as a form of protectionism to
exclude developing-nation exports.

These labor and environmental concerns may have been among the most
important of the motivations that led to the 1999 protests in Seattle, and
they may have been envisioned by many of the protestors as working on
behalf of developing nations. But the protestors' positions were absolutely
rejected by the developing nations. Developing nations were disturbed by
the fact that President Clinton appeared to accept the demonstrators' arguments and to be willing to push for international arrangements that would
establish labor and environmental standards for the developing nations.
The leaders of developing nations feared that such restrictions would be
used for protectionist purposes, and would keep them from increasing their
exports in competition with the better-mechanized industries of the developed nations. In addition, the agenda proposed by the United States was
too narrow to respond to developing-nation concerns such as the likelihood that U.S. antidumping law was being used to exclude exports in those
sectors where the developing nations did have a comparative advantage.
And, on top of all, they feared that the Green Room mechanism was being
used against them.

Just as the Washington consensus altered the ideological framework of
a debate begun as a critique of hegemonic control by the developed world,
unquestioned support for global free trade began to wane at the end of
the century. Under James Wolfensohn, the World Bank began to focus
more on the poor and on equity. The International Monetary Fund began
to doubt some of its traditional responses after seeing them work with,
at best, mixed success in economic crises in Indonesia, Korea, and Thailand in 1997. Reflecting this same ideological adjustment, the WTO's
meeting of the ministerial conference at Doha in November 2001 was far
more sensitive to the needs of the developing world. The most politically

contentious issue was that of drug patents and TRIPS. Many critics of the international pharmaceutical industry argued that patents led to high drug prices in the developing world and made it impossible for patients in that world, especially HIV patients in sub-Saharan Africa, to obtain medicine. Although there were many other problems in the national health systems involved, the point became one of high controversy during 2001, and some argued that TRIPS itself should be amended or repealed. However, a compromise was found, based on drafts negotiated by Brazil and a strong African group that had been well briefed by NGOs; a separate statement endorsed an interpretation of TRIPS that would make it easier for developing nations to deal with patents in the health care area.[28]

The agenda ultimately agreed at Doha for the new negotiations reflected a compromise between interests of developed and developing nations. The question of labor standards had been considered at an earlier Singapore ministerial in 1996. At that ministerial, the parties indicated that they would respect "core labor standards," but made clear that any discussions would be referred to a collaboration with the International Labour Organization; that collaboration, however, barely existed. Doha reaffirmed that labor standards would not be on the negotiating agenda. The environmental issue would be, but it was kept narrow, and the negotiations in this area were initiated "without prejudging their outcome," that is, without a presumption of success. The fact that environmental negotiations were launched but labor negotiations were not implied a possible split in the anti-WTO coalitions in the North. And on an entirely different front, the United States agreed at Doha to negotiate clarifications on antidumping rules, an acceptance that was beneficial to developing nations but politically surprising because of the importance of antidumping law to U.S. steel and semiconductor industries. Further, the negotiations in many areas were to reflect "special and differential treatment" for developing nations, though it was not yet clear how effective such declarations would be. Finally, there was to be discussion of stronger market access for the least-developed countries.

6.4. Different Perspectives and Coalitions

Although economists generally agree that free trade is in the interest of developing nations, leaders in these nations often eschew the policy. Ambivalence toward liberal trade has encouraged coalitions and loose groupings of developing countries within the WTO structure. Three such groups are discussed here, though their membership is not always easy to define.

For some of the poorest nations, including much of sub-Saharan Africa and the poorer nations of Asia and the Caribbean basin, free trade may provide capital imports at a low price, but these nations may have little to export (save, in some cases, commodities, which have been the least dynamic of the export areas), and may lack the resources needed to produce anything to export. Free trade is never a sufficient condition for development, although it may be a necessary condition. These poorer nations are likely to be harmed by TRIPS if they are required to create patent systems that lead them to pay higher prices for such products as pharmaceuticals; the benefits of patent rights are likely to be unavailable in their own markets since the nations are so small that few new products are likely to be developed for their benefit.[29]

The next economic tier of nations has more to gain immediately from a liberal trading regime because it can take advantage of the benefits of trade in low-wage exports. Here there is a clear benefit in international trade, and we have seen nations manage to convert a comparative advantage in very low-wage production (e.g., textiles) into a comparative advantage in successively higher-value activities such as automotive and then precision equipment manufacture. However, this process is probably more difficult than it was in the past, for the competition is so fierce. There are competitive pressures to keep wages low, so that employment may not flow to the next nations down the economic ladder, making it harder to maintain social equity across nations. Open markets increase competition for the more sophisticated products that might be produced by a more skilled labor force, making it more difficult to enter such more advanced areas.[30] And, because of free trade and globalization of production, the traditional infant-industry approach may no longer be available (even in those few economic situations in which it may be wise).

A third group of issues arises as nations move to develop their own more sophisticated industries. Here, the questions are whether the globalization that has arisen under the GATT/WTO trade boom and under the new nontrade provisions of the WTO affects the competitiveness of the developing-nation firms or reduces them to subsidiaries of multinationals based in the traditional developed world. These are issues for the more scientifically and industrially advanced developing nations such as Brazil, China, and India, and for the former socialist nations such as Russia. It may be difficult for these countries to compete with existing firms that are operating at global economies of scale in the production of capital goods or automotive components. Or new firms may be precluded from entry into a market through the intellectual property portfolios held by the existing leaders. And there is always the fear that developed-world firms, operating with economies of scale, are likely to force out developing-world firms in the service sectors such as banking, insurance, and telecommunications. These issues are not problems for the economies of these areas themselves—the investment and employment will be there— but in some places it will be investment controlled by global multinationals, and it may be hard for new multinationals to emerge in the less-developed countries.

The developing-world traditionally lacks bargaining power in international trade negotiations. Power in the trade regime parallels market power—the countries who have the ability to threaten to close large markets or who offer opportunities through access to their markets have traditionally held power in the organization, despite the one-nation, one-vote system. Though the formal principle is one of consensus, the obvious base of real power within the WTO is import market size, for power in bargaining and in dispute settlement depends on the threat not to give an exporter access to a particular market. Hence, the real power is with the United States and Europe, who have every economic incentive to make deals with the developing world that provide the developing world a smaller share of the benefits of trade than is received by the developed-world partners.[31]

The enlargement of the agenda of the WTO had an incidental effect of exposing the limits to the power of the United States and Europe. While previously market size alone had dictated who sat "at the table," the developing world's policies and interests were now at the center of debate. Thus the earlier power balance that underlay "Green Room" procedures now became crucial and dictated a change in access to the inner circle. Indicatively, at Doha, the African nations formed an effective bloc, and were given greater representation in the inner negotiations.

This is not to suggest that the power balance has been re-equilibrated. Moreover, in the key area of sanctions available in the trade dispute and dispute settlement process, power remains lodged with countries with large markets. What does a developing nation that is dependent on the U.S. market do when it wishes to make a legal challenge to the United States under the WTO rules? The formal WTO process is available, and may well provide a positive decision—but the nation may wonder whether it is worth the risk to antagonize the United States. In addition, the imposition of sanctions by a developing country on a developed country that declined to implement a decision could very well be to the disadvantage of the developing country itself.

The developing nations face additional asymmetries in the WTO. They have long complained that they lack the information and professional expertise necessary for effective participation in the trade-negotiating system. In trade talks in such technical areas as TRIPS, international banking or telecommunications rules, and trade-environment questions, the United States can allocate a large delegation of specialists who are well trained in both the economic and political issues on the table; most developing nations, in contrast, will send whatever representative they have in the city where the negotiations are held, often someone with no expertise in the area. Indeed, twenty developing-nation members of the WTO have no regular representative in Geneva, and the average size of a developing-nation mission in Geneva is half that of a developed-nation mission;[32] this is in the face of an average of well over forty WTO meetings per week. As negotiations increasingly reach "behind the border," affected agencies may not learn of the outcome of the negotiations until they are all over. A small nation, or a nation with a small number of qualified people, simply cannot afford the human resources to prepare for and staff all the important international negotiations, at the regional and multilateral levels, in which it has a genuine stake.

Finally, the changing scope of the regime has presented developing nations with enormous difficulties in compliance. When the center of the regime's activity was negotiating tariff levels, members faced the relatively simple task of amending their tariff schedules. But now, for the poorer nations, the demands are much greater. For example, there must be a patent office established to set up a national (or negotiate a regional) patent regime. Compliance with the WTO rules in areas like services demands the equivalent of an administrative law system and requires the development of specific regulatory rules in higher technical areas. In an economy with many state-owned enterprises, it is necessary to develop elaborate deregulation procedures or other arrangements to permit foreign firms to compete with the national institutions.[33] Compliance is expensive in terms of human resource demands and can engender political difficulties when the regime demands fundamental changes in governance structures.

6.5. Responding to the Concerns of the Developing Nations

The trade regime has attempted several types of internal reforms in response to the concerns of the developing nations. First, as suggested above, the regime has long sanctioned special economic arrangements to help these nations. The important historical examples include preferences and efforts to increase the returns to the developing world from the commodities it exports. Such programs led to the two-speed system abandoned in the "single undertaking." However, remnants of this approach remain in the multispeed aspects of the various Uruguay Round agreements, such as variable transition periods for countries to comply with agreements. Thus, for example, TRIPS gave poorer nations a later deadline than more developed nations to put pharmaceutical patent laws in place, and the Doha ministerial expanded the time still further for the poorest nations. There are similar forms of explicit discrimination in certain of the codes.

Second, there have been various schemes to improve developing nations' ability to participate effectively in the WTO. Probably the most important are efforts by international donors and NGOs to assist developing nations in capacity building. For example, the WTO has developed training programs, including courses on trade policy, complete with simulations of trade negotiations and of dispute settlement panels. It has also organized workshops and conferences to help developing nations build understanding of the issues that may be discussed in forthcoming negotiations. This is included in an integrated framework with other organizations such as UNCTAD and the World Bank. The World Intellectual Property Organization (WIPO), not a member of the integrated effort, has extensive training and finance programs to assist nations in complying with TRIPS. There is always, with such programs, a concern with whether they are truly in the developing nations' interests and when they are presenting the goals of the developed nations that contribute most of the financing of the programs.[34] The total WTO funding for such activities had not grown, as of 1999, to reflect the increased number of developing-nation members of the organization, but there was a significant increase in the training course component between 2001 and 2002. The WTO did resurrect the Committee on Trade and Development in 1995, along with a Subcommittee on Least Developed Countries.[35] That committee (of member states) meets regularly and discusses a variety of issues, including special and differential treatment, capacity building, and the approaches to be used in trade policy reviews for developing nations. It might serve as an additional forum for discussions of improvements in such areas.

One of the most important responses to the asymmetric power of the developed world is the Advisory Centre on WTO Law, which is, in essence, an internationally supported law firm in Geneva designed to provide developing nations both training in WTO law and legal advice with respect to specific disputes. It was established through a treaty, negotiated in 1999 by a number of developing nations, the United Kingdom and Canada, and a number of the smaller nations of Europe.[36] The official opening was held in 2001.

Third, the developing world has sought better ways to coordinate and develop its positions. By forming effective coalitions, the developing world has been able not only to pool efforts to develop rational positions, but also to build a bloc with more negotiating power at Geneva. This is difficult, not only because of stress on national policymaking systems, but also because the interests of developing nations differ from nation to nation. Interests may be even more diverse than they were when the G-77 was formed. Nevertheless, it may be the most important direction for developing countries, and the role of the African bloc at Doha was an initial indication of the value of the approach. The ability to form credible coalitions will be crucial for developing countries, because the pattern of negotiations in future rounds is likely to involve trade-offs between developing and developed nations. This became apparent at the Cancún ministerial and is confirmed by the assertive role played since by the larger developing countries.

6.6. Preferential Trade Arrangements and Developing Countries

Since the creation of the multilateral trade regime, countries have negotiated a large number of bilateral, regional, and plurilateral agreements in the same areas of trade policy covered by the GATT/WTO. This growth in regionalism may not reflect problems with the multilateral system but may be part of the way that regime members resolve problems of political support for free trade in a democratically acceptable way.

The development of the European Union, as pointed out in chapter 2, mirrored that of the GATT, in tackling first the removal of quantitative import restrictions and then reducing (or eliminating) tariffs. Eventually, the focus shifted to nontariff barriers and contingent protection, and finally to the whole range of trade-related areas of policy, including intellectual property and services, as well as harmonizing and reconciling standards.

Regionalism in the Latin American region also developed in parallel to the evolution of the GATT, but the nature of the integration process differed from that in Europe. Economic development in that region was thought by many to be stimulated by protection against industrial imports and the allocation of regional production by deliberate investment decisions rather than through the liberalization of internal trade. The import-substitution economic paradigm posed a direct challenge to the liberal orthodoxy of the GATT trade system, but ambiguities in the GATT rules left room for divergences among economic policies. The limited nature of the internal trade liberalization kept the trade groups from developing strong, regionally integrated economies. The main pressures on the multilateral trade system came from the Latin American countries themselves, for commodity agreements and other devices that would at least stabilize and at best expand their export markets. But when the region underwent a conversion to neoliberal economic policies in the 1980s, the GATT/WTO system and its permissive approach to regionalism were tailor-made for its new outward orientation (*apertura*). The countries of the region, individually and through the proliferation of trade agreements, embraced the philosophy of open trade and emphasized that their brand of regionalism was also "open" to imports from other regions as a result of the lowering of MFN tariffs. The most significant of these new agreements was MERCOSUR, joining Brazil and Argentina, along with their smaller neighbors Uruguay and Paraguay, and attracting Chile and Bolivia as associate members. Though buffeted by macroeconomic instability, MERCOSUR still survives, and links with the Andean Pact countries are being actively discussed.[37] Mexico has also been active in seeking agreements with countries in the region, including Colombia and Venezuela, and with MERCOSUR. Support for the multilateral process may have been weakened somewhat by Latin regionalism, but the benefits of global institutions are still fundamental to the trade policies of the region.

Regionalism in Asia has not historically posed any particular problems for the global trade system. The two most active PTAs in the Asia-Pacific region are the Association of South-East Asian Nations (ASEAN) and the Closer Economic Relations Agreement (CER) between Australia and New Zealand.[38] ASEAN is a relative newcomer to trade policy, having been a security grouping in its early years. Its cautious approach to trade liberalization, even within the group, has made it somewhat of a laggard in regional integration.[39] By contrast, after a slow start, the CER is now one of the most complete free trade agreements in the world, and appears to be a successful illustration of the fact that one can integrate many aspects of trade and economic policy without either disturbing the social and political fabric of the constituent societies or engaging in excessive supranational institution building.

The United States throughout much of the postwar period maintained its stance firmly against such regional economic entanglements, limiting its bilateral trade agreements to a free trade arrangement with Israel. A dramatic shift in U.S. trade policy occurred in the mid-1980s, as the United States began to look more closely at ties with its northern and southern neighbors. Canada, long the largest trade partner of the United States, wanted to set bilateral trade policy on a more secure footing. An increase in legal structures would benefit the Canadians in their unequal power relationship with the United States. The Canada-U.S. Free Trade Agreement offered considerable benefits to the smaller country and was hardly considered significant by the U.S. political groups. This then encouraged Mexico in 1990 to ask for a similar agreement, with Canada then deciding to join to make it into a trilateral pact, the NAFTA. But the NAFTA nearly overstepped the political boundaries of trade policy, and awoke a wide range of domestic interests that had previously been little concerned with trade agreements. President Clinton had to "pull out all the stops" to get NAFTA-enabling legislation through Congress. To a greater extent even than the Uruguay Round agreement and the establishment of the WTO, the NAFTA debate took trade policy to the center of political argument. In many ways, U.S. political attitudes toward the WTO are shaped by positions taken on NAFTA. Thus NAFTA is an important part of the context of North American trade politics and of any political disequilibrium that has emerged. Even so, the United States appears committed to further regional trade initiatives, including the recently concluded NAFTA-like agreements with Chile, and to expanding the concept of NAFTA to a Free Trade Area of the Americas (FTAA).

A further, more recent, twist to the saga of regionalism is exemplified by a number of countries, led by Singapore and New Zealand, who are actively negotiating bilateral free trade agreements. The United States has shown an active interest in such agreements, and has reached an agreement with Australia, as well as with Central America and the Dominican Republic (CAFTA). Agreements with Jordan and Singapore have already been signed, and the agreement with Israel from the 1980s is still in existence. Talks with Morocco, Thailand, South Africa, and the Andean countries are under way. Free trade areas have been suggested with countries of the Middle East as a part of the reconstruction of the region for greater security and democracy, and with ASEAN as part of a wider Pacific initiative.

The EU has free trade agreements with more than twenty-five countries and is in the process of renegotiating its preferential Cotonou agreement into a series of reciprocal free trade pacts that will include more than eighty countries. Talks between the EU and MERCOSUR are ongoing, and Canada has signed agreements with Chile as well as with the European Free Trade Association (EFTA) countries. Thus free trade pacts are becoming commonplace and have become a significant adjunct to the multilateral system.

Members appear not to heed the economic argument against regionalism. By definition, any discrimination in favor of supplies from one country risks the diversion of lower-cost supplies from another. And it is never easy to define and enforce "rules of origin" to distinguish goods produced within the trading area from those simply transshipped through the trading area. But the extent of the diversion is directly linked to the height of the MFN tariff: if the multilateral system can reduce tariff levels, the scope for discrimination is lessened and the cost can be controlled. Moreover, where trade agreements lead to internal reforms, all may benefit from them. But even if the risk of trade diversion is low, regionalism may lead to an "attention diversion"; that is, it is not easy for the government of a small or medium-sized country to be negotiating in more than one trade forum at the same time. Even large countries in effect make choices as to which set of negotiations to pursue with priority. Regional trade negotiations tend to be advanced between rounds of multilateral talks, or when those talks are proceeding slowly. This suggests that they are alternatives and may on occasions help the progress of the global talks by reminding countries with fewer regional choices that they may become "less favored nations" if such talks fail.

One aspect of this experimentation in the PTAs is particularly relevant. As the WTO has moved well beyond the regulation of trade policies at the border, a deficit of agreed principles to guide rule-making has developed, contributing to weaker political support for the system. The principles that have been used in guiding regional trade pacts are in many cases worthy of consideration by those seeking to strengthen the WTO regime. These include the principle of harmonization, or rather the limits of harmonization; mutual recognition of the policies, standards, and procedures of other countries; reducing the transaction costs of trade where differences do not reflect underlying conditions; host-country or home-country control, where the decision is made as to which jurisdiction should be responsible for enforcing regulations; and the value of side-payments to facilitate adjustments that have an adverse distributional consequence.

A major issue examined in this book is whether the trade system is out of balance, in part as a result of the success of the judicial structures and the relative weakness of the political or legislative processes. This can cause a disconnect between the domestic political support for the trade system in the major countries and the international requirement to enforce legal judgments that conflict with those interests. Among the drivers of this imbalance have been the number and type of countries that have acceded to the multilateral agreement. While the original decision-making system may have been well suited for its early members, the organization has had an increasingly difficult time adjudicating the variety of demands new members have made for economic benefits. The result has been a number of different approaches within the organization and the need to sanction extra-WTO solutions to trade problems through the creation of PTAs.

Earlier chapters have emphasized that size of market and other proxies for bargaining power play a key role in multilateral trade agreements. Although PTAs may in part be a reaction to a sense of powerlessness among the smaller GATT/WTO members, the effect of market power is evident within these regional organizations. Brazil, and to a lesser extent Mexico and Argentina, dominated LAFTA and led to the decision of the Andean countries to form their own PTA. The United States dominates NAFTA both in economic and political terms. Regionalism in Asia has always had to grapple with the inclusion of Japan and now has to consider the economic potential of China. The original EEC was dominated by France and Germany, and political decisions were (and sometimes still are) made by agreement between those two countries. Although the GATT/WTO system was largely the construction of the transatlantic partners, ironically, in some ways, the small countries have benefited from a rule-based rather than a power-based system. So the tension, in both the regional systems and the global system, is between the interests of those countries that gain in influence as a result of having a structure of rules to restrain the power of the big players and the willingness of the big players to go along with some appearance of "sovereignty sharing" in order to pursue domestic objectives of growth and stability, and entice smaller countries into accepting substantive rules preferred by the bigger players.

Perhaps the most surprising development in regional trade agreements in the past two decades is developing and developed countries' success in coexisting in the same PTA. Rather than postponing the opening up of markets to industrial countries until the economy was considered mature and competitive, the order has been reversed. For a developing country, opening up to imports is a way of developing competitive industries: coupled with macroeconomic policies that take care of inflation, payments imbalances, and excessive government spending, trade reform has allowed many developing countries to sign reciprocal agreements with developed countries. But perhaps even more important, the developing countries gain from improved market access to developed countries. The United States has been particularly open to such trade (save in certain carefully protected areas such as sugar), and its consumers have greatly benefited.

Looking back at the first fifty years of the GATT/WTO, we note that regionalism has not yet slowed the emergence of an open trading system, nor has the expansion of the organization itself. Rather, the inherent realities of unequal growth and noncommensurate power have made it difficult for the regime to accommodate the variety of interests of members. Using the metric of numbers of members, the GATT/WTO has become a truly global regime; the proliferation of regional and bilateral agreements indicates that it does not satisfy all the trade regime requirements of its members. Devising universal policies to accommodate the interests of this enlarged membership, however, has proved to be a difficult task. Regional pacts have in many cases stepped in to fill that need.

Notes

1. From the inception, there had been developing countries in the GATT, but their influence on the agenda was generally limited.

2. Russia is not yet a member, but a number of the former socialist nations of eastern Europe and Central Asia have joined over the past decades.

3. The term *PTA* is used as a shorthand for all schemes that reduce tariffs or otherwise discriminate in favor of imports from another country. Many but by no means all of these arrangements are "regional" and involve mutual free trade within the group. But in the context of the impact on the GATT/WTO principles their common feature is the premise of discrimination among countries.

4. Japan was one of the few WTO members not associated with any regional or bilateral agreement, but has recently negotiated FTAs with Singapore and Mexico to rectify that omission. Well over one hundred agreements have been notified to the GATT and the WTO, though many are no longer active.

5. The Netherlands, for instance, accepted disciplines on behalf of Indonesia and the Netherlands' Caribbean territories, and Belgium, Portugal, and the United States did the same for the countries for which they were at that time responsible. France, Denmark and the United Kingdom did the same, with some temporary exceptions.

6. Protocol of terms of accession of Japan to the General Agreement on Tariffs and Trade, June 7, 1955, at Bank of International Settlement Documents (4th Supp.) 7 (1956). Existing members were also able to retain restrictions on Japanese exports under Article XXXV.

7. WTO Document WTO/ACC/1 (March 24, 1995), available at www.wto.org.

8. More than sixty countries have made use of Article XXXV or its equivalent provision in the WTO to deny access to about thirty acceding countries, including Japan, as mentioned previously.

9. The original 1947 text of the GATT required unanimity, but this standard was relaxed the next year to a two-thirds majority so as to avoid the use of a veto by one contracting party, and Article XXXV was added to preserve the principle of consent.

10. There is an obvious analogy with the "domino" theory of membership of free trade areas, as described by Baldwin (1995), that links the attraction of membership with the "depth" of integration.

11. China was one of the original members of the GATT, but the Peoples' Republic of China renounced its membership in 1949. Taiwan (Chinese Taipei) was not permitted to retain the status of a contracting party of the GATT but for many years kept its trade policy in line with GATT members. It too became a member in 2001, within hours of the membership of China.

12. More detail on these issues is found in Steinberg 1998.

13. Accession of Russia raises some of the same issues of the legal and administrative capacity of the country to comply with WTO regulations, but the issue of the central control of the economy is not relevant. Despite the significance of some state-owned enterprises, Russia is now a relatively unregulated economy.

14. "State-invested enterprise" includes state-owned enterprises, state-trading enterprises, and any joint venture or other enterprise in which the state has invested.

15. For this kind of analysis applied to state-trading enterprises, see Jackson (1990).

16. Arguments have, of course, been made that democracy and freedom are related *indirectly* to the proper functioning of capitalism. See, e.g., Friedman 1962.

17. See, as evidence of demand for this linkage, the yearly use of Title IV of the Trade Act of 1974, as amended (the "Jackson-Vanik Amendment"). While its language deals with emigration, the statute has been used in recent years to deal with human rights broadly.

18. Article XVIII allowed countries to keep quantitative trade barriers to promote import substitution policies and in cases where extreme balance-of-pay-

ments problems were encountered. As trade deficits are common, and indeed essential, for countries requiring capital inflows, this effectively meant that developing countries could keep quota systems in place without restriction.

19. The analysis of long-term trends in the terms of trade between manufactured imports and agricultural exports for developing countries was pioneered by Hans Singer, and the notion that the terms of trade move chronically against developing countries is known as the Prebisch-Singer thesis.

20. The impact of escalation of tariffs with the stage of processing is known as "effective protection." For instance a low or zero tariff on cattle hides and a higher tariff on the shoes made from the cattle hides can protect the "value added" in the shoe sector to a greater degree than the height of the tariff would suggest.

21. In common with the UNCTAD, the G-77 is still in existence, though with many more members.

22. The key documents are the Declaration on the Establishment of a New International Economic Order; the Programme of Action on the Establishment of a New International Economic Order, General Assembly Resolutions 3201 (S-VI) and 3202 (S-VI), May 1, 1974; and the Charter on the Economic Rights and Duties of States, General Assembly Resolution 3281 (XXIX), December 12, 1974.

23. The countries of Central America had formed the Central America Free Trade Area (now the Central American Common Market, CACM) the previous year.

24. "Differential and more favourable treatment, reciprocity and fuller participation of developing countries" (Decision of November 28, 1979, L/4903).

25. The policy of "import-substitution industrialization" was widely practiced in Latin America until the mid-1980s, in contrast to the "export-led industrialization" more common in East and Southeast Asia.

26. For a careful review, see Finger and Schurknecht 1999.

27. There were, however, certain provisions within the individual codes that gave special protection to developing-nation interests, e.g. certain delays within TRIPS and rights for "special and differential treatment" in some situations.

28. Declaration on the TRIPS agreement and public health, WT/MIN(01)/DEC/2, Adopted on November 14, 2001.

29. These countries make up the bulk of what is known as the Group of 90, which were firmly against the start of negotiations on the Singapore issues at Cancún. A smaller coalition, of four African countries, had earlier tabled a paper on the removal of cotton subsidies in developed countries. This cotton initiative also figured prominently in the discussions at Cancún.

30. Consider how difficult, for example, it would be for a new nation, perhaps a Latin American one, to enter the semiconductor world that was such an important growth mechanism for Korea and Taiwan.

31. In this case both power and domestic politics act in the same direction. See Goldstein and Martin 2000.

32. As reported by World Wildlife Fund et. al. (2001).

33. One estimate of the total cost of implementing the Uruguay Round regulations gave a figure of $150 million per country (Finger 2000). This is a large—possibly prohibitive—sum of money for a least-developed country, and the needed expenditures may not be high on the agendas of donor nations and institutions.

34. In addition to the official activity, there are enormous efforts by NGOs to provide background papers putting forward what they believe are the developing nations' interests and to provide education and practical assistance to developing-world negotiators, as well as to lobby developed-world negotiators. In many cases, the value of such efforts is quite substantial; in others, the assistance may reflect the concerns of the NGOs more than those of the developing nations themselves.

35. The Committee on Trade and Development had been set up at the time that Part IV was added to the GATT, in 1966, but had not been particularly active.

36. The United States has so far not participated in the establishment of the Centre.

37. Numerous other trade agreements litter Latin America, under the auspices of the Latin American Integration Association (ALADI), often on the face of it inconsistent with GATT rules.

38. The Asia-Pacific Economic Cooperation (APEC) process is not a regional trade agreement, as no preferences are offered to other members. It is better seen as an ad hoc plurilateral institution that has relevance to the issues of the global system more through its coordinated work-plan of national trade policy changes than through its specifically regional initiatives.

39. ASEAN has discussed an agreement that would include China, Japan, and South Korea, in a bloc (ASEAN + 3) that would have global significance. Asian regionalism could under these circumstances have a much more significant impact on other countries.

Seven

Accommodating Nonstate Actors: Representation of Interests, Ideas, and Information in a State-Centric System

Trade policy, in the view of many groups, has become too important to be left to governments. So while governments discuss and negotiate on matters such as the lack of power, unfair processes, and unfavorable outcomes of the GATT/WTO for developing countries, new *nonstate actors*—namely, environmentalists, organized labor, and antiglobalization activists—voice similar complaints about lack of influence. Some developing countries emphasize that the processes are fundamentally "undemocratic." And so these NGOs and developing countries often support each other in their complaints about the WTO.

These new nonstate actors are not, of course, the only nongovernmental organizations in the system—business has always played a significant role in setting the international trade agenda. This chapter examines both the old and the new nonstate actors and disentangles the web of claims about the WTO made by them and on their behalf. It considers the need to reform institutions of representation, at the national and WTO levels, so that the voices of these actors are represented and intermediated in trade politics, without undermining the political logic of existing institutional arrangements.

That political logic is premised on the notion that the WTO will remain a state-centric institution for the foreseeable future. The two-level system of trade policymaking described in chapter 1—competing interests intermediated at the domestic level into a national bargaining position, and competing national interests intermediated at the WTO level—will not die anytime soon. Moreover, as shown in chapter 2, delegation to the state has been crucial to the success of trade liberalization over the past seventy years (Bailey, Goldstein, and Weingast 1997). In this system, the state plays a central role as a gatekeeper of information, ideas, proposals, and policy.

This chapter argues that *domestic* institutional processes of trade policymaking may suffer from a democratic deficit and may be improved by institutionalizing new avenues for the articulation of interests by the new nonstate actors. At the international level, however, complete democratization is infeasible. In the international context, improved representation of ideas and information from the new nonstate actors may strengthen the WTO, provided that participatory changes do not undermine secrecy in contexts where secrecy performs important functions. The challenge facing the WTO is therefore to modify trade institutions so as to accommodate the representation of new nonstate actors' interests, ideas, and relevant information in a way that is more democratic at the domestic level and functional at the international level.

Section 7.1 describes and explains the interests and motivations of the old and new nonstate actors and their substantive demands. Section 7.2 describes and analyzes their procedural complaints—including the popular claim of a "democratic deficit" at the WTO. Section 7.3 considers *domestic* institutional processes for representation and intermediation of the new nonstate actors' interests, highlighting recent changes that have enhanced the legitimacy and political sustainability of domestic trade policymaking. Section 7.4 examines proposals for more direct voice by nonstate actors in WTO legislative deliberations, suggesting intractable obstacles to their direct participation but identifying some merits of increased indirect participation. Section 7.5 considers more direct participation by NGOs in the WTO dispute settlement process, suggesting that there are informational and legitimacy reasons to favor continued reforms in this area. Section 7.6 concludes that there are several procedural reforms that could better accommodate the new nonstate actors; however, many developing countries oppose those reforms, and procedural change needs to be accompanied by substantive reform if the WTO is to garner the support of the new nonstate actors.

7.1. The Role of Nonstate Actors

Business interests have, of course, long been active in shaping trade diplomacy. But, beginning in the late 1980s, and accelerating through the 1990s, three new groups of nonstate actors became active in trade politics: environmental groups, organized labor, and the antiglobalization movement. Their simultaneous emergence is not coincidental. The issues raised by each of the groups may be considered "spillovers" from trade liberalization: the trade-related interests of each of these groups increased in salience as trade barriers fell to the lowest levels since the early twentieth century. To the extent that the interests of organized labor and environmentalists are represented at the WTO, they are championed by the advanced, industrialized countries—and resisted by the developing countries.

There are important distinctions between the interests of these different nonstate actors. For example, environmentalists and labor unions typically make concrete proposals for substantive and procedural reforms at the WTO, whereas antiglobalization activists more frequently oppose altogether the freer movement of goods and capital. Moreover, at their core, the issues raised by environmentalists are rooted in global cooperation problems requiring international solutions, whereas the issues raised by organized labor do not necessarily require international solutions. Therefore, it is useful to consider the substantive concerns of each group separately and the extent to which the WTO currently addresses those concerns, and then to consider these groups' procedural complaints. But before exploring these newer actors, it is essential to look at the role of business.

7.1.1. Business—the Traditional Nonstate Actor

Business has been the traditional nonstate actor in trade diplomacy, going back to pre–Civil War debates between protectionist industry in New England and free-trade agriculture in the South. Its concerns are reflected through a variety of mechanisms: formal electoral politics, campaign contributions, lobbying, and government's perception of the national economic interest (Grossman and Helpman 2002). Business is, of course, the key target of critics of the WTO, who see the organization as dominated by multinational corporations. Business interests do not, however, speak with one voice. Each specific business community has always lobbied for those trade arrangements that would support its exports or protect it from imports. There have long been national coalitions favoring specific exports, such as, in the case of the United States, manufactured goods, and resisting imports, such as, again in the case of the United States, the steel interests supporting antidumping rules. To a great extent, business groups in the United States have worked with business groups in Europe to free trade in areas where they see mutual benefit. In large measure, the success of GATT/WTO trade liberalization is attributable to the formulation of packages that curry favor with a coalition favoring specific exports and that is more powerful than the coalition resisting imports. However, the success of free trade in areas like automobiles and electronics derived from a group of industries able to find economies of scale by reorganizing themselves on a global level during the last part of the twentieth century (and it is no accident that intracorporate trade has grown much more rapidly than intercorporate trade). Even the new service industries, for example, banking and telecommunications, are, in large part, seeking global economies of scale. Where this was not feasible, as with steel or agriculture, or where the beneficiaries were in the developing world, as with textiles, the move to market opening was less effective. The economic drive underlying the success of the GATT/WTO derived in significant part from a specific subgroup of developed-world industries.

But there is likely to be major change from the coalitions that marked the earlier years of the GATT. Admittedly, predicting international negotiating coalitions is as difficult as predicting future political coalitions—agendas and constituencies evolve together, and there are often surprises in the competition among different issues and their constituencies, but there are many reasons to expect change. Part of the change comes from the nature of business—many more businesses are today global, in contrast to the national businesses of the early days of the GATT. These global businesses generally seek not just trade measures that open markets to their products, but also measures that decrease their costs by permitting the free movement of their inputs—not only raw materials but also capital and labor.

The new issues (which of course evolve in part endogenously) also involve new coalitions. For example, the role of services and of information (as in intellectual property, information products such as movies, and the Internet and computer industries) suggests a northern coalition among intangible and information-based industries. For some issues, it may be hard to find appropriate constituencies. Thus, the antitrust negotiations envisioned by some countries as a part of the Doha Round are likely to be seen as threats to—rather than benefits to—some of the industries that are interested in global trade. Similarly, efforts to bring environmental concerns into the WTO are likely to be unappealing to some of the industries that have traditionally supported the GATT/WTO. Consumers shared in the benefits of lowering traditional trade barriers, for prices typically fell, and therefore consumer movements (to the extent that they have been able to organize) supported trade negotiations. The consumer effects are very different for TRIPS, which tends to raise prices (Drache and Ostry 2002).

The new coalition structure is likely to be shaped by the fact that the relationship between the developing and the developed worlds is becoming more important in the WTO. This is because some of the topics being discussed under the Doha agenda, for example, intellectual property, antidumping, and environmental protection, involve systematic differences between developed- and developing-nation interests. Hence the WTO has called the Doha Round a Development Agenda. U.S. trade objectives, as embodied in the Trade Act of 2002, include even further goals relating to corruption and regulatory reform—and many of these goals reflect the desires of U.S.-based business.

7.1.2. Environmental Organizations

Environmentalists have raised three sets of substantive trade-related concerns. First, the most persistent concern of environmentalists has been that cross-national variance in the stringency and enforcement of environmental measures may be leading to an international "race toward the bottom" in environmental regulation (Stewart 1977; Esty and Geradin 2001). Economic logic suggests that decisions on where to invest will be influenced by the relative stringency of environmental regulations in different countries: all other things being equal, a manufacturer would prefer to locate its operations in a jurisdiction with low costs of compliance with environmental regulations. Empirically, there is little evidence that the level of foreign direct investment in a country is related to the stringency or enforcement of its environmental regulations, nor evidence of a "race toward the bottom" in environmental regulation (Esty and Geradin 2001). However, there is considerable anecdotal evidence that investment relocation decisions are influenced by environmental regulation in extremely "dirty" sectors (such as metal reclaiming from batteries), and the economic logic of the claim is compelling. Moreover, right or wrong, in politics the perceptions of environmentalists matter.

Environmentalists' preferred method of addressing this problem has been to implore the EC and the United States to impose trade restrictions against goods produced abroad under less environmentally stringent rules. Research has shown that economic development, which may be fostered by free trade, is correlated with more stringent environmental regulation, but this is a long-term phenomenon that offers little satisfaction to environmentalists (Grossman and Krueger 1994). Moreover, environmentalists find natural domestic political allies in efforts to use trade restrictions for environmental purposes: import-competing producers are often happy to support these policies, forming a "Baptist-bootlegger" coalition with environmentalists (DeSombre 2000).

But such trade restrictions have often run afoul of GATT/WTO rules. Article XX(g) excepts some trade measures taken for the "conservation of exhaustible natural resources." For example, early GATT dispute settlement panel decisions on Article XX(g) suggested that the natural resources in question must be located within the territory or jurisdiction of the country imposing the trade measure, but *United States—Import Prohibition of Certain Shrimp and Shrimp Products (2000)*, a more recent and more authoritative WTO Appellate Body decision, can be read as eliminating that jurisdictional requirement for invocation of Article XX(g). Nonetheless, that decision is not entirely clear on the jurisdictional scope of Article XX(g), and it establishes a labyrinth of difficult legal hurdles in order to sustain the WTO-legality of any trade measure imposed for environmental purposes (Grunbaum 2002). Perhaps most disturbingly for environmentalists, dicta in the earlier GATT cases and the logic of those decisions have suggested that WTO members that are parties to a multilateral environmental agreement (MEA), such as the Convention on International Trade of Endangered Species (CITES), may not be able to maintain trade restrictions mandated or permitted by that MEA against WTO members that are not parties to that MEA.[1]

Second, environmentalists have been concerned that WTO rules might preclude governments from imposing import restrictions intended to protect against contamination of the domestic environment. Two GATT exceptions provide the primary bases for restricting imports to protect the domestic environment: Article XX(g), described above, and Article XX(b), which permits some trade measures to protect human, animal, or plant life, health, or safety. While these exceptions may appear on their face to be broad, there are significant limitations on their successful invocation. For example, as stated in *United States—Reformulated Gasoline Rule (1996),* the trade measure in question must normally offer the least burdensome means of achieving the objective described by the Article XX exception. To be justified under Article XX(b), the measure in question must be "necessary" for the protection of life, health, or safety. The burden of making those showings rests with the member maintaining the challenged measure. Moreover, one of the WTO agreements intended to elaborate these exceptions—the Agreement on Sanitary and Phytosanitary Measures (SPS agreement)—requires scientific evidence of a harm to be avoided by a trade-restrictive SPS measure; this requirement was used in *EC—Measures Concerning Meat and Meat Products (Hormones) (1998)* to successfully challenge an EC directive banning the importation of beef from hormone-treated cattle, outraging many environmentalists and consumer groups.

While the foregoing environmental concerns have been persistent at the GATT/WTO since the late 1980s, a third set of broader trade-environment issues has also been raised. For example, environmentalists advocate lowering tariffs and trade restrictions on environmentally sound products and services (such as solar energy products). They have advocated more effective regulation of fisheries as part of WTO negotiations. They have rallied against government subsidies for environmentally unsound practices, such as alleged subsidies to the Canadian softwood lumber industry. They have championed the inclusion of transborder cleanup projects in trade negotiations. And they have argued for a clarification of trade rules to expressly permit "green labeling" of consumer products (Steinberg 2002c).

While environmentalists' positions on these issues have engendered substantial political opposition, none of their proposals is fundamentally incompatible with the policy goal of trade liberalization that is central to the WTO system. Only the most extreme environmental activists have argued against trade liberalization, ignoring arguments that free trade leads to more efficient utilization of resources and so less environmental degradation and emphasizing instead that freer trade leads to a greater scale of global production and environmental degradation.

Until the Doha Round was launched in 2001, the GATT/WTO did very little to incorporate these concerns of environmentalists into its negotiating agenda. Last-minute changes to the Uruguay Round agreements offered hortatory and vague commitments to "sustainable development" and the environment. But developing-country negotiators resisted any substantive proenvironmental commitments in those agreements. While the Uruguay Round did establish a Committee on Trade and the Environment (CTE) to explore the possibility of future commitments on the topic, that committee deadlocked along North-South lines (Shaffer 2002). Finally, in 2001, the Doha Work Program included a specific mandate to begin negotiating on three trade-environment topics: (1) the relationship between existing WTO rules and specific trade obligations in MEAs; (2) procedures for regular information exchange between MEA secretariats and the relevant WTO committees; and (3) the reduction or elimination of tariffs and nontariff barriers to environmental goods and services.

Substantively, another bright spot for environmentalists might possibly be two sets of WTO Appellate Body decisions. One concerns a U.S. law that bans the importation of shrimp from countries that do not mandate the use of turtle excluder devices in shrimp-fishing nets. The Appellate Body decision discussed above did hold the U.S. law WTO-inconsistent, but it established criteria by which the law might be held WTO-legal and could be read as having weakened earlier panel decisions that had imposed stringent jurisdictional limitations on Article XX(g), described above. Following U.S. modifications to regulations that implemented the statute in question, and U.S. efforts to negotiate a plurilateral agreement on the topic, the Appellate Body held in 2001 in *U.S.—Import Restrictions on Shrimp Turtle—Recourse to Article 21.5 of the DSU by Malaysia (2001)* that the U.S. shrimp-turtle law, as revised, was WTO-consistent, at least as long as the plurilateral negotiations were under way. In a second decision favored by many environmentalists, *European Communities— Measures Affecting Asbestos and Asbestos-Containing Products (2001),* the Appellate Body held that a French ban on the importation of asbestos-containing cement did not discriminate in favor of cement that excludes asbestos, because the public health effects of asbestos implied that the two forms of cement were not "like products" within the meaning of GATT Article III.

7.1.3. Labor

Organized labor raises three trade concerns. First, like environmental organizations, organized labor is concerned about a race toward the bottom involving national labor standards. As in the environmental context, the economic logic seems compelling: all other things being equal, investment location decisions will be influenced by the relative stringency of labor regulations in various countries; and this phenomenon should put downward pressure on labor standards in countries concerned about attracting foreign direct investment. However, the evidence of a race toward the bottom in labor standards is weak, and there is only weak evidence of any statistically significant relationship between the relative stringency of labor regulations and the level of foreign direct investment (Flanigan 2002). Like environmentalists, organized labor would like to use trade measures to countervail a possible race toward the bottom.

Second, many labor activists view "core labor standards" as basic human rights that should be enforceable through trade measures. There is a strong argument under international law that certain labor standards are now widely regarded as basic human rights with a universal character, including the right to collective bargaining and freedom of association; the right not to be enslaved; the abolition of child labor; and equality of opportunity in employment for men and women (Cleveland 2002). These rights are now affirmed in the June 1998 International Labour Organization (ILO) Declaration on Fundamental Labor Rights.

Third, some labor activists argue that it is unfair that some countries can achieve comparative advantage by maintaining relatively weak labor standards. The argument here is not one of a dynamic that is leading to suboptimal global welfare, but simply that it is inequitable that blue-collar jobs are lost in countries with stringent labor standards—such as the United States and most western European nations—as a result of trade liberalization. From an economic perspective, such arguments may be dismissed: free trade increases global welfare and welfare in each liberalizing nation; adverse distributive consequences within each trading nation should be remedied through tax and social policies. However, as a political matter, it is understandable that labor representatives would complain about trade liberalization in countries—like the United States—that maintain weak trade adjustment assistance programs.

Many labor activists would like to use trade measures against products from countries with low labor standards, but for the most part current WTO rules preclude doing so. Article XX(e) of the GATT permits trade restrictions aimed at goods produced by prison labor, but there is no general right to impose trade measures against goods from a country with a poor human rights record, weak child labor standards, a lack of respect for freedom of association or rights to collective bargaining, patterns of discrimination in employment, or a low or nonexistent minimum wage. Some have suggested the possibility that the WTO Appellate Body might offer broad interpretations of various GATT exceptions (such as those permitting trade measures to protect public morals in Article XX(a) or human health and safety in Article XX(b)) in order to accommodate labor concerns (Cleveland 2002), but such radical lawmaking seems unlikely. Moreover, any such lawmaking would likely lead to a crisis at the WTO precipitated by developing countries, which have consistently opposed a right to use trade measures against countries with weak labor standards.

Subsequent to the creation of the WTO, the EC was joined by U.S. Democratic party leaders and the Clinton administration in championing organized labor's position at the WTO. This at times pitted the transatlantic powers against developing countries, which oppose including labor issues on the WTO agenda. Developing countries were concerned that purportedly labor-based trade measures would be used for protectionist purposes. Moreover, they rejected arguments based on theories of a "race toward the bottom" and the purported inequity that may result from comparative advantage rooted in weak labor standards. In the early WTO years, it appeared that Europe and the United States were making some headway on labor issues in the WTO: in December 1996 in the Singapore Ministerial Conference, WTO ministers declared their renewed "commitment to the observance of internationally recognized core labor standards," while at the same time declaring that the International Labour Organization is "the competent body to set and deal with these standards" and rejecting the use of labor standards for "protectionist purposes." This turned up heat on the ILO, which adopted the 1998 Declaration on Fundamental Labor Rights, described above. But with the Democratic party's loss of the U.S. presidency in 2000, the EC was left alone to champion labor rights at the WTO. Therefore, labor issues were effectively excluded from the Doha negotiating mandate, which restated what had been said earlier at Singapore, and took note of the work being done at the ILO.

There are other trade-related avenues for advancing labor interests. Antidumping, countervailing duty, and safeguards actions have been used to protect labor interests in contexts defined by statute and relevant WTO agreements. Regionally, the North American Commission on Labor Cooperation provides a means by which organized labor and others may petition to initiate a process that can publicize certain antilabor actions by any of the North American governments. Similarly, all EC member states and those countries trying to accede to the EC must participate in the European human rights regime, which offers some legal protection of labor interests. Domestically, various U.S. statutory schemes, such as the Generalized System of Preferences (GSP) and the African Growth and Opportunity Act, permit the suspension of preferential treatment of goods from certain developing countries if they stop respecting core labor standards. Similarly, the EC's GSP conditions the extent of its preferences on a country's implementation and enforcement of particular ILO conventions, although India initiated a challenge to that measure in December 2002.[2] In addition, Congress can always offer increased trade adjustment assistance to support and retrain workers who have lost their jobs as a consequence of trade liberalization. Privately, social labeling schemes may be established and adopted, corporations may adopt codes of conduct for their global operations, and transnational litigation may promote compliance with international labor standards (OECD 2000; Koh 1991; Compa 2002). Finally, economic development would appear to create domestic political conditions that favor the adoption of improved labor standards; while economic development is a slow process, it will likely facilitate a solution to the trade-labor problem in the long run (OECD 1996b).

7.1.4. Other Movements, Including the Antiglobalization Movement

In addition, there are a variety of special-purpose actors that have sought influence in international trade negotiations. Among the most significant in the preparations for the Doha summit were the developing-world medical assistance community, centered on institutions such as Oxfam and Médécins sans Frontiers, which argued that patents raised drug prices in sub-Saharan Africa. They used a kind of pincer movement, working both to create political support for their position in developed countries, especially in Europe, and to assist developing-world delegations in proposing negotiating outcomes. With the increasing scope of WTO activity, there are likely to be many other such special-focus efforts, looking, for example, to other intellectual property issues, to genetically modified foods, and also to fundamental structural concerns such as the adequacy of representation of the developing world in WTO negotiations.

The antiglobalization movement, which has played a role in the street demonstrations at Seattle and at various other international conferences and meetings since, has aggregated all of the critiques of the more particularistic new nonstate actors into a general attack on the WTO—and often on any other entity that promotes the freer movement of goods or capital. In addition to embracing the substantive concerns of environmentalists and organized labor, as described above, antiglobalization protestors complain, for example, that freer trade destroys local enterprise by confronting it with a global market; displaces the diversity of indigenous and national cultures; facilitates the spread of the most mediocre attributes of American culture; exacerbates global and domestic economic inequality; and operates exclusively to benefit multinational corporations and banks. Efforts to distill these complaints into their analytically distinct components are sometimes eschewed by the movement as fruitless acts, which fail to recognize that the system cannot be fixed—it must be junked.

7.2. Complaints about Process: "Underrepresentation" of New Nonstate Actors' Interests

As discussed briefly in chapter 1, some new nonstate actors and commentators complain broadly of a "democratic deficit" at the WTO, focusing on the lack of external transparency (i.e., its "secrecy") and limited opportunities for NGO participation in trade policymaking and dispute settlement (Wallach 2000; Atik 2001; Raustiala 2000; Charnovitz 2002).[3] One commentator has argued, for example, that the WTO is both "generative" and "insular." Generativity occurs when international institutions "produce new substantive rules that modify or extend a given legal agreement," and the subsequent analysis focuses on judicial lawmaking at the WTO. Insularity is characterized by institutional operation with relatively low "transparency and . . . non-executive branch (for example, legislative/public) participation in the international institution and its decisions." This critic views WTO rules as "emanating from inaccessible tribunals in Geneva" and argues that the WTO decision-making processes should more closely resemble the "accepted and the legitimate practices that are broadly shared by liberal democratic states" (Raustiala 2000).

Empirically, these claims of the WTO's generativity are contestable. As shown in chapter 3, while the WTO Appellate Body does engage in lawmaking, its "generativity" is constrained by its discourse of appropriate methods for international legal interpretation of treaty texts—and by politics. Member' signals do not suggest that the Appellate Body has been radically activist or that it has fundamentally shifted the balance of WTO rights and responsibilities. Only a handful of Appellate Body decisions have dealt with labor or environment issues. Moreover, in most countries (including the United States and the EC member states), neither an adverse WTO dispute settlement decision nor a new WTO agreement can be implemented in national law without an affirmative legislative act. Hence, not all analysts would agree that the WTO's judicial system is highly generative.

Conceptually, the relevant locus of insularity in trade policymaking may just as easily be at the domestic level as at the WTO. The WTO is just as insular (i.e., nontransparent and exclusionary) with respect to business interests as to nonbusiness NGO interests, yet it is the nonbusiness NGOs that complain about WTO insularity, not multinational corporations. The core of the problem could be seen as domestic governmental processes and politics favoring the representation of business interests over nonbusiness interests in WTO negotiations. Hence, "insularity" is at least as much a domestic political defect as a defect in the international institution.

More broadly, without disaggregating "democracy," "democratic deficit" is a problematic way to frame procedural problems at the WTO. Robert A. Dahl has concluded that "international organizations are not and are not likely to be democratic." He argues that, in order for an international organization to be democratic, there must be an international *demos*, which is impossible to identify in the absence of a sense of global political community. Politics within states, where political communities exist, may be democratic, but an international organization like the WTO should be seen essentially as an instrument that states use to achieve common purposes (Dahl 1999, 32). Moreover, as an organization operating on the principle of the sovereign equality of states, the WTO respects each state as a sovereign entity and gives formally equal voice to countries with radically different population sizes (Steinberg 2002b). To expect such an international organization to be fully democratic is to engage in what philosophers call a category mistake (Keohane and Nye 2003).

Sophisticated analysts of democratic shortcomings at the WTO disaggregate "democracy" in order to measure performance and prescribe solutions. For example, Robert Howse focuses his democratic critique of the WTO on the problem of agency costs, that is, the problem that agents may act to represent their own interests rather than those of their principals (Howse 2003). More broadly, Keohane and Nye frame their concerns as related to attenuated accountability of international organizations like the WTO (Keohane and Nye 2003).

Nevertheless, it is certainly true that the increased importance of the GATT/WTO has been accompanied by a shift of power towards executive agencies of governments, who, after all, shape the final package that emerges from the negotiations and create international rules that might otherwise be created with different balances by national legislatures. The trade representatives of the world are now making a significantly greater portion of the world's decisions than they did a generation ago. Through the TRIPS negotiation, for example, the USTR made decisions that might once have made by the Patent and Trademark Office (albeit in consultation with that office)—and the point is valid for every agency and sector of negotiation: agriculture, banking regulation, and so on. This need to coordinate international diplomacy across all sectors is unavoidable in a globalizing world. Because the WTO is the forum for package negotiations, it has become the focus for this coordination, and the president and USTR therefore, along with their negotiating partners, make the key trade-off decisions that determine which bodies of international regulation—and therefore national regulation—will be strengthened.

From the perspective used in this book, "underrepresentation" characterizes the central procedural problem created by the rise of the new non-

state actors. Underrepresentation limits the extent to which national governments and the WTO incorporate the new nonstate actors' interests,
ideas, and information, diminishing political support for national trade
policy and for the trade regime, and depriving national trade policymakers and the WTO of useful information and ideas. The concept of underrepresentation captures the essence of a democracy problem in national
political systems insofar as participation and contestation—the two dimensions of Dahl's polyarchy—are diminished by limits on representation (Dahl 1971). Even if institutions of representation were perfected in
domestic trade policymaking institutions, there could be a value to direct
representation of nonstate actors' interests at the WTO in particular contexts. For example, in some contexts examined below, it could be useful
for nonstate actors to bypass the state as a gatekeeper of representation
at the international level in order more efficiently to provide certain types
of information to the WTO.

Underrepresentation at home is a valuable way to frame the procedural
problem raised by the rise of the new nonstate actors. Environmentalists
and organized labor have substantive trade concerns—examined above—
for which there are potential solutions, but the failure to provide institutional processes through which their interests, ideas, and information may
be represented and intermediated has helped drive them into alliance with
antiglobalization activists. The resulting increase in political opposition
to trade liberalization presents the global system of trade institutions (at
the domestic and WTO levels) with one of its greatest challenges. The
new nonstate actors have demanded new institutionalized avenues for
representation and intermediation of their interests in U.S. domestic trade
policymaking. In international processes, some new forms of institutionalized participation have been demanded by which nonstate actors may
transmit useful information or ideas. Some of these changes have been
made, many of which are improving the functionality of the system without undermining its political logic. We consider below representation and
intermediation problems created by the rise of the new nonstate actors at
the domestic and international levels, respectively, and how those problems have been addressed.

7.3. Domestic Institutional Processes of Interest Representation and Intermediation

In the United States, constitutional theory views many of the issues considered by the WTO as being appropriate for decision by both Congress
and the president. In practice, many decisions are effectively made by

the executive branch after informal consultations with key members of Congress, and then approved under a fast-track process that formally denies opportunity for congressional amendment. In parliamentary systems, key political leaders can be kept involved in the negotiations, and the parliament is routinely expected to approve the cabinet's proposals. These processes pose an issue with the public in constitutional democracies, however, and there are also important institutional issues in developing nations, where there may be less analytical capability to evaluate the possible trade-offs.

Historically, labor unions and environmentalists have not been among the core interest groups that have participated in U.S. trade policymaking. Hence, when trade became a highly salient issue to these actors in the late 1980s, their exclusion from domestic trade policymaking processes had been effectively institutionalized. Consider for example the institutional structure of U.S. trade policymaking. As described in chapter 2, in the last century Congress increasingly delegated authority over trade policy to the executive branch, giving it some authority to negotiate reciprocal tariff reductions starting in 1934, and delegating more complete authority to negotiate modern, multi-issue trade agreements in 1974 (subject to subsequent congressional approval). Since then, the executive branch has had primary responsibility for trade policymaking, subject to congressional oversight. But the executive branch agencies and congressional oversight committees involved in that process have not been entities that are fundamentally concerned with the interests of the new nonstate actors.

In the United States, it has been difficult to define a constitutionally sound way for the Congress and president to cooperate in making trade policy. At one time a legislative veto was used, under which Congress could, by vote (sometimes in one house, sometimes in both houses) strike down a presidential foreign policy decision. This procedure was first used in the 1930s and greatly expanded during the 1970s, when Congress was particularly concerned about presidential authority. The Supreme Court declared the approach unconstitutional in *Immigration and Naturalization Service v. Chadha* in 1983.

An alternative, however, has survived: the fast-track procedure first included in the Trade Act of 1974. Under this procedure, referred to since 2002 as "trade promotion authority," Congress agrees in advance to consider as a whole the president's legislative package implementing a trade agreement and to vote yes or no on it within a defined time without amendment. The Congress thus still has a review, while the president naturally shapes the details and trade-offs of the package in order to build a congressional majority in each House. This clearly gives the president more authority than under the traditional system of congressional shaping of legislation to be presented to the president. At the same time, it enables the president to submit a package that includes both the gains and the concessions made in the trade negotiations and to be confident that the package cannot be amended to exclude those items that Congress might dislike but that may be important parts of the overall package from the viewpoint of foreign negotiating partners. The process is, for the present, a reasonable accommodation of interests—but it does transfer power from Congress to the executive, and certainly raises fundamental constitutional issues should the scope of WTO agreement continue to grow.

The congressional committees with primary oversight responsibility are the House Ways and Means Committee and the Senate Finance Committee. As long as tariff reductions were the primary focus of trade negotiations, it made sense to put these two revenue committees in charge of trade policy. But as shown throughout this book, particularly in chapter 5, trade is no longer only about tariffs. When it became clear that the Uruguay Round agreements would cover a host of nontariff topics, a half dozen committees in each House had to begin engaging in congressional oversight: for example, the judiciary committees held hearings on the TRIPS agreement, and the agriculture committees held hearings on the Agreement on Agriculture. For environmentalists and labor unions to enjoy representation and intermediation of their interests in Congress, the committees with jurisdiction over environmental and labor union issues, respectively, would have to be afforded a formal role in the process. Environmentalists and labor unions have established channels of communication with those committees, whose members enjoy expertise on these topics.

The Trade Act of 2002 established a Congressional Oversight Group intended to expand the breadth of participation by congressional leaders in areas beyond the traditional topics of tariffs and other border measures. To the extent that the group includes members of Congress with interests in environmental and labor issues, that organizational innovation will enhance the representation and intermediation of the new nonstate actors' interests along with those of more traditional trade interests. This approach, which finds precedent in the UK House of Commons EU Scrutiny Committee, should also reduce some of the duplication of work associated with multiple congressional oversight hearings by each interested committee.

The executive branch suffers from similar institutional shortcomings. Established by an executive order, the Office of the United States Trade Representative (USTR) has coordinated U.S. trade policy since 1963 (originally as the Office of the Special Representative for Trade Negotiations). In that capacity, USTR has chaired the main interagency committees that are established by statute to decide the executive branch's position on trade issues. Since 1975, the Trade Policy Committee (TPC) has been the most senior interagency group that considers trade policy; it is composed of the USTR as chair, and the secretaries of Commerce, State, Treasury, Agriculture, and Labor. Given the political salience of environmental issues in trade politics today, it should be of some concern that agencies traditionally focused on environmental and health issues are not automatically included on the TPC. In the late 1980s, when these issues first began to appear in Uruguay Round negotiating texts, the administrators of the Environmental Protection Agency (EPA) and Food and Drug Administration (FDA) were surprised that they had been excluded from the interagency process. USTR has since then increasingly exercised its authority to invite these and other agencies to participate in the interagency process, as appropriate.

Within USTR, there is an elaborate advisory group process—yet it is not very transparent, and it is dominated by special interests, as can be seen by looking at the membership of the various groups on the USTR website. There has been some organizational change to accommodate new nonstate actors. The Clinton administration established an Office for the Environment and Natural Resources, which stood alongside offices on agriculture, industry and telecommunications, services, investment, intellectual property, textiles, and various regions of the world. Moreover, since 1995, USTR has established a Trade and Environment Policy Advisory Committee, regularly released its dispute settlement briefs and public information on its negotiating position on various issues, and regularly included environmentalists and organized labor representatives on the Advisory Committee on Trade Policy and Negotiations. Yet there is still no USTR office responsible for labor issues. In short, the executive branch is moving in the direction of modifying its internal processes and structures to better accommodate the new nonstate actors (Stokes and Choate 2001).

Europe faces the difficulty of defining a negotiating position acceptable to its members. Trade policy is within the competence of the EU and thus is an integral part of the "first pillar" and hence subject to the institutional processes of decision making involving the European Commission and the Council of Ministers. The European Commission has the responsibility for negotiating trade agreements, subject to a mandate from the Council of Ministers. The European negotiation process, based on an "Article 133 Committee" of trade representatives of the member nations, is even more obscure than its U.S. analogue and, at least in the judgment of some critics, became still more opaque with the reforms that were proposed in the 2000 Nice summit of the European leaders and entered in force in 2002.[4]

As the negotiating decisions are effectively made by representatives from member state governments in the Council of Ministers, they are subject to internal horse-trading. Trade decisions can be held up until domestic (EU) arguments are settled. Thus the "two-level game" of domestic and trade policy becomes a "three-level game" with the EU level intervening (Patterson 1997).[5] More importantly, there is no general European constitutional requirement for either national or European parliamentary ratification of the trade agreements; hence, although there is a practice of consultation with the European Parliament, and national governments may need to vote on implementation measures, there is only a weak analogue to the congressional vote under fast track. Countries have tended to resist the involvement of the parliament: although it would enhance legitimacy and improve transparency, it would also make deals more difficult to conclude.

7.4. Representation at the WTO: The Legislative Process

Business and NGOs normally engage the WTO legislative process primarily through attempting to affect initial national (and EU) bargaining positions. Thus, their primary lobbying focus is on trade representatives and on any legislation that authorizes negotiations. For example, the Trade Act of 2002 reflected extensive congressional discussion attempting to shape the USTR's negotiating position on such issues as the environment, labor, and intellectual property.

These interest groups also lobby at the international negotiations, but as outsiders seeking to affect an inside, nation-to-nation negotiation. One form of lobbying is aimed primarily at affecting public opinion in order to encourage consideration of desired positions. Thus, the U.S. and European intellectual-property-based industries have expended great effort to obtain global support for their views that certain kinds of copying of goods, inventions, and creative expression should be globally condemned, not just in the United States. Their hope is to make it easier for the negotiators to reach the positions the industries desire; they may be concerned about many other negotiations as well as those conducted under the WTO umbrella.

Clearly, access to negotiators is also an important part of the lobbying process and is sought by both business and NGO interests. The extent of access depends on both the interest and the specific negotiator, as well as on the country involved. In some cases business or NGO interests produce drafts of proposed agreement terms; in others, they may suggest changes in proposed language; in still others, they may urge acceptance or rejection of a specific proposal. Business and NGOs may also be particularly well suited to providing certain types of information and ideas otherwise unavailable to WTO negotiators. The success of these efforts depends on the political importance of the particular community to the particular negotiator, as well as on the ability of negotiators or lobbyists to build a coalition around the positions they support. It has been argued that in some international contexts, the NGOs have, relative to business, more power than in domestic consultations (Kellow 2002).

This process interacts in a complex way with the secrecy typical of WTO negotiations. The more open the process, one might assume, the greater the likelihood of public "buy-in" to the result. And openness makes it possible to find ways to modify agreements in minor ways to respond to a group's concern and make the overall package more broadly acceptable. Further, it is clear that negotiations are, in reality, rather open—a person interested in the negotiations on a particular issue can readily learn the positions of the major nations. What is not easy to learn is the likely outcome of the horse trading that will be conducted in secret by major actors.

At the same time, uncertainty about the contents of international negotiating texts can be valuable to negotiators in forestalling the mobilization of domestic interests until trade round packages are complete (Koremenos 2002). Increased transparency would diminish that uncertainty, mobilizing domestic political battles before conclusion of the agreement. For psychological and economic reasons, groups losing trade protection as a result of liberalization are more likely to mobilize in opposition to an agreement than groups gaining export markets are likely to mobilize in support (Goldstein and Martin 2000). For example, when GATS requests (but not offers) were leaked to NGOs in April 2002, environmental NGOs protested vehemently against the content of the requests and the GATS liberalization exercise (Bridges 2002a). Hence, transparency can precipitate decisive, organized opposition to a trade agreement earlier than otherwise—even if the final agreement is a net benefit to the country as a whole.

7.5. Representation at the WTO: The Judicial Process

Whether a nation initiates WTO dispute settlement proceedings may be a highly lobbied decision—an example in the United States is the 2003 decision to initiate dispute settlement over European actions with respect to genetically modified foods, an action long sought by U.S. agricultural and biotechnology interests. Once the proceeding is initiated, direct participation by business and NGOs in the WTO's judicial process is much more limited.

Although business may complain about particular decisions, it is NGOs who have most strongly criticized the WTO panel decision process. They view it as secretive and expert-dominated rather than as open and participatory. Indeed, their criticism may reflect a trend in the national and regional regulatory processes in both the United States and Europe. In the past, domestic regulatory decisions were delegated to expert agencies with the expectation that the experts would make a decision, certainly after a hearing (at least in the United States), but with primary reliance on their own expertise. Today, the issues are now delegated to agencies with the expectation that the decision making will include participation by all, including both industry and NGOs. The expert agencies may make a decision in the face of deadlock, but the preference is for negotiation. Expertise is being replaced by representation and negotiation. WTO dispute settlement panels perform a judicial function that differs in important ways from the functions of domestic agencies, which are largely administrative or quasi-legislative. Nonetheless, some complain that panels operate in an expert fashion, with the decisions made by trade experts, who have the possibility of consulting scientific experts, such as those called in the beef hormone case. And the proceedings are closed. While this is judicial, this process is similar to the older expert-oriented regulatory pattern.

The factors affecting change differ in the judicial context from the legislative context: there are better reasons to favor direct outsider participation in the judicial process. First, the role of information is different. Information is crucial to the proper operation of enforcement and dispute settlement functions. NGOs may offer a "fire alarm" approach to information generation for the dispute settlement process that may complement a state-centric "police patrol" approach (McCubbins and Schwartz 1984; Raustiala 2002). NGOs may be better than states at generating certain types of information. Second, organizing by NGOs that unravels a potential logrolled output would be rarely problematic in the judicial process, which takes place after legislative politics have been concluded. Third, although the GATT dispute settlement system benefited from secrecy, which allowed negotiators and lawyers to frankly recommend solutions to panelists that might be politically acceptable yet not legally elegant or robust, the WTO dispute settlement process is so legalized and cases are so deeply lawyered that legal accuracy and robustness are central and the political functions once served by secrecy are now far less relevant (Roh 2002). For these reasons, and because of the legitimating effects of increased transparency, EC and U.S. negotiators have supported measured, increased transparency in the WTO judicial process.

Nonetheless, parts of the dispute settlement process still benefit from secrecy. In consultations between members, there is a value to maintaining secrecy so that the parties can be free to brainstorm and consider settlement alternatives, without worrying that the nascent alternatives will be leaked, taken out of context, mischaracterized, or only partly revealed to the public in a way that emphasizes shortcomings. Moreover, insofar as settlement discussions involve a package of solutions, transparency would subject settlement negotiations to the same risks of premature opposition and unraveling that exist in the legislative context.

During the phase of formal proceedings, there is also a value to limits on transparency. The national political acceptability of dispute settlement decisions is enhanced to the extent that member disputants have a venue for communicating to panelists and the Appellate Body without the presence of nonstate actors. For example, member disputants have in the past suggested to panels and the Appellate Body alternative legal formulations likely to be acceptable in domestic politics. Similarly, just as NGO end-runs around the position of powerful governments are unproductive and politically damaging in the legislative context, these end-runs would be damaging and politically counterproductive in the judicial context.[6]

The WTO has embraced one institutional innovation that has yielded the benefits of greater NGO involvement in the dispute settlement process, without diminishing secrecy in contexts in which secrecy is important. The right of a panel to consider *amicus curiae* submissions by NGOs, which was established in the *U.S.—Shrimp-Turtle* Appellate Body decision, creates an avenue along which important information and ideas might be conveyed to panels and the Appellate Body. That decision made clear that panels may (but are not required to) accept amicus submissions, providing leeway for panels to reject amicus briefs or arguments in politically sensitive contexts, such as efforts by NGOs to end-run government positions they dislike.

7.6. Conclusions

The most important procedural questions raised by the role of business and of new nonstate actors are these: how national institutions of trade policymaking should ensure that the various nonstate actors have adequate opportunities for participation and contestation in domestic trade politics; and how WTO institutions should change to ensure that the same actors have an opportunity to provide relevant information and ideas in ways that do not undermine the effective operation of those institutions. If the new nonstate actors are unable to participate in revamped domestic political processes of trade policymaking, particularly in countries like the United States where they are an active political force, they will spill into the streets. In addition, ideational, informational, and legitimacy benefits could be reaped from the indirect participation of NGOs in the WTO legislative process and from their more direct participation in the dispute settlement process.

Developing-country negotiators have, however, tended to argue against more direct NGO participation in part because their countries lack active, indigenous NGOs and in part because they perceive active NGOs as representing interests rooted in Western, advanced, industrialized countries. This position may be changing in some areas, as a result of the successful coalitions between NGOs and developing countries that have emerged around TRIPS and medical policies. Even so, it is still difficult for the WTO to accept greater external transparency, even in the dispute settlement system, and the EC and U.S. governments would likely have to "pay" for further external transparency with commercial concessions to the developing countries.

Ultimately, procedural changes alone will not be enough. These new actors have identified substantive trade-related issues as important policy priorities. The persistence of these new actors since 1990 suggests that they will not disappear from trade politics in Europe and the United States anytime soon. If anything, as trade barriers fall further, international environmental and labor issues, along with human rights, will become even more salient to these NGOs. If the domestic political consensus favoring trade liberalization is to be reestablished and sustained in Europe and the United States, then substantive changes to WTO rules will have to be made to accommodate, at least in part, the interests of the new nonstate actors.

Notes

1. These cases were *United States—Restrictions on Imports of Tuna*, August 16, 1991 (WTO 1991), and United States—*Restrictions on Imports of Tuna*, June 16, 1994 (WTO 1994). Neither panel report was adopted.

2. The Indian challenge actually specified the "Drug Arrangements" of the EU's GSP, which had been extended to Pakistan but not India, thus raising the issue as to whether the scheme was consistent with the Enabling Clause and its requirements of nondiscrimination. The panel agreed that the EU's GSP was deficient, and the main findings were upheld on appeal (though with the justification somewhat modified). It remains to be seen whether this will lead to a gradual shift in the GSP schemes operated by other countries.

3. Including NGOs in WTO decisions does not, however, solve the democratic deficit if these organizations themselves are unelected and unaccountable.

4. As the scope of trade rules expanded, as described in chapter 5, the appropriate range of EU and national competence became blurred. Service trade negotiations, for instance, influenced national regulatory decisions. After the Uruguay Round a judgment in the European Court of Justice was needed to clarify who could ratify the agreement. The Nice Treaty clarified somewhat the ECJ decision, but still left "shared competencies" in certain areas of trade (Woolcock 2000).

5. This is most noticeable in contentious areas of EU policy such as agriculture, where the debates about trade negotiations often occur at the same time as debates about CAP reform (Coleman and Tangermann 1999).

6. A May 2002 amicus brief submitted by indigenous tribes in a Canadian-U.S. softwood lumber dispute exemplifies this risk. The indigenous tribes claimed that the Canadian government was effectively subsidizing its lumber industry by failing to have adequately compensated the tribes for forestland seized by the government. The brief effectively challenged the WTO panel to penalize the Canadian government for a domestic political decision that was taken for reasons unrelated to trade. Neither party to the dispute—Canada nor the United States—would want the panel to accept the argument made in the amicus brief because doing so would upset delicate domestic political decisions that are essentially unrelated to trade (Bridges 2002b).

Eight

Conclusions

The vast increase in the cross-national movement of goods and services in the years following World War II was both a cause and a manifestation of the globalization of the world economy. This increase in trade dwarfs that which occurred a century earlier and represents a new era in which production and commerce became intricately intertwined. To explain this phenomenon, analysts have looked at innovations in transportation, communication, and productive techniques; as important, however, is the change in national policy that accompanied these technological changes. The ability and willingness of governments to open borders to goods and services produced outside their polity is the political phenomenon discussed in the preceding pages. We argue that this policy shift could not have occurred in the absence of the GATT/WTO. The organization facilitated liberalization by fostering the creation of pro-free-trade coalitions and by increasing the costs of *ex post* opportunistic and nationalistic behavior.

We offer four observations as way of conclusion. First, we examine the extent to which our analysis of the trade regime is consistent with that suggested by the literature on international cooperation. We suggest that the functions we assume necessary to generate cooperation in trade were present—the organization undermined information asymmetries, thereby allowing countries to worry less about ex post cheating by trading partners. The result was a willingness to enter into beneficial trade agreements. Going further, however, we suggest that the organization's ability to get countries to the negotiating table was as much, or more, a result of power politics as it was due to the interest of nations in striking efficient trade deals. Trade cooperation occurred not apart from, but in the shadow of, power politics.

We next look at the extent to which the transition in 1995 from the GATT to the WTO was a fundamental reform of the trade regime. Although the WTO is a new legal entity, and re-equilibrated the balance of substantive undertakings with the underlying power relations, our study confirms March and Olsen's contention that "efforts to reform political institutions are often unsuccessful in accomplishing precisely what was intended" (1989, 53). Built on top of the GATT structure, the WTO is an example not of revolutionary but evolutionary change. The transformation, however, has had a number of unintended effects, often making it more difficult to generate cooperative trade agreements than during its GATT days.

Third, we examine the issue of delegation in international trade politics. Given the rapid growth of membership in the WTO, with an accompanying variation in members' preferences, we would expect nations to find it increasingly convenient to delegate power to the center. This has not occurred in the GATT/WTO. Rather, members neither grant the secretariat nor the elected director-general autonomous power. Such a lack of delegation, an interesting anomaly, exists because it serves the interests of the powerful members.

Last, we ask how analysts should assess the success of an international organization. The international community is littered with international treaties, institutions, and organizations. Most analysts argue that the trade regime has been as successful as any of the other postwar institutions. Did the GATT/WTO have its intended effects on trade flows? We suggest that the GATT/WTO was successful on two dimensions. First, the organization led to an increase in trade, a result of both a reduction in tariff and nontariff barriers of members and the diffusion worldwide of trade-expanding agreements. Second, the organization made it difficult for nations to "backslide" during hard economic times. By agreeing to a set of rules of conduct and specific procedures for when and how a country can renegotiate an agreement, members undermined the political volatility of their own trade policies, creating a predictable market for commerce.

8.1. Is Trade Politics "Low" Politics?

In the 1970s, it was still common to think about economic interactions as "low" politics and security politics as "high" politics. In one case, decision makers sought to solve collective problems through diplomacy; in the other, politics occurred in the shadow of force. The distinction, however, made less and less analytic sense over time (Keohane and Nye 1977). Trade and monetary politics were subject to the same "power politics" as were security issues, even if countries rarely threatened military action when diplomacy failed. Throughout this study we found international economic cooperation to operate in the shadow of power politics—trade cooperation has been part of, and not apart from, the underlying power relationships among participating countries. From the creation of the GATT through its rebirth as the WTO, the choice of international rules and the procedures by which those rules were incorporated into policy reflected the interests of the larger economies.

Considerations of power, however, sit uncomfortably with the conventional understanding of trade politics. Cooperation in the trade regime is based on the premise of mutually beneficial exchange, made possible through lowering transaction costs and alleviating sources of market failures, especially those due to information asymmetries. This "liberal" logic, associated with Robert Keohane's pathbreaking book *After Hegemony*, suggests a lesser role for power relations in the trade regime. Although a hegemonic nation may be more willing than others to provide the resources necessary for regime creation, power itself is rarely assumed a factor in the liberal view of market exchange. The regime is a collective good, which explains its vast increase in membership over time.

Our study suggests that power asymmetries cannot be ignored. As Lloyd Gruber has argued, nations may be better off in the regime once the GATT/WTO is created, but they may have been best off in a world absent this international institution (Gruber 2000). Developing nations comply with the rules of the WTO not out of enlightenment, but because the regime has changed their choice set. They can join and be subject to rules not of their choosing or stay out and be precluded from opportunity for economic gain. Power is always present. Still, while our study confirms that trade agreements were made in the shadow of power, it is less clear that a simple division between the "winners" who created the regime and the "losers" who are forced to comply with rules not of their choosing is a helpful distinction.

On a fundamental level, this study reinforces an explanation for trade policy as part of, and not distinct from, politics. Repeatedly, our explanation for the structure of the organization and the behavior of members relies on an understanding of the preferences of those who have market power. Although the voting rules suggest a principle of national equality, all decisions were made in the light of actual trade flows. In the immediate aftermath of World War II, this gave the United States overwhelming advantage. As Japan and West Germany recovered from World War II and became increasingly important trading partners, their power in the regime increased. The creation of the EEC and eventually the expanded EU created a market akin to that of the United States, granting the Community increased voice.

The importance of U.S. power in the constitution of the trade regime cannot be overstressed. Although it is true that the regime facilitated cooperation by lowering transaction costs and alleviating information asymmetries among all members, as argued in chapter 2, the manner in which the regime chose to address these problems reflected America's history with bilateral trade treaties more than the conference that drew up the ITO charter. The reconstitution of the regime into the WTO, the single undertaking, the expansion of the regime to regulatory issues, and the empowerment of the dispute settlement system would not have occurred without U.S. guidance and support. Similarly, the timing of trade rounds as well as their depth and breadth cannot be explained without reference to political events within the United States. In the history of the regime, the United States is one without equals.

Establishing the importance of American consent to any trade innovation does not mean that in any simple sense, the regime responded to changes in American interests. Over time, the United States has found less support for the ideas that it brought to the table. Opposition has not only come from a new and coherent Europe but also from a better-organized developing world. In general, the United States has had a more and more difficult time controlling the regime's agenda. The battle that occurred over the director-general position in 1999 indicates the deep divisions in the organization, both between the United States and Europe but also between the developed and developing world. Given that the term of the director-general was fungible, a compromise was reached, splitting the term of office between the two candidates. Not all issues on the agenda can be resolved in this manner—King Solomon would have found it impossible to overcome the stalemate that occurred at the Cancún ministerial meeting in 2003. The United States could neither motivate Europe to agree to give up agricultural export subsidies nor command support from the developing world on any further entry into their markets. The ability to craft particularistic solutions to American trade problems has eluded America's negotiating team, as indicated in chapter 5, even in areas of great interest such as genetically modified products.

Uneven economic wealth among members, juxtaposed with a rule system that grants each country one vote, has made decision making within the regime a difficult task. Although power relations are evident throughout our study in examples from principal supplier bargaining to invitations to the "Green Room," they have not always been decisive. Both the weak and the strong adhere to the rules of the regime, not out of fear of punishment, but because predictable rules and accessible markets serve their interests. The extent to which the more powerful are willing to be "bound" by the will of the majority depends on what interests, domestic and international, are served by such policies.

Most obvious from this study is that market opening is a political act, reaching deeply into the fabric of societies. Finding a coalition in support of trade openness is often difficult; maintaining open borders during hard economic times is a challenge for all elected officials. Underlying any view of power politics among nations must be a more disaggregated view of who wins and loses within each nation. Power relations are not just reserved for the negotiating table but, as centrally, are found in the ability of leaders to forge protrade alliances at home.

8.2. What Is New about the WTO?

Looking at the spate of contemporary critiques of the trade regime, it would seem that the trade regime had been radically transformed in 1995 with its more legalized form granting new power to constrain nations. Our investigation cannot corroborate this perspective; rather, we find far more continuity than change in the regime over time. The differences between the GATT and WTO are limited. As in its early days, the organization remains a loose contract signed by almost 150 nations that facilitates bargaining among members. In practice, these agreements are successful to the extent that they are self-enforcing. The heart of the organization remains its ability to facilitate mutually advantageous economic bargains, not its ability to punish cheaters, akin to domestic courts. The changes in the organization were evolutionary, not fundamental, layering often-contradictory rules on top of a normative structure created in response to problems facing the trading system in the years after World War II.

The expansion of the organization occurred in two areas. First, as detailed in earlier chapters, the WTO includes a significant number of agreements that were not part of the GATT and that challenge long-standing norms. The original organization valued flexibility--nations were obligated to follow the rules only to the extent politically feasible. The result was a myriad of obligations, not all of which were common to all members. The WTO embraces a more conventional understanding of compliance. Where the GATT agreements were voluntary, signing onto the WTO obligated nations to agreements that they did not participate in creating. Second, a shift occurred in the vision of the scope of the organization's regulatory purview. The GATT regulated trade at the border. The WTO's range is far broader, and the arena of trade regulation now includes its micro-foundations, whether in the arena of labor, environmental, or production standards.

These changes are illustrated in earlier chapters through the examination of three aspects of the post-1995 regime. First, the WTO is a *single undertaking*, meaning that almost all rules apply to all members. While the GATT allowed countries to sign on to new agreements only if they found it politically feasible to be obligated by the new rule, the WTO eschewed this flexibility in favor of more even application of rules across all members. Second, the organization created a more formal judiciary and an Appellate Body with implications for the development of a "common law" on international trade. While the GATT used dispute settlement as a means to convince nations that compliance was in their "enlightened self interest," the new system does not allow nations to veto a finding when politically inconvenient. The result is a system that encourages punishment, whether through retaliation or through an expansive judicial process. Finally, in particular, by incorporating the TRIPS agreement into the WTO, the organization changed its domain from issues at the border, such as tariffs and quotas, to issues of the production of the good that is traded. It is not that regulatory issues were avoided in earlier years—a number of agreements, including subjects as broad as intellectual property rights and environmental production controls, had been discussed and regulated. What occurred with the TRIPS agreement that distinguishes the WTO from the earlier GATT is that the organization no longer considers regulatory policies as an adjunct to a larger concern about border trade barriers. "Behind the border" issues are now within the realm of the WTO's jurisdiction.

The WTO, with its broader agenda and expanded dispute settlement system, is a hybrid institution—it has a new mandate but retains the fundamental structures of the GATT years. The GATT was created to encourage nations to adhere to basic principles in their trading relations. Trade was to be nondiscriminatory. When a subset of nations concluded a bilateral liberalization agreement, all nations benefited. Of course, nations understood this merely as a principle—exceptions were contemplated from the start, both in the form of regional trading areas and more favorable access for developing countries. Even so, the principle of nondiscrimination, enshrined in MFN agreements, diffused rapidly throughout the trading world. The principle of nondiscrimination was adopted by the new structure to the expanded set of trade policies. However, the practice of nondiscrimination remains problematic, as evidenced by the vast increase in the number of preferential trading agreements in the decade following the WTO's creation and the growing realization that the developing world will not be able to comply with regulations in a timely manner.

As well as discouraging discrimination, the trade regime encouraged nations to adopt more liberal, open trade policies. The GATT encouraged liberalization by organizing trade rounds in which countries bargained for mutual access to each other's markets. Open borders, however, was never a prerequisite for membership. Except at time of accession, no country was forced to participate in a tariff round, and the expectation of reciprocity in return for tariff reductions never extended to the developing world. The GATT was less a "liberal" organization than a regime attempting to regularize expectations about the trade policies of other nations. Much of the actual GATT text was an attempt to make explicit when exceptions to trade rules were allowable and what sets of policies were inconsistent with membership. A range of discriminatory practices, ranging from dumping to export subsidization, was regulated, not precluded. The WTO is a far more "liberal" trade organization, demanding deep concessions from members upon accession and requiring all members to agree to far-reaching rules of conduct, even when there is little chance that the rules will be followed.

What explains the restructuring of the GATT into the WTO, a more legalized and expansive institution? The simple answer is that the expansion was in the interest of powerful participants. The United States and the European Union have benefited greatly from the international trading regime created by the WTO. It is not only a source of their economic strength; it is also a mechanism to help them achieve their national policy goals, including the strengthening of intellectual property systems protecting their products and the opening of markets for their exporters of goods and services. This is not to say that benefits are not shared, for a group of developing nations have also grown rapidly and effectively during this period; it is rather to say that the growth in trade has been of the form desired by the powerful nations.

In part, the more developed countries' policies were influenced by fundamental changes in production patterns, leading to pressures to expand what could be "horse-traded" at the bargaining table. Save for the Council of the European Union, and perhaps for the summits of the G-7 and G-8, there are few other international negotiating forums in which a cross-sector trade-off can be negotiated. Intellectual property can be traded against agricultural and textile trade—something feasible nowhere else in the international system. TRIPS could not have been negotiated in the World Intellectual Property Organization, nor could agricultural subsidy reform have been negotiated in the Food and Agricultural Organization.

In addition to seeing their interests served by expanding the purview of the trade regime, the larger trading nations assumed they would benefit from a more effective dispute settlement system. The major trading nations—United States, EU, Canada, and Japan—all agreed to reform the dispute settlement system in the late 1980s. Each believed it would benefit from the judicial system, seeing itself more often in compliance with trading rules than its trading partners. The WTO's dispute settlement process is, by far, the most used and most effective international dispute settlement process. Although it is natural that some of its decisions and processes are criticized, few would say that it is not a basically fair process or that there has been corruption. The system uses high-quality decision-makers, has the power to enforce a significant and specific body of international law, and has control over a trade sanction that seems to be of just the right strength both to be politically acceptable and to generally induce compliance. This has encouraged the international community to place more and more issues under the WTO. An efficient judicial system, however, was never a concern for the founders of the GATT. Politics often precludes "justice" when it comes to domestic matters that relate to jobs and electoral support. While the legal experts who wrote the DSU paid close attention to rules and compliance, the GATT's founders set their sights on domestic constraints and local politics.

The WTO was created as a result of a confluence of interests and power. Areas like intellectual property and trade in services entered because the United States and Europe favored them. The GATT/WTO decision-making process was reformed and expanded because all parties believed that they, as opposed to their trading partners, had policies consistent with regime rules. Perhaps most fundamentally, the expansion of the rules to all members was an outgrowth of the expansion of the trading agenda. New issues reflected new production patterns and required "horse trading," not only between developed nations but also among all members.

8.3. An International Bureaucracy

Although members of the secretariat are quick to say that the organization is member driven, the professional bureaucracy has played a key role in the trade regime. Analysts should not be surprised to note the importance of the secretariat. All complex organizations require some degree of delegation to "agents." Agency relationships are pervasive in modern society, and although principals may attempt to control the behavior of these actors, such controls are always imperfect. "Given information asymmetries, agents typically know more about their task than their principals do" (Pratt and Zechhauser 1984, 3). Knowing this, principals attempt to monitor their agents.

In the context of the trade regime, the fear of agents' autonomy has led members to keep the bureaucracy far smaller and less well funded than any other international organization of comparable importance. The secretariat at the GATT/WTO has been granted limited independence from the membership, and the director-general, elected by the members, is granted little real authority. The members fear that autonomy might lead the organization to promote policies inconsistent with political pressures at home, a problem of particular importance for the relatively more powerful nations participating in the regime. As a result, the members of the secretariat rarely chair committees, and the growth in the number of professionals, as opposed to support staff, has been far less than expected, given the rapid increase in membership. Still, logic suggests that the growth of the organization and its increasing complexity should grant the secretariat authority, even given these constraints. Our review suggests a number of ways in which the secretariat influences outcomes, although it would be difficult to characterize this role as an example of "agency slack."

First, the secretariat is the keeper of information. It collects and disseminates data provided by members to others in the organization; members responded to the need to upgrade data systems in the late 1970s to facilitate tariff rounds by moving data collection to the center of the organization. The benefit was a significant expansion of common knowledge about trade flows and the status of trade restrictions.

Second, the secretariat plays a key role in dispute settlement. Even though members have refused to allow cases to be based on formal precedent, the secretariat assures the intellectual continuity of panel decisions. Even with no formal legal role, members of the secretariat influence decisions, through advice to panel participants and informal recommendations on written reports. The effect has been generally consistent panel reports and far fewer decisions that are politically difficult to administer. The secretariat is the collective memory of the organization—understanding the political pressures of members, it mediates the dispute process and tries to assure that decisions resonate with political realities.

Third, the secretariat provides support for small developing nations. The regime provides training for government officials on interpretation of rules and compliance with them. Training sessions both transfer information and socialize trade officials of new members to support the underlying purposes of the regime. Past employees of the secretariat advise developing countries on a range of activities, from dispute panel processes, to the collection of appropriate information for trade talks, to proposals to increase their voice in the organization. While the larger nations can rely on expertise at home, smaller and developing economies rely more extensively on the secretariat for support.

While the first directors-general were selected because of their expertise as international civil servants, the most recent appointees have political rather than technical backgrounds. The lack of expertise at the top of the organization, either in economics or in international law, has created a widening division between the professional staff and the political leadership. Needing to rely upon the permanent staff for support, the relationship between the Office of the Director-General and the civil service has become increasingly strained. This is not to suggest that power resides in the director-general's office. He and his staff are as constrained by the membership as is the secretariat. Still, the relationship between the professional staff and the director-general's office has evolved with changes in the organization. Where the early secretariat saw the director-general as its representative to the membership, the more politicized relationship of recent years has led the secretariat to view the director-general's office as pursuing interests often at odds with the policies being promoted by the professional staff.

The mantra among the staff and the members of the WTO is that the organization is "member driven;" the reality of a complex organization supported by an educated and sophisticated staff is not entirely consistent with this image. Institutional change has had unanticipated effects on the organization. "Concurrent intentional changes of prima facie intelligence may combine to produce joint outcomes that are not intended by anyone and are directly counter to the interests motivating the individual actions" (March and Olsen 1989, 57). Given that the rules of the WTO became more complex and inclusive, some agent had to be entrusted with the job of both interpretation and monitoring of compliance. Unintentionally, the role of the secretariat has expanded, even as the membership attempts to keep the bureaucracy in a subservient role and as the director-general has become more a political position and less one entrusted to an individual with trade expertise.

8.4. Measuring Success

Among analysts of international institutions, the GATT/WTO is the most often cited as the premier example of successful international cooperation. The proof of the claim is found in the organization's longevity, its ability to reinvent itself in 1995, and the vast increase in membership. However, few social scientists have attempted to measure its success against the standard set for itself in the preamble to the GATT, that is, to increase commerce by having nations enter "into reciprocal and mutually advantageous arrangements directed to the substantial reduction of tariffs and other barriers to trade" (Article I). Has the trade regime really increased trade among participants? One of the first large-scale statistical analyses of trade patterns, conducted by Andrew Rose in the *American Economic Review* (2004), suggests that the answer is "no." Rose finds no evidence that membership in the organization increases trade—in fact, some of his findings suggest that nations who were not members may have had a larger increase in their trade than did members.

Our analysis suggests the opposite conclusion. Compared to other post–World War II international institutions, the GATT/WTO remains the most successful. This success must be understood not only by an economist's metric of trade openness but also by the ability of the organization to do two things. First, trade agreements have been honored, even in the face of economic downturns. The GATT/WTO was created to stop "backsliding," not just to assure free trade. Second, the GATT/WTO has created a set of both normative and "legal" standards for international trade that has diffused widely throughout the globe. The trade regime can be viewed as having created a "focal point" on trade policy that members and non-members alike find convenient to follow. The scope of shared understandings about the role of politics in trade is far broader today than at the time of the organization's creation. Although states may not have chosen to pursue unconditional free trade, they are far less likely to think intervention in the market is legitimate. It is this understanding of what is and is not legitimate, not necessarily consistent behavior, that is a key metric of the success of the institution.

Still, it is important to examine the basis of Rose's findings, cited extensively in the press (*Economist*, November 21, 2002; *Financial Times*, November 7, 2002). Although well argued and analyzed, Rose's data reveals a key problem with analyses that do not pay close attention to the institutional details of an organization. In order to assess the effects of the GATT/WTO, we must look at the trade patterns of all participants, not just the formal members. As we explain in an earlier chapter, the regime's membership included countries not on the membership list but who adhered to the rules of the organization and granted and were given MFN status. When a colonial power, such as England, France, or Portugal, entered the GATT, all of its colonies were also participants. When these countries became independent, they obtained de facto membership. When they joined, they did not go through an accession process akin to that of other new members but were granted membership based on the tariff schedules used in the past. When we measure trade of these participants as well as formal members, the data suggests that the GATT/WTO has, in fact, increased trade among members dramatically (Goldstein, Rivers, and Tomz 2005). Rose failed to include these countries in his study, assuming participation began only on the date listed on the WTO website.

This is not to argue that the GATT/WTO has eradicated all trade barriers. Although the regime facilitated the lowering of many tariff and nontariff barriers, the benefits were uneven. In certain sectors, especially those that rely on labor-intensive production measures, barriers to trade remain high. Similarly, almost all trade in agricultural products is constrained, a significant problem for the developing world. We have argued throughout this book that the organization's purposes were more regulatory than liberal: although the organization attempted to open up markets, as important, or more important, was the creation of rules of conduct that would allow predictability. The lesson of the Great Depression was not only that high barriers to trade lead to economic misfortune but also that unregulated policies lead decision makers to turn to trade barriers to solve domestic ailments. The GATT/WTO did not open up all borders to trade, but it did remove tariff hikes from the tool kit of leaders in member countries. The GATT/WTO has made trade more predictable, even if not truly free.

8.5. In Conclusion: Trade Relations in the Twenty-first Century

Given the structure of the WTO, can it remain a viable vehicle for the regulation of world trade? As noted in chapter 3, the dispute settlement system is making decisions that evoke strong political responses in both

Europe and the United States. As seen in chapters 4 and 5, the principles of the WTO now reach areas of commerce, such as product standards and agricultural subsidies, where the traditional assumptions of reciprocal benefit may no longer hold. And as seen in chapter 7, as membership has expanded, a more diverse set of interests must be reconciled at the negotiating table. What was created as a small club of developed-world traders has now become an organization of diverse negotiators dealing with highly technical, complex, and sensitive issues. The old club style of GATT is gone. The issues are no longer just the domain of governments, but are now subject to the influence of NGOs working to shape national policies and the international negotiations themselves. The trade ministries that once managed GATT negotiations are now working in a much more complex political matrix. All these factors have combined so that governments have relatively little political flexibility in facing the issues now in dispute in the international trade system.

In this century, the organization will face an increasingly complex trading environment that will make it difficult to craft politically acceptable deals. To survive, the organization must face three challenges. First, the organization must find coalitions of supporters within member states. This will be difficult. The coalition structure that marked the earlier years of the GATT is gone. The success of free trade in areas like electronics derived from the support of industries that found openness a convenience, allowing them to exploit economies of scale by reorganizing themselves on a global level during the last part of the twentieth century. Confronted by international competition and outsourcing, both blue- and white-collar workers in these sectors have become increasingly wary of globalization. In their place, the new service industries such as banking and telecommunications, again seeking global economies of scale, have become the backbone of the contemporary free-trade coalition. Finding support for their position, however, has become increasingly difficult. National producers in the developed world often find it difficult to compete with foreign firms; when industry responds by moving production abroad, the move engenders antiglobalization sentiment among labor. In many developed countries a "Baptist-bootlegger" coalition of the Right and the Left—nationalists, labor, and environmentalists—has created new and powerful veto players in the political arena, making it difficult to find any majority that supports new trade initiatives.

Second, the expansion of the trade agenda may make it impossible to craft majority support among the membership for any new policy initiative. New areas of regulation, such as antitrust, are likely to be seen as threats to—rather than benefits to—some of the industries that are interested in global trade, while environmental issues are unlikely to be appealing to some of the industries that have classically supported the GATT/

WTO. Many of the new topics now central to trade, such as intellectual property, antidumping, and environmental protection, involve systematic differences between the interests of developed and developing nations. It is the developing world that is being forced to change its practices to comply with standards in the developed world, even as its membership in the organization increases dramatically. Tensions exist not only between countries at different levels of development but within the developed world, as evidenced by the disputes over beef-hormones and bananas.

Finally, we must consider challenges to multilateralism. Countries will make choices in the twenty-first century. They can participate in a universal organization that attempts to create common standards and practices, or they can choose smaller, often regional, trading institutions. Regionalism arises from a variety of factors, including the ability to be more open to trade than is feasibly negotiated at the global level. Such agreements can increase trade, and trade diversion may be small compared to the amount of trade growth. In addition, the mechanisms of opening developed at the regional level may provide experience useful in similar opening at the global level. But there are risks, and regionalism may well undermine the global trade regime. Every preferential or regional arrangement contradicts the MFN principle, and one of the fundamental benefits of MFN is that it makes economic access to markets a less effective tool with which to seek broader political concessions.

Our review suggests that the impetus for regional arrangements may be found in the WTO itself. The notion of universal rules may be too utopian. It is nearly impossible to imagine that even with time, nations will move toward identical trade structures, given the vast differences in legal and political traditions. The organization can choose to look aside, reinstitute a multispeed approach, or negotiate special treatment within common rules. The alternative of using dispute settlement or other means to force compliance may prove counterproductive, pushing the South into more politically viable regional arrangements. Yet for the South to eschew universalism is shortsighted—the acceptance of WTO agreements provides greater access to investment and markets, increases the visibility and importance of the South, and provides a basis for future North-South negotiation. Further, in some areas, regionalism makes little sense; it is hard to envision ways for nations to opt out of agreements regulating product or environmental standards without undercutting the possibility of global economies of scale.

Trade liberalization depends upon the WTO being viewed as a legitimate agent. At the heart of its legitimacy problem is that many old assumptions about the role of the trade regime no longer fit. It was once oriented toward free trade—and thus gained the legitimacy of serving a goal known to be globally beneficial. But as it entered into other areas, it became a rule-oriented institution—and therefore needed a new form of legitimacy, since there are politically significant trade-offs involved in writing rules, and it can no longer be assumed that the rules are mutually beneficial. The organization now seeks a more development-oriented goal, but that vision is still inchoate. The WTO as an institution has become one of the centerpieces of the international economic order—and that order is changing rapidly. The WTO must respond to these changes to maintain its relevance.

Bibliography

Abbott, Kenneth W., Robert O. Keohane, Andrew Moravcsik, Anne-Marie Slaughter, and Duncan Snidal. 2000. "The Concept of Legalization." *International Organization*. 54:401.

African Group. 2002. "Negotiations on the Dispute Settlement Understanding, Proposal of the Africa Group in the WTO." October. (On file with authors.)

Alt, James, and Michael Gilligan. 1994. "Survey Article: The Political Economy of Trading States: Factor Specificity, Collective Action Problems and Domestic Political Institutions." *Journal of Political Philosophy* 2:165.

Alter, Karen J. 2000. "The European Union's Legal System and Domestic Policy: Spillover or Backlash?" *International Organization* 54:489.

Atik, Jeffery. 2001. "Democratizing the WTO." *George Washington Internation Law Review* 33:451.

Bagwell, Kyle, and Robert W. Staiger. 2002. *The Economics of the World Trading System*. Cambridge: MIT Press.

Bailey, Michael A., Judith Goldstein, and Barry R. Weingast. 1997. "The Origins of American Trade Policy: Rules, Coalitions, and International Politics." *World Politics* 49:309–38.

Baldwin, Richard E. 1995. "A Domino Theory of Regionalism." In Richard Baldwin, Pertti Haaparanta, and Jaakko Kiander, eds. *Expanding Membership of the European Union*. Cambridge: Cambridge University Press. 25–48.

Barfield, Claude. 2001. *Free Trade, Sovereignty, Democracy: The Future of the World Trade Organization*. Washington, D.C.: AEI Press.

Barton, John H. 2001. "The Economics of TRIPS: International Trade in Information-Intensive Products." *George Washington International Law Review* 33:473.

Bauer, Raymond A., Ithiel de Sola Pool, and Lewis Anthony Dexter. 1963. *American Business and Public Policy: The Politics of Foreign Trade*. New York: Atherton Press.

Beier, Friedrich-Karl, and Gerhard Schricker, eds. 1989. *GATT or WIPO? New Ways in the International Protection of Intellectual Property*. New York: VCH Publishers.

Bello, Judith Hippler. 1996. "The WTO Dispute Settlement Understanding: Less is More." *American Journal of International Law* 90:416.

Bhala, Raj. 1999a. "The Myth About *Stare Decisis* and International Trade Law (Part I of a Trilogy)." *American University Law Review* 14:845.

———. 1999b. "The Precedent Setters: *De Facto Stare Decisis* in WTO Adjudication (Part Two of a Trilogy)." *Journal of Transnational Law and Policy* 9:1.

———. 2001. "The Power of the Past: Towards *De Jure Stare Decisis* in WTO Adjudication (Part Three of a Trilogy)." *George Washington Journal of International Law* 33:837.

Bidwell, P. W., and W. Diebold Jr. 1949. "The United States and the International Trade Organization." *International Conciliation* 49:187.

Blackhurst, Richard. 1998. "The Capacity of the WTO to Fill Its Mandate." In *The WTO as an International Organization*, ed. Anne O. Krueger. Chicago: University of Chicago Press. 31–58.

———. 2001. "Reforming WTO Decision-Making: Lessons from Singapore and Seattle." In Klaus Gunter Deutsch and Bernhard Speyer, eds., *Freer Trade in the Next Decade: Issues in the Millennium Round in the World Trade Organization*. New York: Routledge. 295–310.

Boddez, T., and M. Trebilcock. 1993. *Unfinished Business: Reforming Trade Remedy Laws in North America*. Toronto: C. D. Howe Institute.

Borrus, Michael, and Stephen Cohen. 1997. "Completing the Circuit: The Transatlantic Initiative in Information Technology." In Richard H. Steinberg and Bruce Stokes, eds., *Partners or Competitors? The Prospects for U.S.-European Cooperation on Asian Trade*. Boulder, Colo.: Rowman and Littlefield.

———. 1998. "Why Now? A Transatlantic Initiative in Information Technology." BRIE Working Paper No. 119, Berkeley Roundtable on the International Economy, Berkeley, Calif.

Borrus, Michael, and John Zysman. 1997. "Globalization with Borders: The Rise of Wintelism as the Future of Industrial Competition." BRIE Working Paper No. 97, Berkeley Roundtable on the International Economy, Berkeley, Calif.

Bradley, A. Jane. 2003. Former Assistant United States Trade Representative for Dispute Settlement, telephone interview by Richard Steinberg, January 14.

Bridges. 2002a. "GATS: Leaked EC Draft Requests Bring Mixed Reactions." *Bridges Weekly Trade News Digest*, April 23, 5.

Bridges. 2002b. "Native Canadian Group to be Heard in Lumber Dispute." *Bridges Weekly Trade News Digest*, May 2, 13.

Bridges. 2002c. "U.S. DSU Proposal Receives Mixed Reactions." *Bridges Weekly Trade News Digest*, December 20, 10.

Brown, William Adams, Jr. 1950. *The United States and the Restoration of World Trade: An Analysis and Appraisal of the ITO Charter and the General Agreements on Tariff and Trade*. Washington, D.C.: Brookings Institution Press.

Burley (Slaughter), Anne-Marie, and Walter Mattli. 1993. "Europe Before the Court: A Political Theory of Legal Integration." *International Organization* 47:41.

Busch, Marc L., and Eric Reinhardt. 2002. "Testing International Trade Law: Empirical Studies of GATT/WTO Dispute Settlement." In Daniel Kennedy and James Southwick, eds., *The Political Economy of International Trade Law: Essays in Honor of Robert E. Hudec*. Cambridge: Cambridge University Press. 457–81.

Cable, Vincent. 1987. "Textiles and Clothing." In J. Michael Finger and Andrzej Olechowski, eds. *The Uruguay Round: A Handbook on the Multilateral Trade Negotiations*. Washington, D.C.: World Bank. 180–90.

Calabresi, Guido, and Douglas Melamed. 1972. "Property Rules, Liability Rules, and Inalienability: One View of the Cathedral." *Harvard Law Review* 85: 1089.

Cameron, James, and Kevin R. Gray. 2001. "Principles of International Law in the WTO Dispute Settlement Body." *International and Comparative Law Quarterly* 50:248.

Charnovitz, Steve. 2000. "Opening the WTO to Non-Governmental Interests." *Fordham International Law Journal* 24:173.

———. 2002. "WTO Cosmopolitics." *New York University Journal of International Law and Policy* 34:299.

Cleveland, Sarah H. 2002. "Human Rights Sanctions and International Trade: A Theory of Compatibility." *Journal of International Economic Law* 5:1.

———. 2003. "Why International Labor Standards?" In Robert J. Flanagan and William J. Gould IV, eds., *International Labor Standards: Globalization, Trade and Public Policy*. Stanford: Stanford University Press. 129–78.

Coase, Ronald. 1960. "The Problem of Social Cost." *Journal of Law and Economics* 3, p. 1.

Cohen, Stephen S. 1998. "Form, Scale and Limits in China's Trade and Development." *Journal of Asian Economics* 8:615.

Cohen, Stephen S., and John Zysman. 1987. *Manufacturing Matters: The Myth of the Post-Industrial Economy*. New York: Basic Books.

Coleman, William, and Stefan Tangermann. 1999. "The 1992 CAP Reform, the Uruguay Round and the Commission: Conceptualizing Linked Policy Games." *Journal of Common Market Studies* 37:385.

Compa, Lance. 2002. "Pursuing International Labour Rights in U.S. Courts." *Industrial Relations* 49:5.

Cowhey, Peter, and Laura Sherman. 1998. "The FCC and the Reform of the International Telecommunications Services Market." *Euromoney*, winter.

Croley, Stephen P., and John H. Jackson. 1996. "WTO Dispute Procedures, Standard of Review, and Deference to National Governments." *American Journal of International Law* 90:193.

Croome, John. 1995. *Reshaping the World Trading System: A History of the Uruguay Round*. Geneva: World Trade Organization.

Curzon, Gerard, and Victoria Curzon. 1973. "GATT: Traders' Club." In Robert W. Cox and Harold K. Jacobson, eds., *The Anatomy of Influence*. New Haven: Yale University Press. 298–333.

Dahl, Robert A. 1971. *Polyarchy: Participation and Opposition*. New Haven: Yale University Press.

———. 1999. "Can International Organizations Be Democratic? A Skeptic's View." In Ian Shapiro and Casiano Hacker-Cordon, eds., *Democracy's Edges*. Cambridge: Cambridge University Press, 19–36.

Dam, Kenneth W. 1970. *The GATT: Law and International Economic Organization*. Chicago: University of Chicago Press.

Davey, William J. 2001. "Has the WTO Dispute Settlement System Exceeded Its Authority?" *Journal of International Economic Law* 4:79.

Davis, Christina. 2003. *Food Fights over Free Trade: How International Institutions Promote Agricultural Trade Liberalization*. Princeton: Princeton University Press.

DeSombre, Elizabeth. 2000. *Domestic Sources of International Environmental Policy: Industry, Environmentalists and U.S. Power*. Cambridge: MIT Press.

Drache, Daniel, and Sylvia Ostry. 2002. "From Doha to Kananaskis: The Future of the World Trading System and the Crisis of Governance." In *Trade Policy Research* 2002. Ottawa: Department of Foreign Affairs and International Trade.

Esty, Daniel, and Damien Gerardin. 2001. "Regulatory Co-Option." In Daniel Esty and Damien Gerardin, eds. *Regulatory Competition and Economic Regulation: Comparative Perspectives*. New York: Oxford University Press. 30–46.

Evans, John W. 1971. *The Kennedy Round in American Trade Policy*. Cambridge: Harvard University Press.

Feketekuty, Geza. 1998. "Setting the Agenda for the Next Round of Negotiations on Trade in Services." In Jeffrey J. Schott, ed., *Launching New Global Trade Talks: An Action Agenda*. Washington, D.C.: Institute for International Economics. 91–110.

Finger, J. Michael. 1993. *Antidumping: How It Works and Who Gets Hurt*. Ann Arbor: University of Michigan Press.

———. 2000. "Implementation and the Integrated Framework." www.worldbank .org/research/trade/finger.htm.

Finger, J. Michael, and Julio J. Nogués. 2001. "The Unbalanced Uruguay Round Outcome: The New Areas in Future WTO Negotiations." World Bank Policy Research Working Paper 2732, December.

Finger, J. Michael, Ulrich Reincke, and Adriana Castro. 1999. "Market Access Bargaining in the Uruguay Round: Rigid or Relaxed Reciprocity?" World Bank Paper No. 2258.

Finger, J. Michael, and Ludger Schurknecht. 1999. "Market Access Advances and Retreats since the Uruguay Round Agreement." September. www-wds .worldbank.org.

Flanigan, Robert J. 2002. "Labor Standards and International Competitive Advantage." Paper prepared for delivery at the Conference on Labor Standards, Stanford Law School, May 21.

Ford, Christopher. 1994. "Judicial Discretion in International Jurisprudence: Article 381c and General Principles of Law." *Duke Journal of Comparative and International Law* 5:35.

Frankel, Jeffrey. 1997. *Regional Trading Blocs in the World Economic System*. Washington, D.C.: Institute for International Economics.

Friedman, Milton. 1962. *Capitalism and Freedom*. Chicago: University of Chicago Press.

General Agreement on Tariffs and Trade (GATT). 1958. *Trends in International Trade: A Report by a Panel of Experts*, October. (Harberler Report)

GATT Legal Affairs. 1968. Selection of Executive Secretary. GATT Archive, Stanford University.

———. 1989. The Drafting of GATT Panel Reports: Internal Note by the Legal Affairs Division, 14.9.1989. GATT Archive, Stanford University.

Gervais, Daniel J. 1998. *The TRIPS Agreement: Drafting History and Analysis*. London: Sweet and Maxwell.

Gibson, Paul, John Wainio, David Whitley, and Mary Bohman. 2001. "Profiles of Tariffs in Global Agricultural Markets." Agricultural Economic Report No. 796, Economic Research Service, U.S. Department of Agriculture, January.

Gilligan, Michael J. 1997. *Empowering Exporters: Reciprocity, Delegation, and Collective Action in American Trade Policy*. Ann Arbor: University of Michigan Press.

Gilpin, Robert. 1981. *War and Change in World Politics*. Cambridge: Cambridge University Press.

Goldin, Ian, Olin Knudsen, and Domininc van der Mensbrugghe. 1993. *Trade Liberalization: Global Economic Implications*. Washington, D.C.: World Bank.

Goldstein, Judith. 1993. *Ideas, Interests, and American Trade Policy*. Ithaca: Cornell University Press.

———. 1996. "International Law and Domestic Institutions: Reconciling North American 'Unfair' Trade Laws." *International Organization* 50:641.

Goldstein, Judith, and Joanne Gowa. 2002. "US National Power and the Post-War Trading Regime." *World Trade Review* 1:153.

Goldstein, Judith, and Lisa Martin. 2000. "Legalization, Trade Liberalization, and Domestic Politics: A Cautionary Note." *International Organization* 54:603.

Goldstein, Judith, Douglas Rivers, and Michael Tomz. 2005. "International Relations: Understanding the Effects of GATT and the WTO on World Trade." Stanford University. Typescript.

Graham, Edward M. 1998. "Contestability, Competition, and Investment in the New World Trade Order." In Geza Feketekuty with Bruce Stokes, eds., *Trade Strategies for a New Era: Ensuring U.S. Leadership in a Global Economy*. New York: Council on Foreign Relations. 204–22.

Graham, Edward M., and J. David Richardson. 1997. *Global Competition Policy*. Washington, D.C.: Institute for International Economics.

Grossman, Gene M., and Elhanan Helpman. 2002. *Interest Groups and Trade Policy*. Princeton: Princeton University Press.

Grossman, Gene M., and Alan B. Krueger. 1994. "Economic Growth and the Environment." National Bureau of Economic Research Working Paper No. 4634.

Gruber, Lloyd. 2000. *Ruling the World: Power Politics and the Rise of Supranational Institutions*. Princeton: Princeton University Press.

Grunbaum, Gustavo. 2002. "Dispute Settlement and U.S. Environmental Laws." In Richard H. Steinberg, ed. *The Greening of Trade Law: International Trade Organizations and Environmental Issues*. Boulder, Colo.: Rowman and Littlefield. 51–80.

Haas, Ernst. 1958. *The Uniting of Europe*. Stanford: Stanford University Press.

Harrison, Glenn W., Thomas F. Rutherford, and David G. Tarr. 1996. "Quantifying the Uruguay Round." In Will Martin and L. Alan Winters, eds., *The Uruguay Round and Developing Countries*. Cambridge, Cambridge University Press. 216–52.

Hart, H.L.A. 1961. *The Concept of Law*. Oxford: Clarendon Press.

Heumeuller, Dirk, and Timothy E. Josling. 2001. "Trade Restrictions on Genetically Engineered Foods: The Application of the TBT Agreement." Paper presented at "Biotechnology, Science and Modern Agriculture: A New Industry at the Dawn of the Century," Ravello, Italy, June 15–18.

Hirschman, Albert O. 1945. *National Power and the Structure of Foreign Trade*. Berkeley and Los Angeles: University of California Press.

Hoekman, Bernard M., and Michel M. Kostecki. 2001. *The Political Economy of the World Trading System: The WTO and Beyond*. Oxford: Oxford University Press.

Howse, Robert. 2002a. "The Appellate Body Rulings in the Shrimp/Turtle Case: A New Legal Baseline for the Trade and Environment Debate." *Columbia Journal of Environmental Law* 27:489.

———. 2002b. "From Politics to Technocracy—and Back Again: The Fate of the Multilateral Trading Regime." *American Journal of International Law* 96:94.

———. 2003. "How to Begin to Think About the 'Democratic Deficit' at the WTO." University of Michigan. Typescript.

Hudec, R. E. 1991. *Enforcing International Trade Law: The Evolution of the Modern GATT Legal System*. Salem, N.H.: Butterworth.

———. 1992. "Judicialization of GATT Dispute Settlement." In Michael Hart and Debra P. Steger, eds., *In Whose Interest? Due Process and Transparency in International Trade*. Ottawa: Centre for Trade Policy and Law. 1–53.

———. 1999. "The New WTO Dispute Settlement Procedure: An Overview of the First Three Years." *Minnesota Journal of Global Trade* 8:1.

Hughes, Layla. 1998. "Limiting the Jurisdiction of Dispute Settlement Panels: The WTO Appellate Body Beef Hormone Decision." *Georgetown International Environment Law Review* 10:915.

Huntington, Samuel. 1968. *Political Order in Changing Societies*. New Haven: Yale University Press.

International Agricultural Trade Research Consortium. 2001. "The Current WTO Agricultural Negotiations: Options for Progress." Commissioned Paper No. 18, September.

International Monetary Fund. 1977. *International Financial Statistics Yearbook*. Washington, D.C.: IMF.

Irwin, Douglas. 2002. *Free Trade under Fire*. Princeton: Princeton University Press.

Jackson, John H. 1969. *World Trade and the Law of GATT*. Ann Arbor, Mich.: Michie Press.

———. 1990. *Restructuring the GATT System*. London: Royal Institute for International Affairs.

———. 1997a. *The World Trading System*. 2nd ed. Cambridge: MIT Press.

———. 1997b. "The WTO Dispute Settlement Understanding—Misunderstandings on the Nature of Legal Obligation." *American Journal of International Law* 91:60.

———. 2000. *The Jurisprudence of the GATT and the WTO*. London: Cambridge University Press.

Josling, Timothy E. 1998. *Agricultural Trade Policy: Completing the Reform*. Washington, D.C.: Institute for International Economics.

Josling, Timothy E., and Allan Rae. 2003. "Processed Food Trade and Developing Countries: Protection and Trade Reform." *Food Policy*, June.

Josling, Timothy E., and Stefan Tangermann. 2003. "Production and Export Subsidies in Agriculture: Lessons from GATT and WTO Disputes Involving the US and the EC." In Mark Pollack and Ernst-Ulrich Petersmann, eds., *Transatlantic Economic Disputes*. Oxford: Oxford University Press, 207–32.

Josling, Timothy E., Donna Roberts, and David Orden. 2004. *Food Regulation and Trade: Toward a Safe and Open Global System*. Washington, D.C.: Institute for International Economics.

Josling, Timothy E., Stefan Tangermann, and Thorald K. Warley. 1996. *Agriculture in the GATT*. Basingstoke: Macmillan.

Kahler, Miles. 2001. *Leadership Selection in the Major Multilaterals*. Washington, D.C.: Institute for International Studies.

Keesing, Don, and Martin Wolfe. 1980. *Textile Quotas against Developing Countries*, London: Trade Policy Research Center.

Kellow, Aynsle. 2002. "Comparing Business and Public Interest Associability at the International Level." *International Political Science Review* 23:175.

Keohane, Robert O. 1982. "The Demand for International Regimes." *International Organization* 36:325.

———. 1984. *After Hegemony*. Princeton: Princeton University Press.

Keohane, Robert O., Andrew Moravcsik, and Anne-Marie Slaughter. 2000. "Legalized Dispute Resolution: Interstate and Transnational." *International Organization* 54:(457).

Keohane, Robert O., and Joseph S. Nye Jr. 1977. *Power and Interdependence*. Boston: Little Brown.

———. 2003. "Democracy, Accountability and Global Governance." In Miles Kahler and David Lake, eds., *Governance in a Global Economy*, Princeton: Princeton University Press. 386–411.

Kock, Karin. 1969. *International Trade Policy and the GATT 1947–1967*. Stockholm: Almqvist and Wiksell.

Koh, Harold H. 1991. "Transnational Public Law Litigation." *Yale Law Journal* 100:2347.

Koremenos, Barbara. 2002. "Open Covenants, Clandestinely Arrived At." October. Unpublished manuscript.

Koremenos, Barbara, Charles Lipson, and Duncan Snidal. 2001. "The Rational Design of International Institutions." *International Organization* 55:761.

Krasner, Stephen D. 1976. "State Power and the Structure of International Trade." *World Politics* 28:317.

———. 1979. "The Tokyo Round: Particularistic Interests and Prospects for Stability in the Global Trading System." *International Studies Quarterly*. 23:491.

———. 1983. "Structural Causes and Regime Consequences: Regimes as Intervening Variables." In Stephen D. Krasner, ed., *International Regimes*. Ithaca: Cornell University Press. 1–22.

———. 1991. "Global Communications and National Power: Life on the Pareto Frontier." *World Politics* 43:336.

Krugman, Paul. 1991. *Strategic Trade Policy and the New International Economics*. Cambridge: MIT Press.

Lanoszka, Anna. 2001. "The WTO Accession Process—Negotiating Participation in a Globalizing Economy." *Journal of World Trade Law* 35:575.

Lavorel, Warren. 1995. Telephone interview by Richard Steinberg, March.

Lawrence, Robert Z. 2004. *Crimes and Punishments? An Analysis of Retaliation Under the WTO*. Washington, D.C.: Institute of International Economics.

Leitner, Kara, and Simon Lester. 2004. "WTO Dispute Settlement 1995–2003: A Statistical Analysis." *Journal of International Economic Law* 7:169.

Leopold, Aldo. 1990. *A Sand County Almanac.* New York: Ballantine.

Lindsey, Brink, and Dan Ikenson. 2002. "Reforming the Antidumping Agreement: A Road Map for WTO Negotiations." CATO Institute Trade Policy Analysis 21, CATO Institute Center for Trade Policy Analysis, Washington, D.C.

Mansfield, Edward. 1993. "Concentration, Polarity, and the Distribution of Power." *International Studies Quarterly* 37:105.

Mansfield, Edward, and Helen Milner. 1999. "New Wave of Regionalism." *International Organization* 53:589.

Marceau, Gabrielle. 1999. "A Call for Coherence in International Law: Praises for the Prohibition Against 'Clinical Isolation' in WTO Dispute Settlement." *Journal of World Trade* 33:87.

March, James, and Johan Olsen. 1989. *Rediscovering Institutions: The Organizational Basis of Politics.* New York: Free Press.

Martin, Lisa L. 1992. *Coercive Cooperation: Explaining Multilateral Economic Sanctions.* Princeton: Princeton University Press.

———. 2000. *Democratic Commitments: Legislatures and International Cooperation.* Princeton: Princeton University Press.

Maskus, Keith. 2000. *Intellectual Property Rights in the Global Economy.* Washington, D.C.: Institute for International Economics.

Matthews, Duncan. 2002. *Globalizing Intellectual Property Rights: The TRIPS Agreement.* London: Routledge.

McCubbins, Mathew D., and Thomas Schwartz. 1984. "Congressional Oversight Overlooked: Police Patrols versus Fire Alarms." *American Journal of Political Science* 28:165.

McRae, Donald. 2003. "Claus-Dieter Ehlermann's Presentation on the Role and Record of Dispute Settlement Panels and the Appellate body of the WTO: Comment by Professor Donald McRae." *Journal of International Economic Law* 6:709.

Michalopoulos, Constantine. 2000. "The Role of Special and Differential Treatment for Developing Countries in GATT and the World Trade Association." Typescript.

Milgrom, Paul R., Douglass C. North, and Barry Weingast. 1990. "The Role of Institutions in the Revival of Trade: The Law Merchant, Private Judges, and the Champagne Fairs." *Economics and Politics* 2:1.

Moravcsik, Andrew. 1991. "Negotiating the Single European Act: National Interests and Conventional Statecraft in the European Community." *International Organization* 45:19.

———. 1997. "Taking Preferences Seriously: A Liberal Theory of International Politics." *International Organization* 51:513.

Narlikar, Amrita. 2001. "WTO Decision-Making and Developing Countries." South Centre, Trade-Related Agenda, Development and Equity, Working Papers 12 November.

Odell, John, and Barry Eichengreen. 1998. "The United States, the ITO, and the WTO: Exit Options, Agent Slack, and Presidential Leadership." In Anne O.

Krueger, ed., *The WTO as an International Organization*. Chicago: University of Chicago Press. 181–209.

Okun, Arthur M. 1975. *Equality and Efficiency: The Big Tradeoff*. Washington, D.C.: Brookings Institution.

Oloka-Onyango, J., and Deepika Udagama. 2000. "The Realization of Economic, Social, and Cultural Rights: Globalization and Its Impact on the Full Enjoyment of Human Rights." U.N. Doc. E/CN.4/Sub.2/2000/13, U.N. Subcommission on the Promotion and Protection of Human Rights.

Olsen, Mancur. 1971. *The Logic of Collective Action: Goods and the Theory of Groups*. Cambridge: Harvard University Press.

Oppenheim, Lassa. 1992. *Oppenheim's International Law*. 9th ed. Ed. Robert Jennings and Arthur Watts, Harlow: Longman.

Organization for Economic Cooperation and Development (OECD). 1996a. *Antitrust and Market Access: The Scope and Coverage of Competition Laws and Implications for Trade*. Paris: OECD.

———. 1996b. *Trade, Employment and Labour Standards*. Paris: OECD.

———. 2000. "Guidelines for Multinational Enterprises." http://www.oecd.org/daf/investment/guidelines.

———. 2003. *Agricultural Policies in OECD Countries: Monitoring and Evaluation*. Paris: OECD, June.

Overseas Development Institute. 1995. "Developing Countries in the WTO." 1995 Briefing Paper No. 3.

Paemen, Hugo, and Alexandra Bensch. 1995. *From the GATT to the WTO: The European Community and the Uruguay Round*. Leuven: Leuven University Press.

Palmeter, David, and Petros C. Mavroidis. 1998. "The WTO Legal System: Sources of Law." *American Journal of International Law* 92:38.

Patterson, Gardner, and Eliza Patterson. 1994. "The Road From GATT to MTO." *Minnesota Journal of Global Trade* 3:35.

Patterson, Lee Ann. 1997. "Agricultural Policy Reform in the European Community: A Three-Level Game Analysis." *International Organization* 51:135.

Pauwelyn, Joost. 2001. "The Role of Public International Law in the WTO: How Far Can We Go?" *American Journal of International Law* 95:535.

Permanent Court of International Justice. 1927. The Case of the S.S. "Lotus." Judgment 9, 1927, PCIJ, Series A, No. 10, p. 19.

Petersmann, Ernst-Ulrich. 1997. *The GATT/WTO Dispute Settlement System: International Law, International Organizations, and Dispute Settlement*. London: Kluwer Law International.

Porges, Amelia. 1995. "The New Dispute Settlement: From the GATT to the WTO." *Leiden Journal of International Law* 8:1.

Pratt, John, and Richard Zeckhauser. 1984. *Principals and Agents: The Structure of Business*. Cambridge: Harvard Business School.

Preeg, Ernest H. 1970. *Traders and Diplomats*. Washington, D.C.: Brookings Institution Press.

———. 1995. *Traders in a Brave New World: The Uruguay Round and the Future of the International Trading System*. Chicago: University of Chicago Press.

Preparatory Committee for the International Trade Organization. 1947. Press Release. GATT Archive, Stanford University.

Prestowitz, Clyde V. 1988. *Trading Places: How We Allowed Japan to Take the Lead*. New York: Basic Books.

Prusa, Thomas. 1999. "On the Spread and Impact of Anti-dumping." National Bureau of Economic Research Working Paper No. 7404.

Putnam, Robert. 1988. "Diplomacy and Domestic Politics: The Logic of Two-Level Games." *International Organization* 42:427.

Raghavan, Chakravarthi. 1995. "WTO Establishes Appellate Body." November 30. http://www.sunshine.org/trade/process/followup/1995/index.htm.

Ragosta, John. 2002. Comments at the American Bar Association/Georgetown University Law Center 2002 International Trade Law Symposium, Washington, D.C., September 12.

Ragosta, John, Navin Joneja, and Mikhail Zeldovich. 2003. "WTO Dispute Settlement: The System is Flawed and Must be Fixed." http://www.dbtrade.com/publications/wto_dispute_settlement_is_flawed.pdf.

Ramakrishna, Hegde. 1998. Statement Circulated by Mr. Ramakrishna, Minister of Commerce, at the second Session of the WTO Ministerial Conference, Geneva, WTO. Doc. WT/MIN (98)/ST/36 (98–2030). May 18.

Raustiala, Kal. 2000. "Sovereignty and Multilateralism." *Chicago Journal of International Law* 1:401.

———. 2002. "Police Patrols, Fire Alarms, and Treaty Review under the NAAEC." In John Knox and David Markell, eds. *The North American Commission on Environmental Cooperation: An Assessment*. Stanford: Stanford University Press. 401–19.

Reif, Tim. 2002. Democratic Chief Trade Counsel, U.S. House Committee on Ways and Means, interview by Richard Steinberg, Washington, D.C., April.

Riches, Cromwell A. 1940. *Majority Rule in International Organization*. Baltimore: Johns Hopkins University Press.

Roberts, Donna, Laurian Unnevehr, Julie Caswell, Ian Sheldon, John Wilson, D. Otsuki, and David Orden. 2001. "Agriculture in the WTO: The Role of Product Attributes in the Agricultural Negotiations." International Agricultural Trade Research Consortium, Commissioned Paper No. 17.

Roh, Chip. 2002. Interview by Richard Steinberg, Washington, D.C., September 11.

Rose, Andrew, 2004. "Do We Really Know That the WTO Increases American Trade?" *American Ecomomic Review* 94:94.

Ruggie, John Gerard. 1983. "International Regimes, Transactions, and Change: Embedded Liberalism in the Postwar Economic Order." In Stephen D. Krasner, ed., *International Regimes*. Ithaca: Cornell University Press. 195–232.

Sauvé, Pierre, and Robert M. Stern, eds. 2000. *GATS 2000; New Directions in Services Trade Liberalization*. Boston: Center for Business and Government, Harvard University; Washington, D.C.: Brookings Institute Press.

Schattschneider, E. E. 1935. *Politics, Pressures and the Tariff: A Study of Free Enterprise in Pressure Politics as Shown in the 1929–30 Revision of the Tariff*. New York: Prentice-Hall.

Schott, Jeffery J. 1994. *The Uruguay Round: An Assessment*. Washington, D.C.: Institute for International Economics.

Shaffer, Gregory C. 2002. "The Nexus of Law and Politics: The WTO's Committee on Trade and Environment." In Richard H. Steinberg, ed., *The Greening of Trade Law, International Trade Organizations and Environmental Issues*. Boulder, Colo.: Rowman and Littlefield. 81–114

Slaughter (Burley), Anne-Marie, and Walter Mattli. 1993. "Europe Before the Court: A Political Theory of Legal Integration." *International Organization* 47:41.

Srinivasan, T. N. 1998a. *Developing Countries and the Multilateral Trading System*. Boulder, Colo.: Westview Press.

———. 1998b. "Regionalism and the WTO: Is Non-discrimination Passé?" In Anne O. Krueger, ed., *The WTO as an International Organization*. Chicago: University of Chicago Press. 329–49.

Stanton, G. 1999. "Review and Implementation of the SPS and TBT Agreements." Food and Agriculture Organization, Rome.

Stein, Arthur. 1993. *Why Nations Cooperate*. Cambridge: MIT Press.

Steinberg, Richard H. 1994. "The Uruguay Round: A Legal Analysis of the Final Act." *International Quarterly* 6(2): 1–44.

———. 1998. "Institutional Implications of WTO Accession for China." California: University of California Institute on Global Conflict and Cooperation. Policy Paper No. 41.

———. 1999. "The Prospects for Partnership: Overcoming Obstacles to Transatlantic Trade Policy Cooperation in Asia." In Richard H. Steinberg and Bruce Stokes, eds., *Partners or Competitors? The Prospects for U.S.-E.U. Cooperation on Asian Trade*. Boulder, Colo.: Rowman and Littlefield. 213–250.

———. 2002a. "Explaining Similarities and Differences Across International Trade Organizations." In Richard H. Steinberg, ed., *The Greening of International Trade Law: International Trade Organizations and Environmental Issues*. Boulder, Colo.: Rowman and Littlefield. 277–309.

———. 2002b. "In the Shadow of Law or Power? Consensus-Based Bargaining and Outcomes at the GATT/WTO." *International Organization*. 56:339.

———. 2002c. "Understanding Trade and the Environment: Conceptual Frameworks." In Richard H. Steinberg, ed., *The Greening of Trade Law: International Trade Organizations and Environmental Issues*. Boulder, Colo.: Rowman and Littlefield. 1–20.

———. 2004. "Judicial Law-Making at the WTO: Discursive, Constitutional, and Political Constraints." *American Journal of International Law* 98:247.

Steinberg, Richard H., and Timothy E. Josling, 2003. "When the Peace Ends: The Vulnerability of EC and US Agricultural Subsidies to WTO Legal Challenge." *Journal of International Economic Law*. 6:369.

Stewart, Richard B. 1977. "Pyramids of Sacrifice? Problems of Federalism in Mandating State Implementation of National Environmental Policy." *Yale Law Journal* 86:1196.

Stokes, Bruce, and Pat Choate. 2001. *Democratizing U.S. Trade Policy*. New York: Council on Foreign Relations.

Stoler, Andrew. 2002. WTO Deputy Director-General, interview by Richard Steinberg, Monterey, Calif. January.

Sykes, Alan O. 1989. "Countervailing Duty Law: An Economic Critique." *Columbia Law Review* 89:199.

Sykes, Alan O. 1991. "Protectionism as a 'Safeguard': A Positive Analysis of the GATT 'Escape Clause' with Normative Speculations." *University of Chicago Law Review* 58:255.

———. 1995. "Regulatory Protectionism and the Law of International Trade." *University of Chicago Law Review* 66:1.

———. 1998. "Comparative Advantage and the Normative Economics of International Trade Policy." *Journal of International Economic Law* 1:49.

———. 2003a. "The Economics of WTO Rules on Subsidies and Countervailing Measures." John M. Olin Law and Economics Working Paper No. 186 (2nd ser.).

———. 2003b. "The Safeguards Mess; a Critique of WTO Jurisprudence." John M. Olin Law and Economics Working Paper No. 187 (2nd ser.).

Tarullo, Daniel K. 2003. "The Hidden Costs of International Dispute Settlement: WTO Review of Domestic Anti-dumping Decisions." *Law and Policy in International Business* 34:109.

Trachtman, Joel P. 1999. "The Domain of WTO Dispute Resolution." *Harvard International Law Journal* 40:333.

Tullock, Gordon. 1975. "The Transitional Gains Trap." *Bell Journal of Economics* 6:671.

Tyson, Laura D'Andrea. 1992. *Who's Bashing Whom? Trade Conflict in High-Technology Industries.* Washington, D.C.: Institute for International Economics.

U.K. Commission on Intellectual Property Rights. 2002. "Integrating Intellectual Property Rights and Development Policy." Intellectual Property Rights Commission, London, September.

United States Government. 1947. Delegation Position Paper. GATT Archive: Stanford University.

U.S. Secretary of Commerce. 2002. "Executive Branch Strategy Regarding WTO Dispute Settlement Panels and the Appellate Body." In Report to the Congress Transmitted by the Secretary of Commerce, December 30.

U.S. Tariff Commission. 1948. *Operation of the Trade Agreements Program: July 1934 to April 1948.* Washington: GPO.

Vogel, David. 1986. *National Styles of Regulation: Environmental Policy in Great Britain and the United States.* Ithaca: Cornell University Press.

Wallach, Lori. 2000. "The FP Interview: Lori's War." *Foreign Policy,* spring, 37.

Waltz, Kenneth. 1970. "The Myth of Interdependence." In Charles Kindleberger, ed., *The International Corporation.* Cambridge: MIT Press. 205–23.

———. 1979. *Theory of International Politics.* Menlo Park, Calif.: Addison-Wesley.

Weil, Prosper. 1997. "The Court Cannot Conclude Definitively . . . *Non Liquet* Revisited." *Columbia Journal of Transnational Law* 36:109.

Weiler, J.H.H. 1991. "The Transformation of Europe." *Yale Law Journal* 100:2403.

———. 2000a. *The EU, the WTO, and the NAFTA: Towards a Common Law of International Trade?* Oxford: Oxford University Press.

———. 2000b. "The Rule of Lawyers and the Ethos of Diplomats: Reflections on the Internal and External Legitimacy of WTO Dispute Settlement." Harvard Jean Monnet Working Paper 9/00, Harvard Law School.

Wilcox, Clair. 1972. *A Charter for World Trade.* New York: Arno Press.

Winham, Gilbert R. 1986. *International Trade and the Tokyo Round Negotiation.* Princeton: Princeton University Press.

Woolcock, Steven. 2000. "European Trade Policy: Global Pressures and Domestic Constraints." In Helen Wallace and William Wallace, eds., *Policy-Making in the European Union.* (2nd ed.) Oxford: Oxford University Press, 373–399.

World Bank. 1972. *World Development Indicators.* Washington, D.C.: World Bank.

———. 1997. *World Development Indicators.* Washington, D.C.: World Bank.

———. 2001. *World Development Indicators.* Washington, D.C.: World Bank.

World Trade Organization (WTO). 1991. "Report of the Panel, United States—Restrictions on Imports of Tuna." Reprinted in *International Legal Materials* 30:1594.

———. 1994. "Report of the Panel, United States—Restrictions on Imports of Tuna." Reprinted in *International Legal Materials* 33:839.

———. 1995. *The Results of the Uruguay Round of Multilateral Trade Negotiations: The Legal Texts.* Geneva: World Trade Organization.

———. 1998a. "Report of the Appellate Body, European Communities—Measures Concerning Meat and Meat Products (Hormones)." WT/DS26/AB/R, WT/DS48/AB/R. World Trade Organization, Geneva.

———. 1998b. "Report of the Appellate Body, United States—Import Prohibition of Certain Shrimp and Shrimp Products." WT/DS58/AB/R. World Trade Organization, Geneva.

———. 2001. "Report of the Panel, United States—Import Prohibition of Certain Shrimp and Shrimp Products, Recourse to Article 21.5 by Malaysia." WT/DS58/RW. World Trade Organization, Geneva.

World Wildlife Fund et al. 2001. "Open Letter on Institutional Reforms in the WTO." October.

Index